X-MEN
AND
SPIDER-MAN

X-MEN/SPIDER-MAN. Contains material originally published in magazine form as X-MEN/SPIDER-MAN #1-4 and X-MEN #35. First printing 2009. ISBN# 978-0-7851-3953-9. Published by MARVEL PUBLISHING, INC., a subsidiary of MARVEL ENTERTAINMENT, INC. OFFICE OF PUBLICATION: 417 5th Avenue, New York, NY 10016. Copyright © 1967, 2008 and 2009 Marvel Characters, Inc. All rights reserved. $19.99 per copy in the U.S. (GST #R127032852); Canadian Agreement #40668537. All characters featured in this issue and the distinctive names and likenesses thereof, and all related indicia are trademarks of Marvel Characters, Inc. No similarity between any of the names, characters, persons, and/or institutions in this magazine with those of any living or dead person or institution is intended, and any such similarity which may exist is purely coincidental. **Printed in the U.S.A.**. ALAN FINE, CEO Marvel Publishing Division and EVP & CMO Marvel Characters B.V.; DAN BUCKLEY, President of Publishing - Print & Digital Media; JIM SOKOLOWSKI, Chief Operating Officer; DAVID GABRIEL, SVP of Publishing Sales & Circulation; DAVID BOGART, SVP of Business Affairs & Talent Management; MICHAEL PASCIULLO, VP Merchandising & Communications; JIM O'KEEFE, VP of Operations & Logistics; DAN CARR, Executive Director of Publishing Technology; JUSTIN F. GABRIE, Director of Publishing & Editorial Operations; SUSAN CRESPI, Editorial Operations Manager; ALEX MORALES, Publishing Operations Manager; STAN LEE, Chairman Emeritus. For information regarding advertising in Marvel Comics or on Marvel.com, please contact Mitch Dane, Advertising Director, at mdane@marvel.com. For Marvel subscription inquiries, please call 800-217-9158.

10 9 8 7 6 5 4 3 2 1

X-MEN
AND
SPIDER-MAN

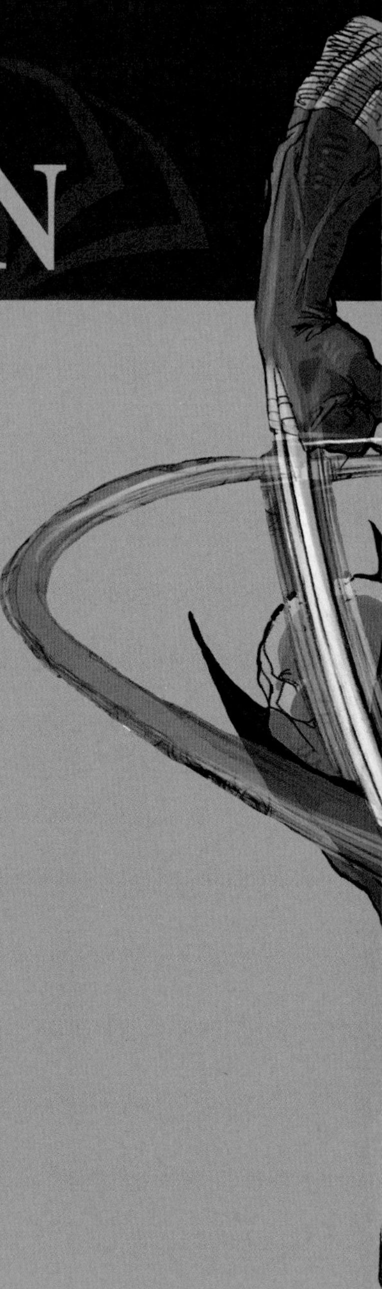

Writer .... Christos Gage
Artist .... Mario Alberti
Letterer .... Jared K. Fletcher
Assistant Editor .... Tom Brennan
Editor .... Stephen Wacker

"ALONG CAME A SPIDER..."
FROM *X-MEN* #35 (AUGUST 1967)

Writer .... Roy Thomas
Penciler .... Werner Roth
Inker .... Dan Adkins
Letterer .... Jerry Feldmann
Editor .... Stan Lee

Collection Editor .... Mark D. Beazley
Editorial Assistant .... Alex Starbuck
Assistant Editors .... Cory Levine & John Denning
Editor, Special Projects .... Jennifer Grünwald
Senior Editor, Special Projects .... Jeff Youngquist
Senior Vice President of Sales .... David Gabriel
Book Designer .... Spring Hoteling
Production .... Jerry Kalinowski

Editor in Chief .... Joe Quesada
Publisher .... Dan Buckley
Executive Producer .... Alan Fine

Special thanks to Andy Schmidt & Paolo Ramella.

Dedicated to Antonio Alberti

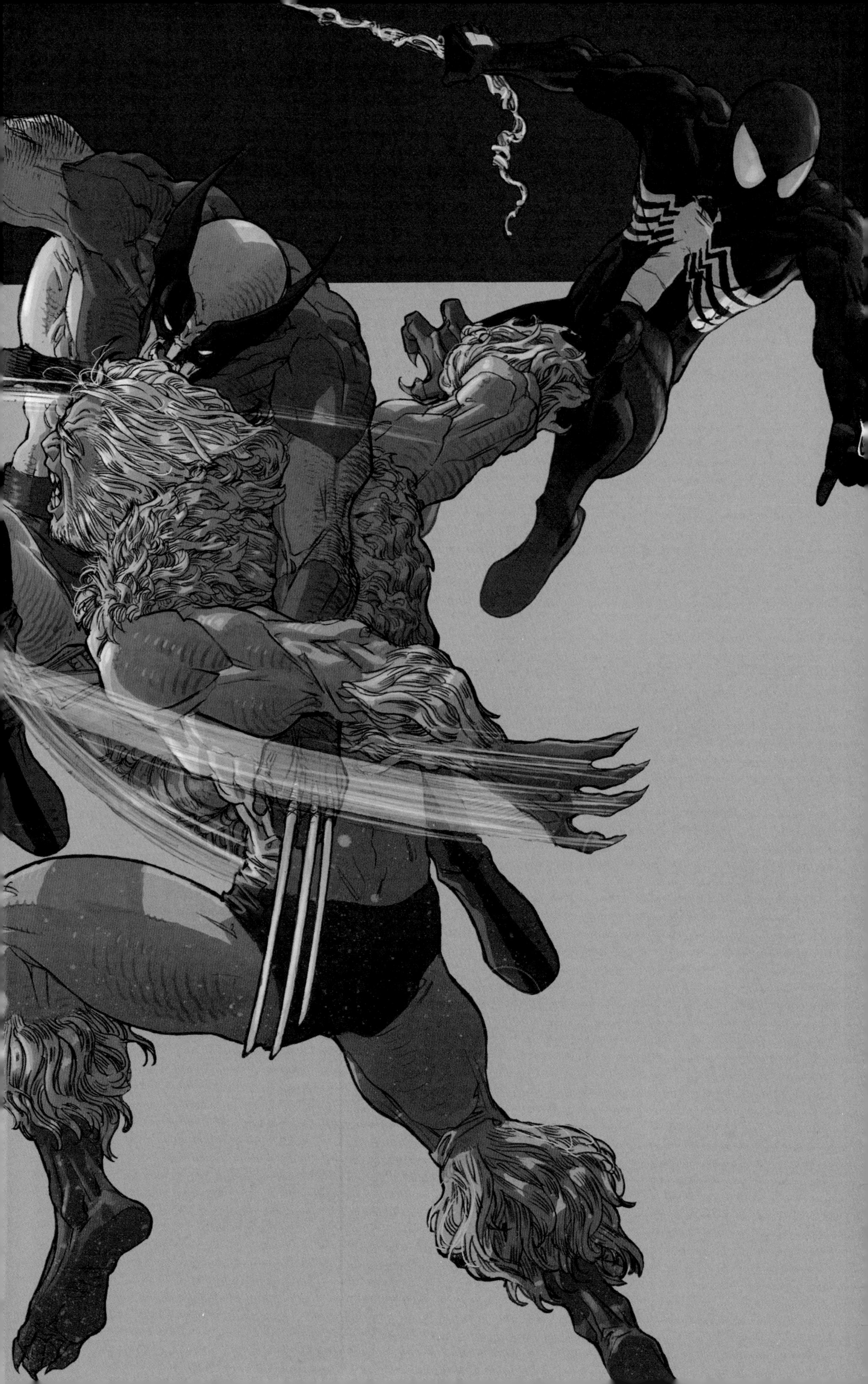

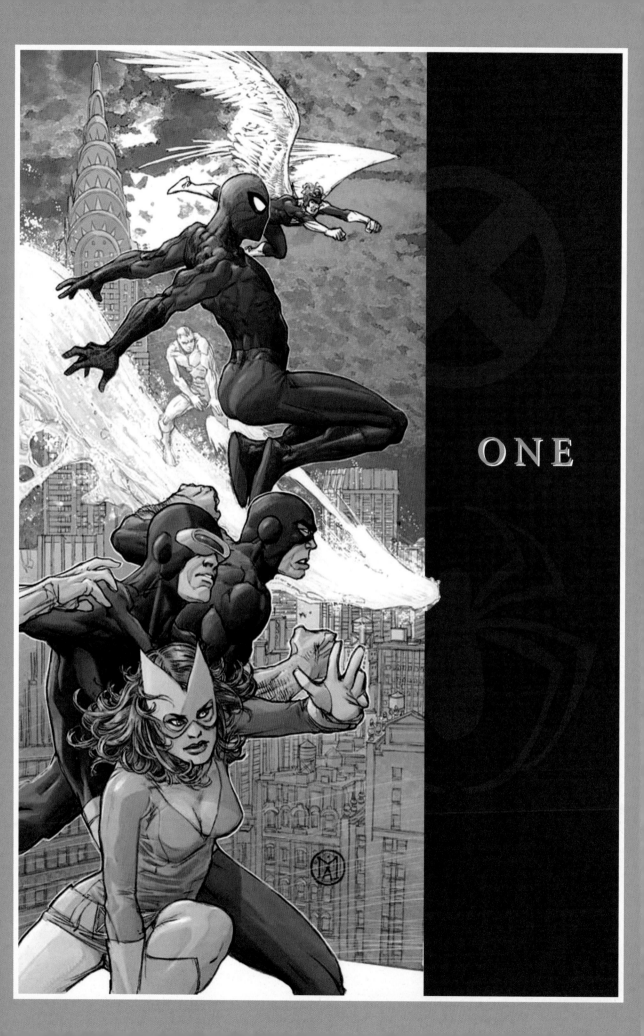

ONE

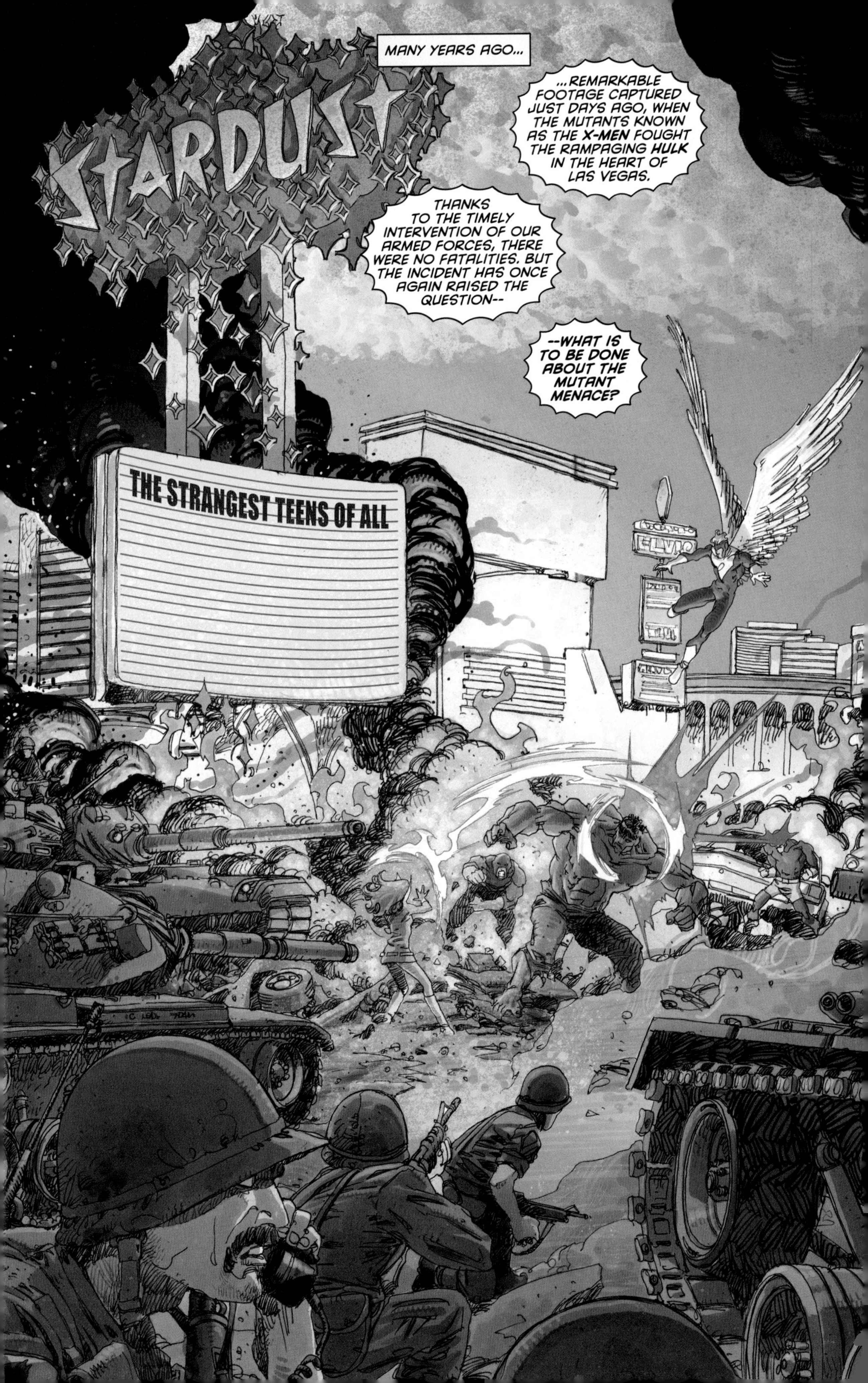
STARDUST
MANY YEARS AGO...
...REMARKABLE FOOTAGE CAPTURED JUST DAYS AGO, WHEN THE MUTANTS KNOWN AS THE X-MEN FOUGHT THE RAMPAGING HULK IN THE HEART OF LAS VEGAS.
THANKS TO THE TIMELY INTERVENTION OF OUR ARMED FORCES, THERE WERE NO FATALITIES. BUT THE INCIDENT HAS ONCE AGAIN RAISED THE QUESTION--
--WHAT IS TO BE DONE ABOUT THE MUTANT MENACE?
THE STRANGEST TEENS OF ALL

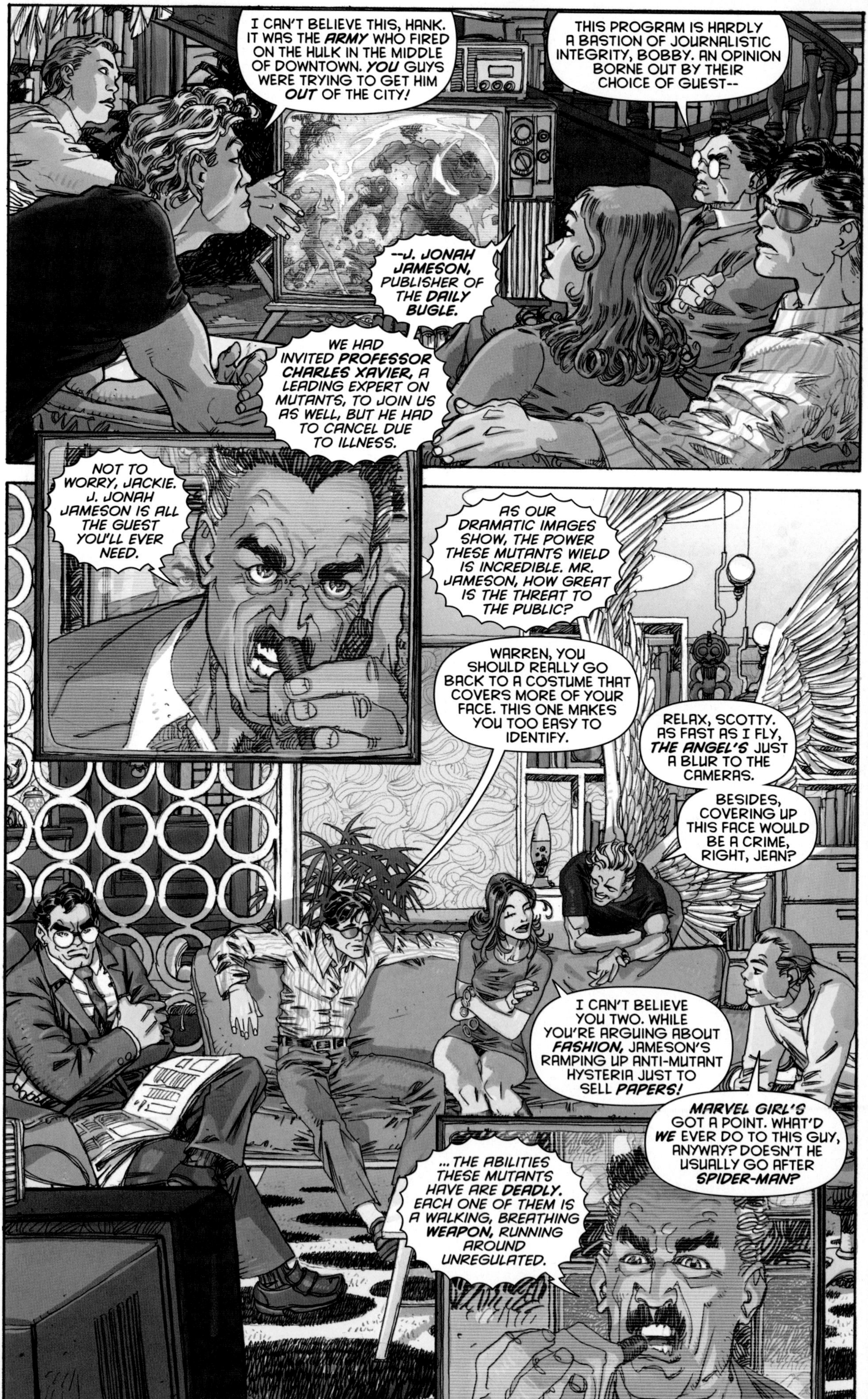
I CAN'T BELIEVE THIS, HANK. IT WAS THE ARMY WHO FIRED ON THE HULK IN THE MIDDLE OF DOWNTOWN. YOU GUYS WERE TRYING TO GET HIM OUT OF THE CITY!
THIS PROGRAM IS HARDLY A BASTION OF JOURNALISTIC INTEGRITY, BOBBY. AN OPINION BORNE OUT BY THEIR CHOICE OF GUEST--
--J. JONAH JAMESON, PUBLISHER OF THE DAILY BUGLE.
WE HAD INVITED PROFESSOR CHARLES XAVIER, A LEADING EXPERT ON MUTANTS, TO JOIN US AS WELL, BUT HE HAD TO CANCEL DUE TO ILLNESS.
NOT TO WORRY, JACKIE. J. JONAH JAMESON IS ALL THE GUEST YOU'LL EVER NEED.
AS OUR DRAMATIC IMAGES SHOW, THE POWER THESE MUTANTS WIELD IS INCREDIBLE. MR. JAMESON, HOW GREAT IS THE THREAT TO THE PUBLIC?
WARREN, YOU SHOULD REALLY GO BACK TO A COSTUME THAT COVERS MORE OF YOUR FACE. THIS ONE MAKES YOU TOO EASY TO IDENTIFY.
RELAX, SCOTTY. AS FAST AS I FLY, THE ANGEL'S JUST A BLUR TO THE CAMERAS.
BESIDES, COVERING UP THIS FACE WOULD BE A CRIME, RIGHT, JEAN?
I CAN'T BELIEVE YOU TWO. WHILE YOU'RE ARGUING ABOUT FASHION, JAMESON'S RAMPING UP ANTI-MUTANT HYSTERIA JUST TO SELL PAPERS!
MARVEL GIRL'S GOT A POINT. WHAT'D WE EVER DO TO THIS GUY, ANYWAY? DOESN'T HE USUALLY GO AFTER SPIDER-MAN?
...THE ABILITIES THESE MUTANTS HAVE ARE DEADLY. EACH ONE OF THEM IS A WALKING, BREATHING WEAPON, RUNNING AROUND UNREGULATED.

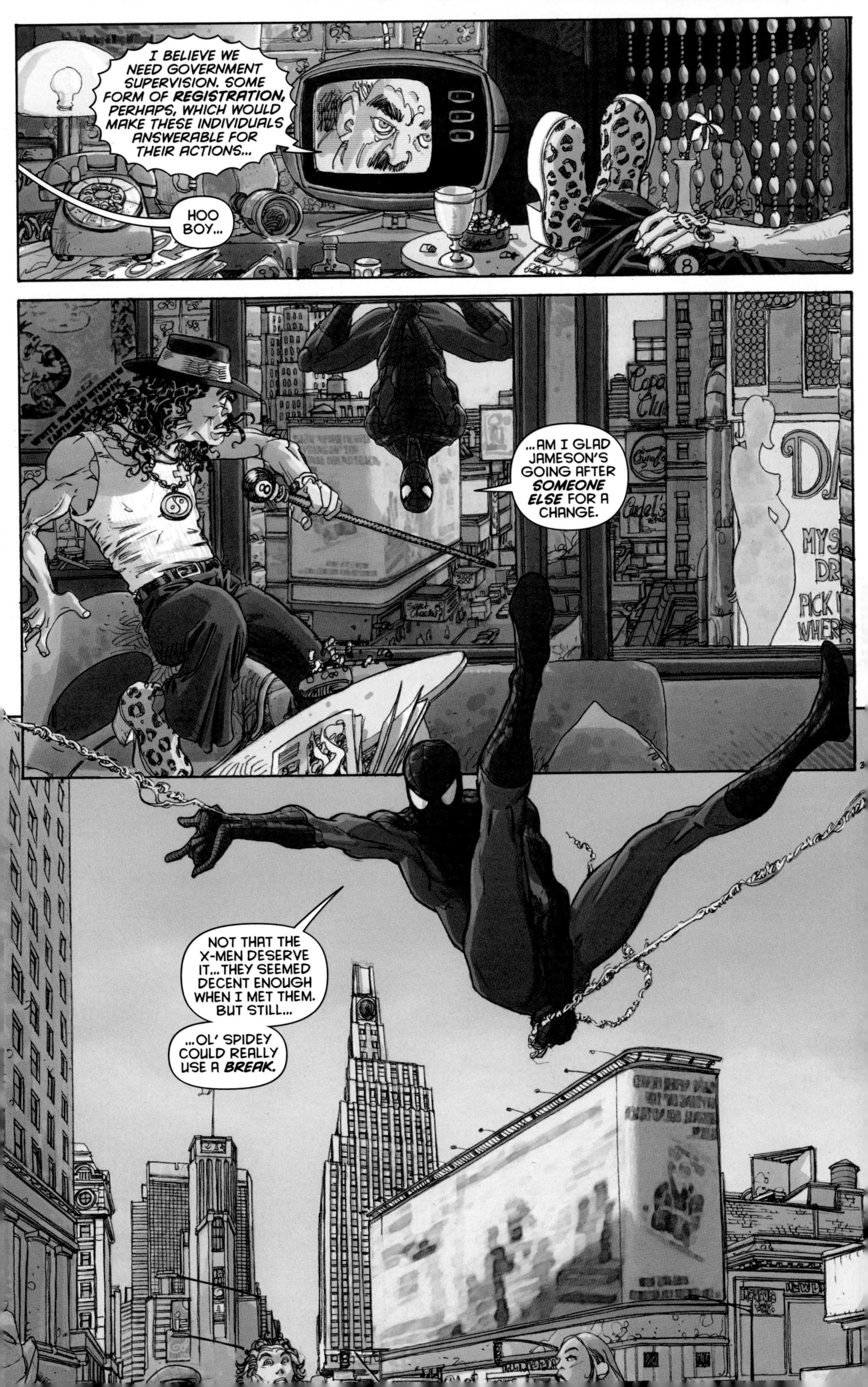
I BELIEVE WE NEED GOVERNMENT SUPERVISION. SOME FORM OF REGISTRATION, PERHAPS, WHICH WOULD MAKE THESE INDIVIDUALS ANSWERABLE FOR THEIR ACTIONS...
HOO BOY...
...AM I GLAD JAMESON'S GOING AFTER SOMEONE ELSE FOR A CHANGE.
NOT THAT THE X-MEN DESERVE IT... THEY SEEMED DECENT ENOUGH WHEN I MET THEM. BUT STILL...
...OL' SPIDEY COULD REALLY USE A BREAK.

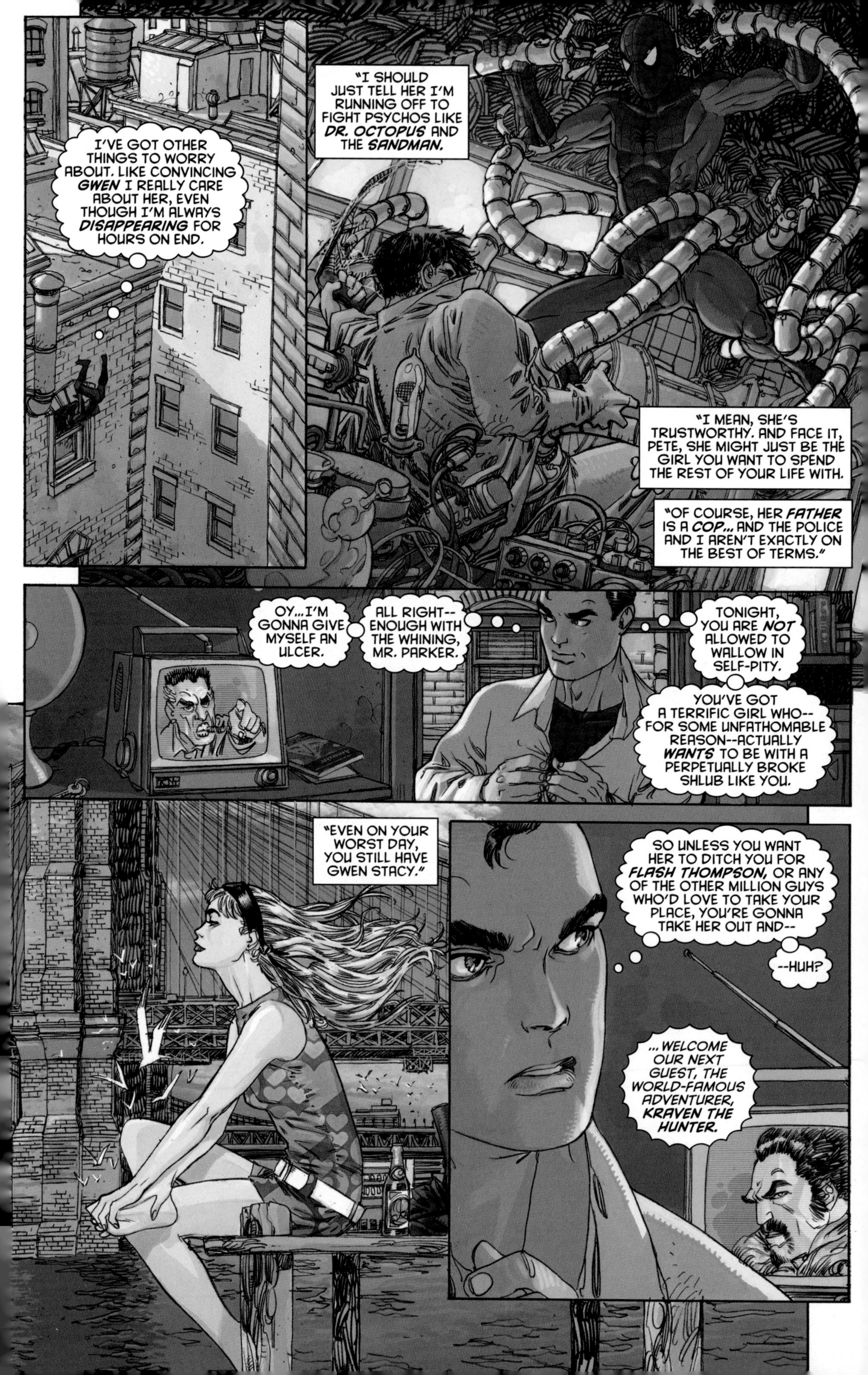
I'VE GOT OTHER THINGS TO WORRY ABOUT. LIKE CONVINCING GWEN I REALLY CARE ABOUT HER, EVEN THOUGH I'M ALWAYS DISAPPEARING FOR HOURS ON END.
"I SHOULD JUST TELL HER I'M RUNNING OFF TO FIGHT PSYCHOS LIKE DR. OCTOPUS AND THE SANDMAN.
"I MEAN, SHE'S TRUSTWORTHY. AND FACE IT, PETE, SHE MIGHT JUST BE THE GIRL YOU WANT TO SPEND THE REST OF YOUR LIFE WITH.
"OF COURSE, HER FATHER IS A COP... AND THE POLICE AND I AREN'T EXACTLY ON THE BEST OF TERMS."
OY...I'M GONNA GIVE MYSELF AN ULCER.
ALL RIGHT--ENOUGH WITH THE WHINING, MR. PARKER.
TONIGHT, YOU ARE NOT ALLOWED TO WALLOW IN SELF-PITY.
YOU'VE GOT A TERRIFIC GIRL WHO--FOR SOME UNFATHOMABLE REASON--ACTUALLY WANTS TO BE WITH A PERPETUALLY BROKE SHLUB LIKE YOU.
"EVEN ON YOUR WORST DAY, YOU STILL HAVE GWEN STACY."
SO UNLESS YOU WANT HER TO DITCH YOU FOR FLASH THOMPSON, OR ANY OF THE OTHER MILLION GUYS WHO'D LOVE TO TAKE YOUR PLACE, YOU'RE GONNA TAKE HER OUT AND--
--HUH?
...WELCOME OUR NEXT GUEST, THE WORLD-FAMOUS ADVENTURER, KRAVEN THE HUNTER.

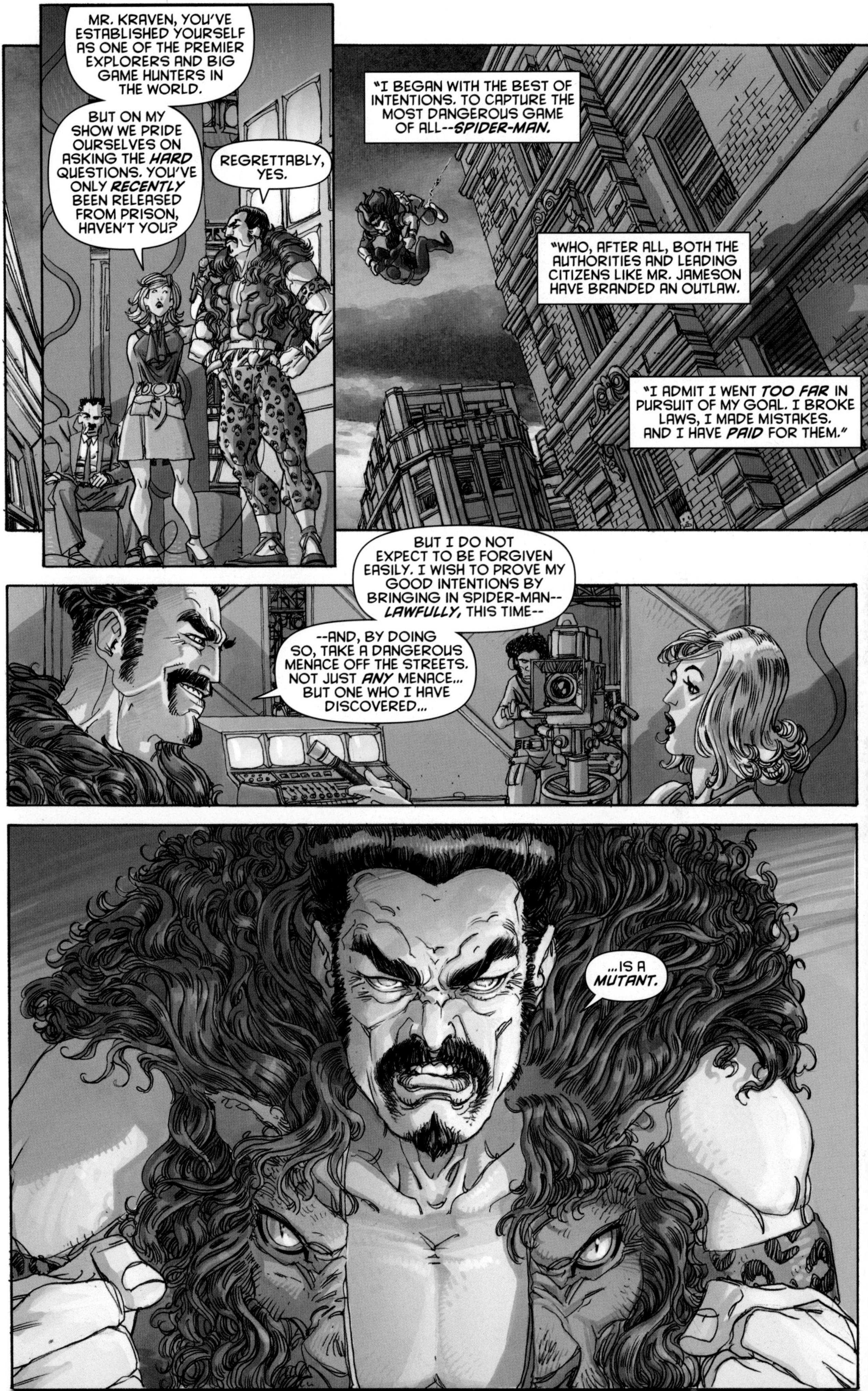
MR. KRAVEN, YOU'VE ESTABLISHED YOURSELF AS ONE OF THE PREMIER EXPLORERS AND BIG GAME HUNTERS IN THE WORLD.
BUT ON MY SHOW WE PRIDE OURSELVES ON ASKING THE HARD QUESTIONS. YOU'VE ONLY RECENTLY BEEN RELEASED FROM PRISON, HAVEN'T YOU?
REGRETTABLY, YES.
"I BEGAN WITH THE BEST OF INTENTIONS. TO CAPTURE THE MOST DANGEROUS GAME OF ALL--SPIDER-MAN.
"WHO, AFTER ALL, BOTH THE AUTHORITIES AND LEADING CITIZENS LIKE MR. JAMESON HAVE BRANDED AN OUTLAW.
"I ADMIT I WENT TOO FAR IN PURSUIT OF MY GOAL. I BROKE LAWS, I MADE MISTAKES. AND I HAVE PAID FOR THEM."
BUT I DO NOT EXPECT TO BE FORGIVEN EASILY. I WISH TO PROVE MY GOOD INTENTIONS BY BRINGING IN SPIDER-MAN--LAWFULLY, THIS TIME--
--AND, BY DOING SO, TAKE A DANGEROUS MENACE OFF THE STREETS. NOT JUST ANY MENACE... BUT ONE WHO I HAVE DISCOVERED...
...IS A MUTANT.

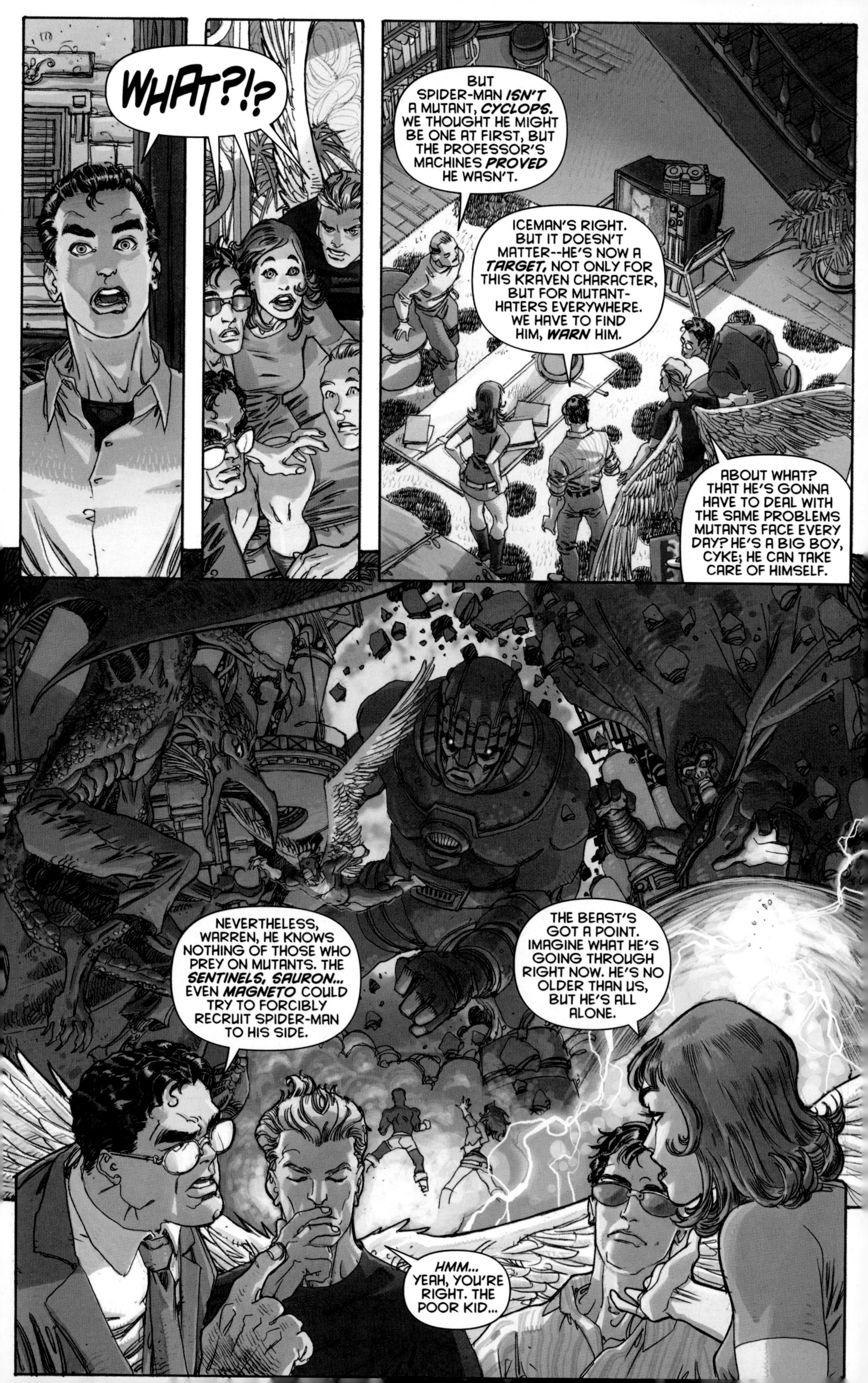
WHAT?!?
BUT SPIDER-MAN ISN'T A MUTANT, CYCLOPS. WE THOUGHT HE MIGHT BE ONE AT FIRST, BUT THE PROFESSOR'S MACHINES PROVED HE WASN'T.
ICEMAN'S RIGHT. BUT IT DOESN'T MATTER--HE'S NOW A TARGET, NOT ONLY FOR THIS KRAVEN CHARACTER, BUT FOR MUTANT-HATERS EVERYWHERE. WE HAVE TO FIND HIM, WARN HIM.
ABOUT WHAT? THAT HE'S GONNA HAVE TO DEAL WITH THE SAME PROBLEMS MUTANTS FACE EVERY DAY? HE'S A BIG BOY, CYKE; HE CAN TAKE CARE OF HIMSELF.
NEVERTHELESS, WARREN, HE KNOWS NOTHING OF THOSE WHO PREY ON MUTANTS. THE SENTINELS, SAURON... EVEN MAGNETO COULD TRY TO FORCIBLY RECRUIT SPIDER-MAN TO HIS SIDE.
THE BEAST'S GOT A POINT. IMAGINE WHAT HE'S GOING THROUGH RIGHT NOW. HE'S NO OLDER THAN US, BUT HE'S ALL ALONE.
HMM... YEAH, YOU'RE RIGHT. THE POOR KID...

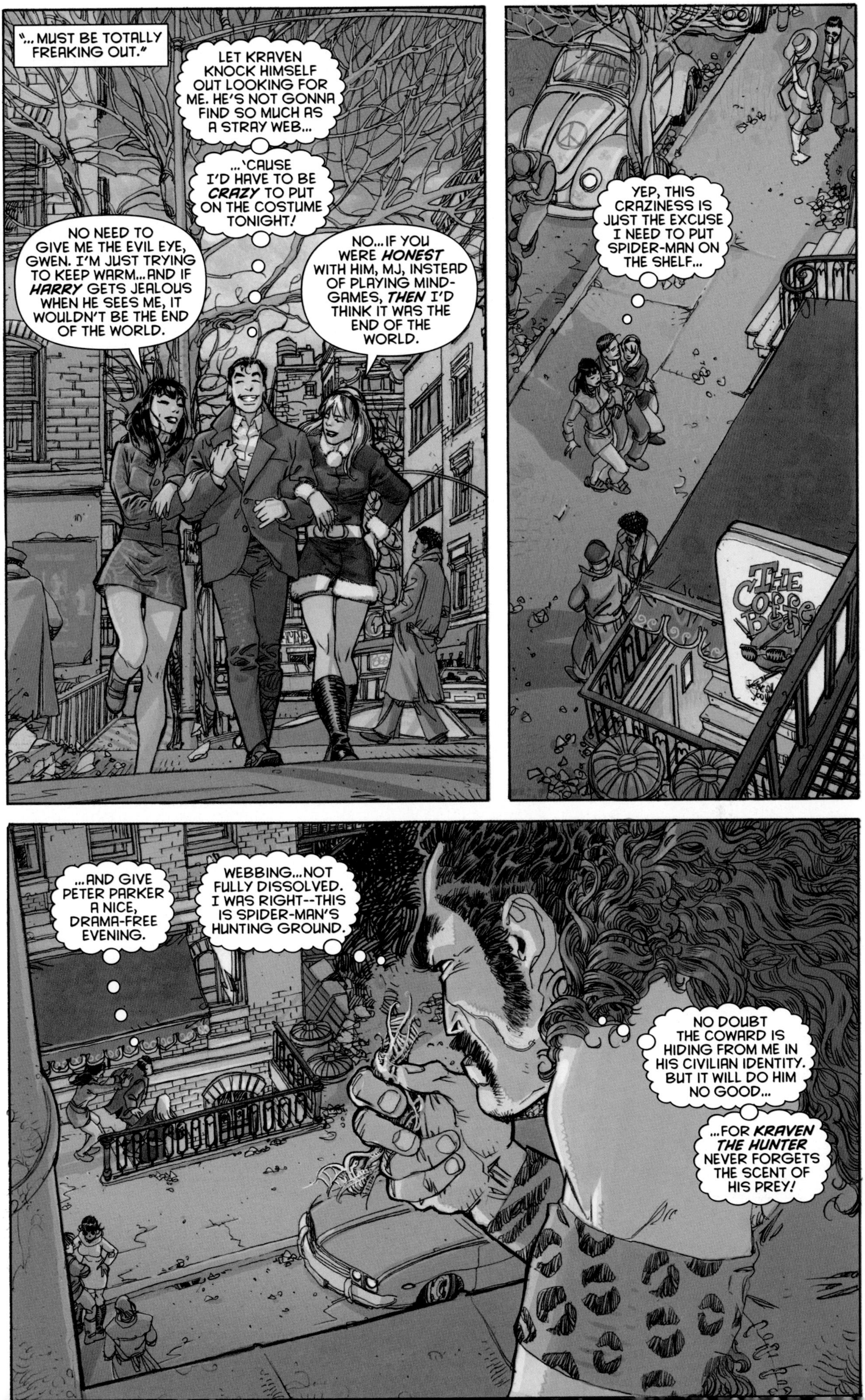
"...MUST BE TOTALLY FREAKING OUT."
LET KRAVEN KNOCK HIMSELF OUT LOOKING FOR ME. HE'S NOT GONNA FIND SO MUCH AS A STRAY WEB...
...'CAUSE I'D HAVE TO BE CRAZY TO PUT ON THE COSTUME TONIGHT!
NO NEED TO GIVE ME THE EVIL EYE, GWEN. I'M JUST TRYING TO KEEP WARM...AND IF HARRY GETS JEALOUS WHEN HE SEES ME, IT WOULDN'T BE THE END OF THE WORLD.
NO...IF YOU WERE HONEST WITH HIM, MJ, INSTEAD OF PLAYING MIND-GAMES, THEN I'D THINK IT WAS THE END OF THE WORLD.
YEP, THIS CRAZINESS IS JUST THE EXCUSE I NEED TO PUT SPIDER-MAN ON THE SHELF...
THE COFFEE BEAN
...AND GIVE PETER PARKER A NICE, DRAMA-FREE EVENING.
WEBBING...NOT FULLY DISSOLVED. I WAS RIGHT--THIS IS SPIDER-MAN'S HUNTING GROUND.
NO DOUBT THE COWARD IS HIDING FROM ME IN HIS CIVILIAN IDENTITY. BUT IT WILL DO HIM NO GOOD...
...FOR KRAVEN THE HUNTER NEVER FORGETS THE SCENT OF HIS PREY!

WHERE TO NOW, JEAN?

I...I'M NOT SURE.

THE PROFESSOR'S STILL TOO SICK TO FIND SPIDER-MAN, AND MY TELEPATHY ISN'T NEARLY AS PRECISE AS HIS.

I...FEEL LIKE HE'S SOMEWHERE IN THIS AREA, BUT I CAN'T PINPOINT HIM.

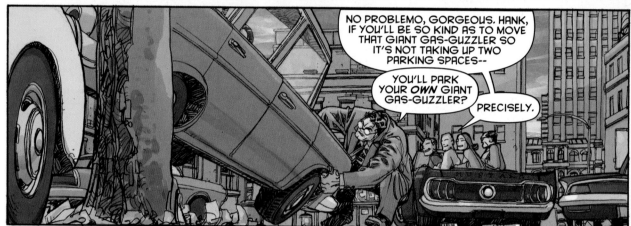

NO PROBLEMO, GORGEOUS. HANK, IF YOU'LL BE SO KIND AS TO MOVE THAT GIANT GAS-GUZZLER SO IT'S NOT TAKING UP TWO PARKING SPACES--

YOU'LL PARK YOUR OWN GIANT GAS-GUZZLER?

PRECISELY.

WHAT ARE YOU DOING, WARREN? WE HAVE TO FIND--

--SPIDER-MAN, I KNOW. BUT THINK ABOUT IT-- HE'S NOT SPIDER-MAN ALL THE TIME. WHEN HE TAKES OFF THE MASK, HE'S A GUY OUR AGE.

SO WE START CHECKING OUT HOT SPOTS FOR THE YOUTH OF AMERICA. MAYBE JEANIE'LL PICK UP A STRAY THOUGHT AND FIND OUR BOY.

IT'S NOT A BAD IDEA, SCOTT.

WELL...ALL RIGHT. BUT TRY TO BE INCONSPICUOUS.

INCONSPICUOUS? A RICH PLAYBOY, A MAN WITH RUBY-RED SUNGLASSES, A FELLOW BUILT LIKE A GORILLA AND A GORGEOUS REDHEAD?

McCOY, IN NEW YORK. NOBODY'LL LOOK TWICE.

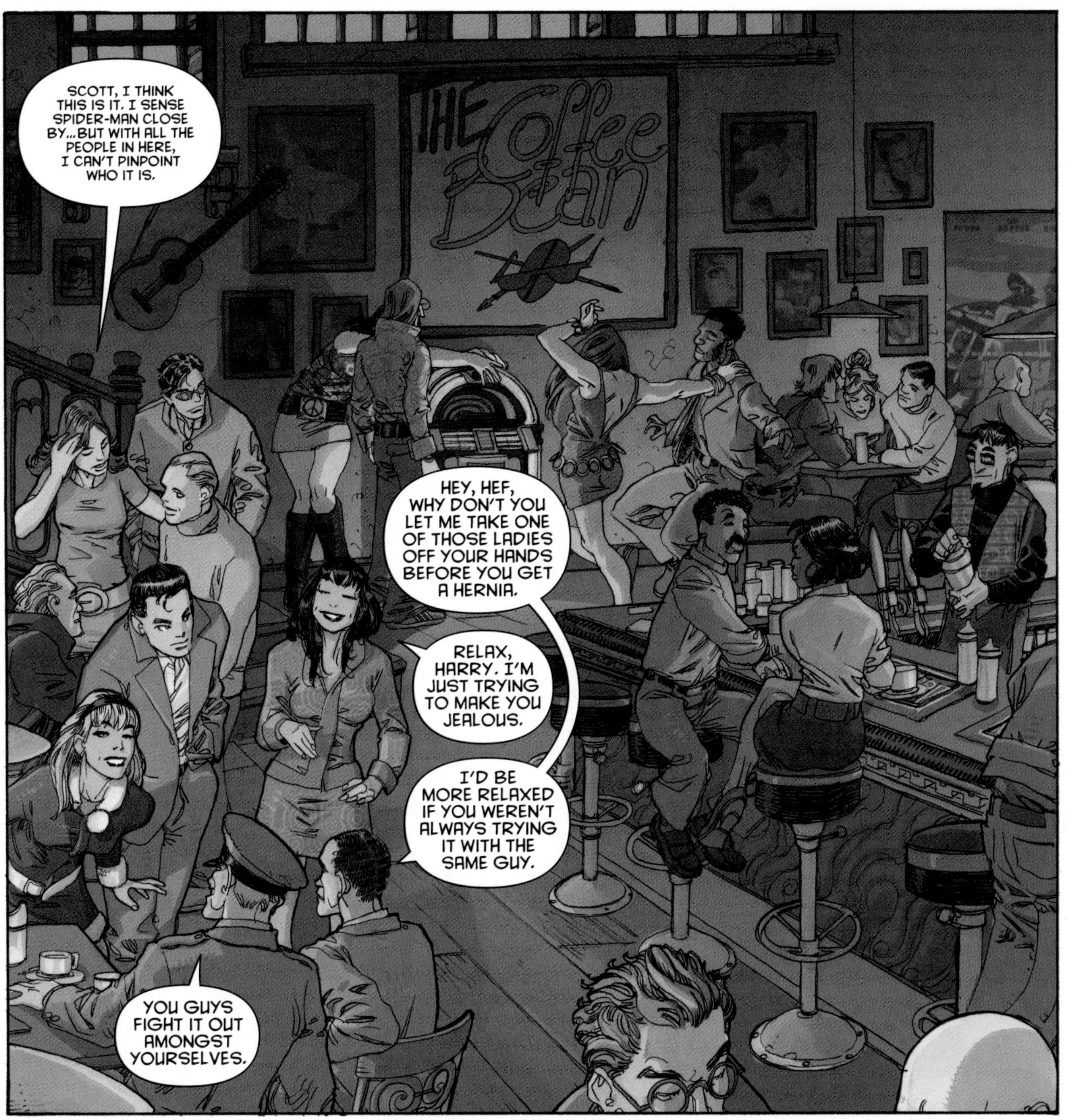
SCOTT, I THINK THIS IS IT. I SENSE SPIDER-MAN CLOSE BY...BUT WITH ALL THE PEOPLE IN HERE, I CAN'T PINPOINT WHO IT IS.
THE Coffee Bean
HEY, HEF, WHY DON'T YOU LET ME TAKE ONE OF THOSE LADIES OFF YOUR HANDS BEFORE YOU GET A HERNIA.
RELAX, HARRY. I'M JUST TRYING TO MAKE YOU JEALOUS.
I'D BE MORE RELAXED IF YOU WEREN'T ALWAYS TRYING IT WITH THE SAME GUY.
YOU GUYS FIGHT IT OUT AMONGST YOURSELVES.

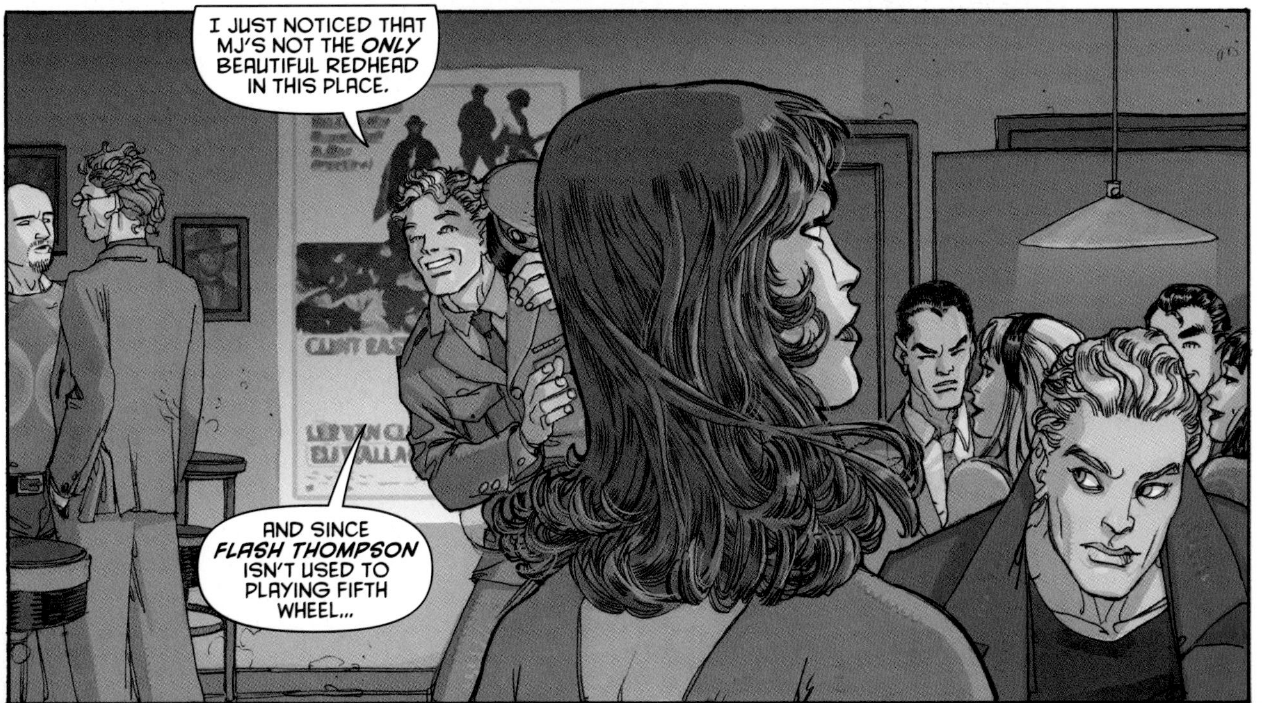
I JUST NOTICED THAT MJ'S NOT THE *ONLY* BEAUTIFUL REDHEAD IN THIS PLACE.
AND SINCE *FLASH THOMPSON* ISN'T USED TO PLAYING FIFTH WHEEL...

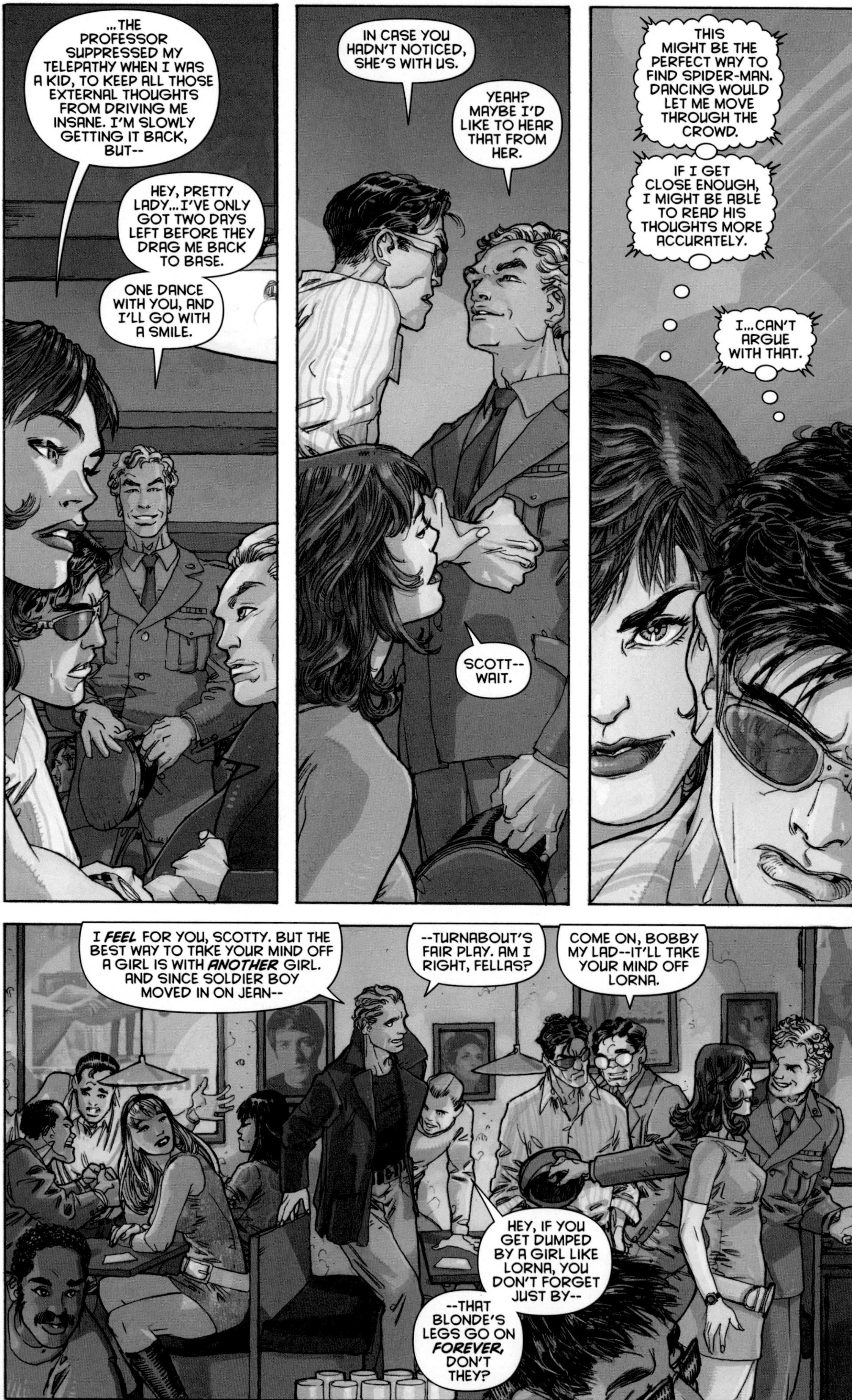
...THE PROFESSOR SUPPRESSED MY TELEPATHY WHEN I WAS A KID, TO KEEP ALL THOSE EXTERNAL THOUGHTS FROM DRIVING ME INSANE. I'M SLOWLY GETTING IT BACK, BUT--
HEY, PRETTY LADY...I'VE ONLY GOT TWO DAYS LEFT BEFORE THEY DRAG ME BACK TO BASE.
ONE DANCE WITH YOU, AND I'LL GO WITH A SMILE.
IN CASE YOU HADN'T NOTICED, SHE'S WITH US.
YEAH? MAYBE I'D LIKE TO HEAR THAT FROM HER.
SCOTT-- WAIT.
THIS MIGHT BE THE PERFECT WAY TO FIND SPIDER-MAN. DANCING WOULD LET ME MOVE THROUGH THE CROWD.
IF I GET CLOSE ENOUGH, I MIGHT BE ABLE TO READ HIS THOUGHTS MORE ACCURATELY.
I...CAN'T ARGUE WITH THAT.
I FEEL FOR YOU, SCOTTY. BUT THE BEST WAY TO TAKE YOUR MIND OFF A GIRL IS WITH ANOTHER GIRL. AND SINCE SOLDIER BOY MOVED IN ON JEAN--
--TURNABOUT'S FAIR PLAY. AM I RIGHT, FELLAS?
COME ON, BOBBY MY LAD--IT'LL TAKE YOUR MIND OFF LORNA.
HEY, IF YOU GET DUMPED BY A GIRL LIKE LORNA, YOU DON'T FORGET JUST BY--
--THAT BLONDE'S LEGS GO ON FOREVER, DON'T THEY?

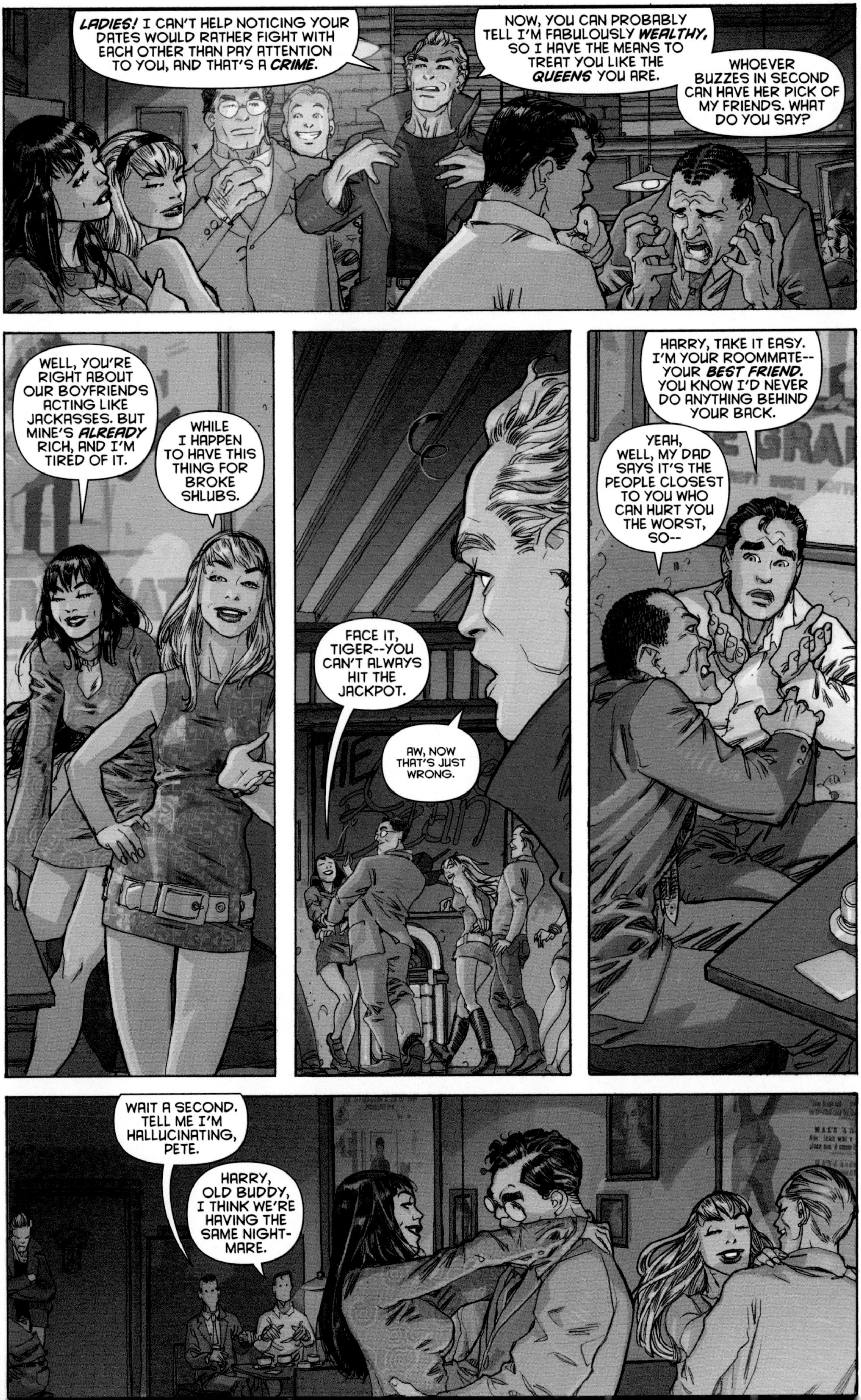
LADIES! I CAN'T HELP NOTICING YOUR DATES WOULD RATHER FIGHT WITH EACH OTHER THAN PAY ATTENTION TO YOU, AND THAT'S A CRIME.
NOW, YOU CAN PROBABLY TELL I'M FABULOUSLY WEALTHY, SO I HAVE THE MEANS TO TREAT YOU LIKE THE QUEENS YOU ARE.
WHOEVER BUZZES IN SECOND CAN HAVE HER PICK OF MY FRIENDS. WHAT DO YOU SAY?
WELL, YOU'RE RIGHT ABOUT OUR BOYFRIENDS ACTING LIKE JACKASSES. BUT MINE'S ALREADY RICH, AND I'M TIRED OF IT.
WHILE I HAPPEN TO HAVE THIS THING FOR BROKE SHLUBS.
FACE IT, TIGER--YOU CAN'T ALWAYS HIT THE JACKPOT.
AW, NOW THAT'S JUST WRONG.
HARRY, TAKE IT EASY. I'M YOUR ROOMMATE-- YOUR BEST FRIEND. YOU KNOW I'D NEVER DO ANYTHING BEHIND YOUR BACK.
YEAH, WELL, MY DAD SAYS IT'S THE PEOPLE CLOSEST TO YOU WHO CAN HURT YOU THE WORST, SO--
WAIT A SECOND. TELL ME I'M HALLUCINATING, PETE.
HARRY, OLD BUDDY, I THINK WE'RE HAVING THE SAME NIGHT-MARE.

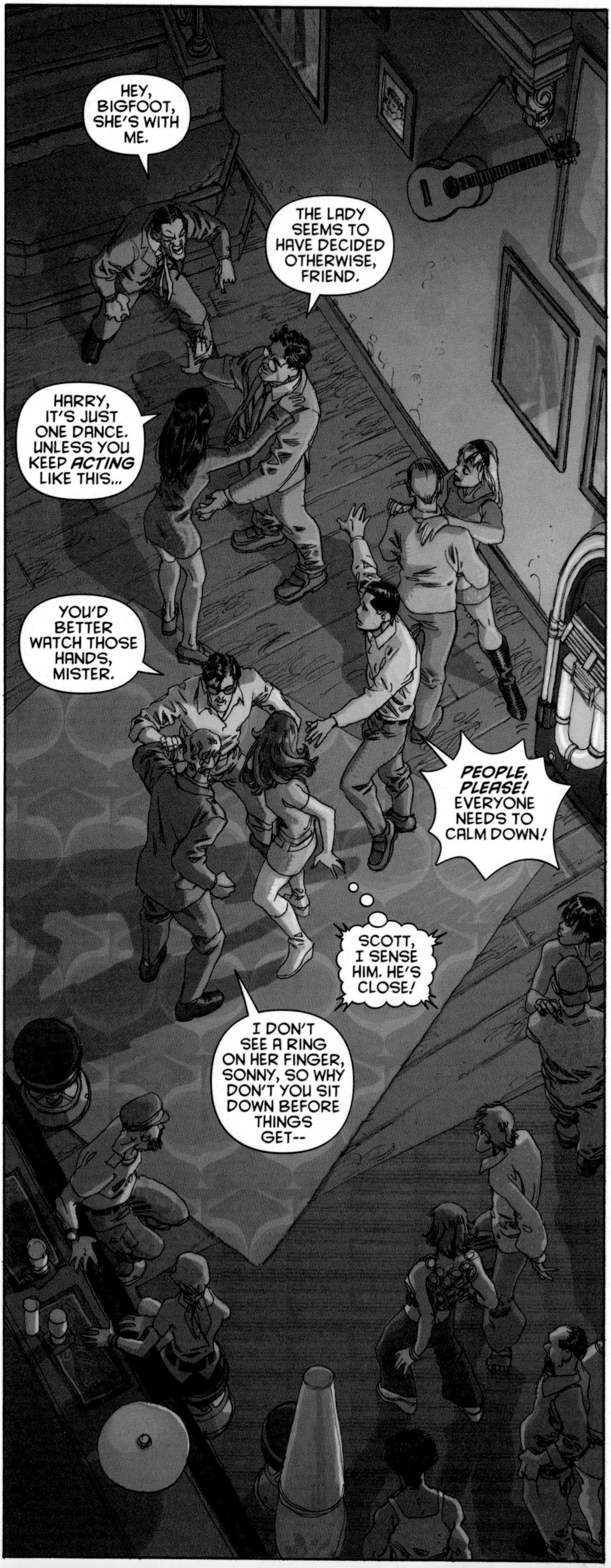
HEY, BIGFOOT, SHE'S WITH ME.
THE LADY SEEMS TO HAVE DECIDED OTHERWISE, FRIEND.
HARRY, IT'S JUST ONE DANCE. UNLESS YOU KEEP *ACTING* LIKE THIS...
YOU'D BETTER WATCH THOSE HANDS, MISTER.
PEOPLE, PLEASE! EVERYONE NEEDS TO CALM DOWN!
SCOTT, I SENSE HIM. HE'S CLOSE!
I DON'T SEE A RING ON HER FINGER, SONNY, SO WHY DON'T YOU SIT DOWN BEFORE THINGS GET--

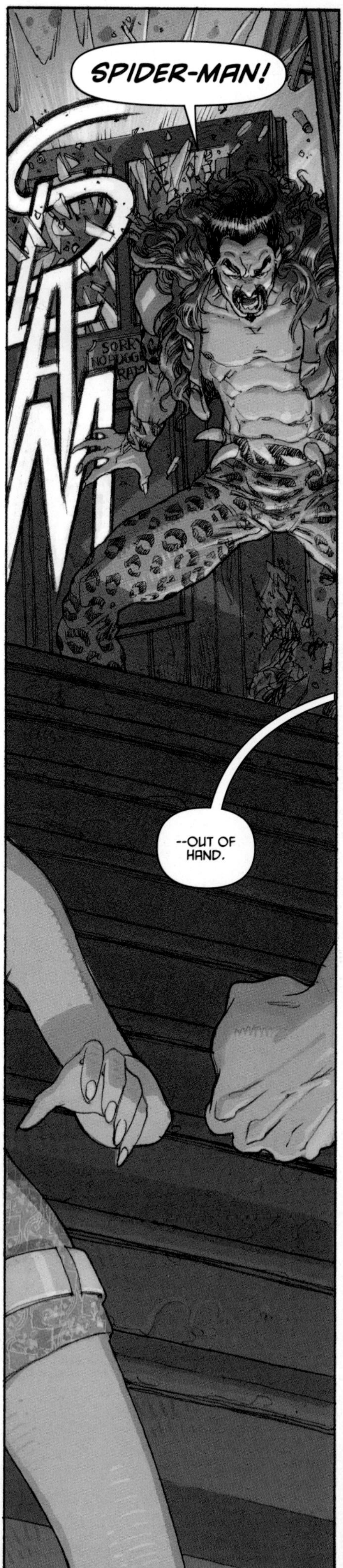
SPIDER-MAN!
--OUT OF HAND.

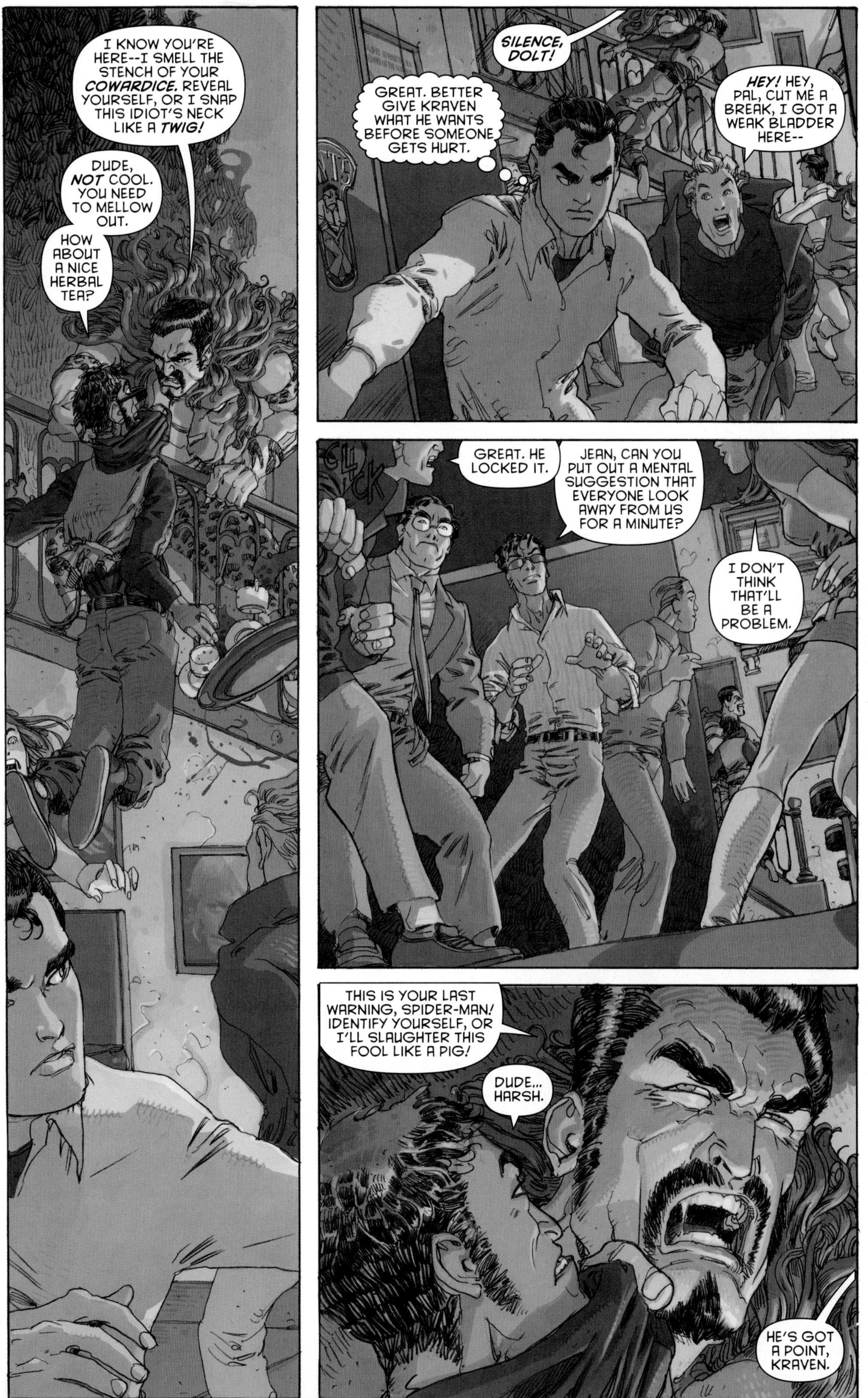
I KNOW YOU'RE HERE--I SMELL THE STENCH OF YOUR COWARDICE. REVEAL YOURSELF, OR I SNAP THIS IDIOT'S NECK LIKE A TWIG!
DUDE, NOT COOL. YOU NEED TO MELLOW OUT.
HOW ABOUT A NICE HERBAL TEA?
SILENCE, DOLT!
GREAT. BETTER GIVE KRAVEN WHAT HE WANTS BEFORE SOMEONE GETS HURT.
HEY! HEY, PAL, CUT ME A BREAK, I GOT A WEAK BLADDER HERE--
GREAT. HE LOCKED IT.
JEAN, CAN YOU PUT OUT A MENTAL SUGGESTION THAT EVERYONE LOOK AWAY FROM US FOR A MINUTE?
I DON'T THINK THAT'LL BE A PROBLEM.
THIS IS YOUR LAST WARNING, SPIDER-MAN! IDENTIFY YOURSELF, OR I'LL SLAUGHTER THIS FOOL LIKE A PIG!
DUDE... HARSH.
HE'S GOT A POINT, KRAVEN.

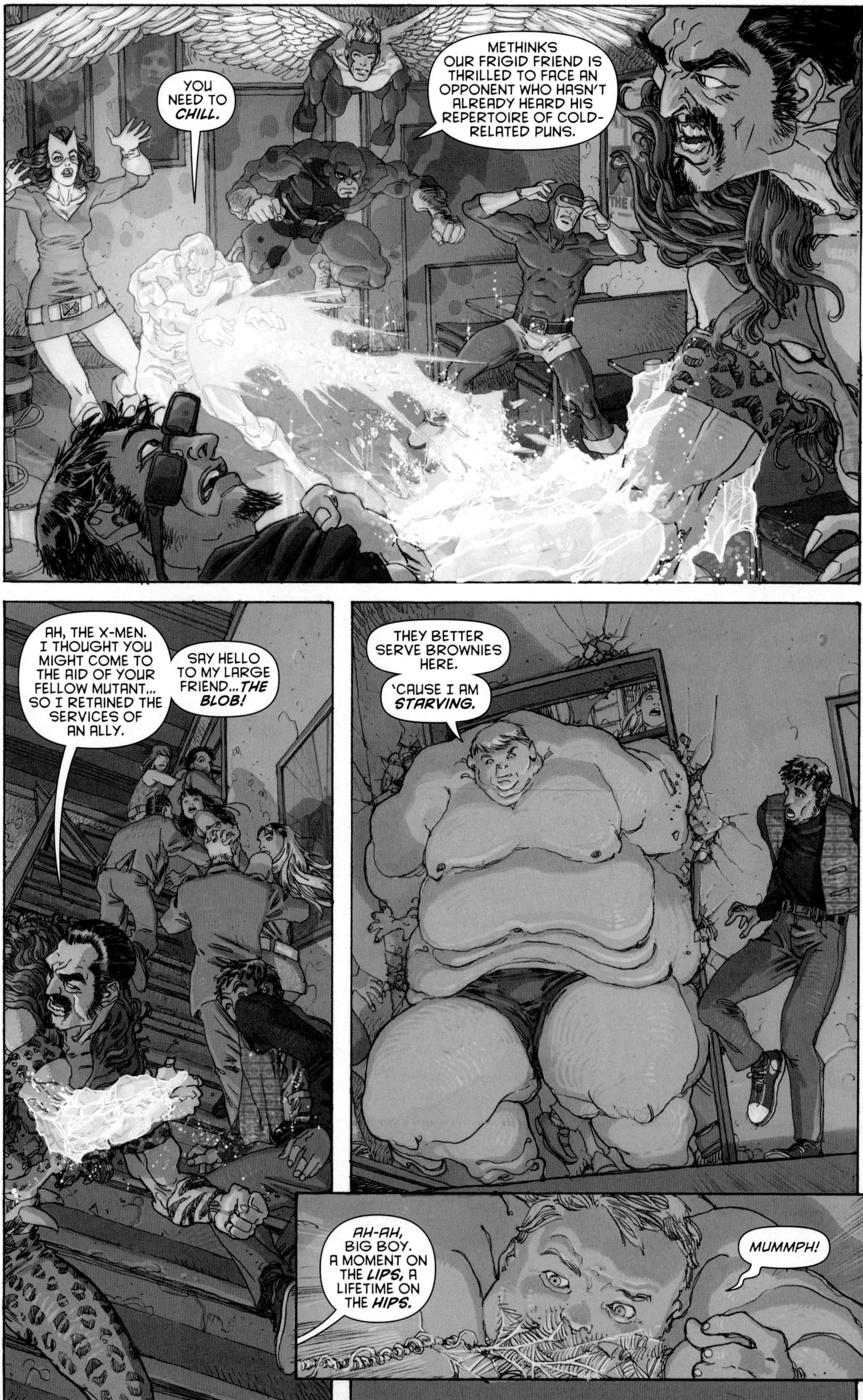
YOU NEED TO CHILL.
METHINKS OUR FRIGID FRIEND IS THRILLED TO FACE AN OPPONENT WHO HASN'T ALREADY HEARD HIS REPERTOIRE OF COLD-RELATED PUNS.
AH, THE X-MEN. I THOUGHT YOU MIGHT COME TO THE AID OF YOUR FELLOW MUTANT... SO I RETAINED THE SERVICES OF AN ALLY.
SAY HELLO TO MY LARGE FRIEND...THE BLOB!
THEY BETTER SERVE BROWNIES HERE.
'CAUSE I AM STARVING.
AH-AH, BIG BOY. A MOMENT ON THE LIPS, A LIFETIME ON THE HIPS.
MUMMPH!

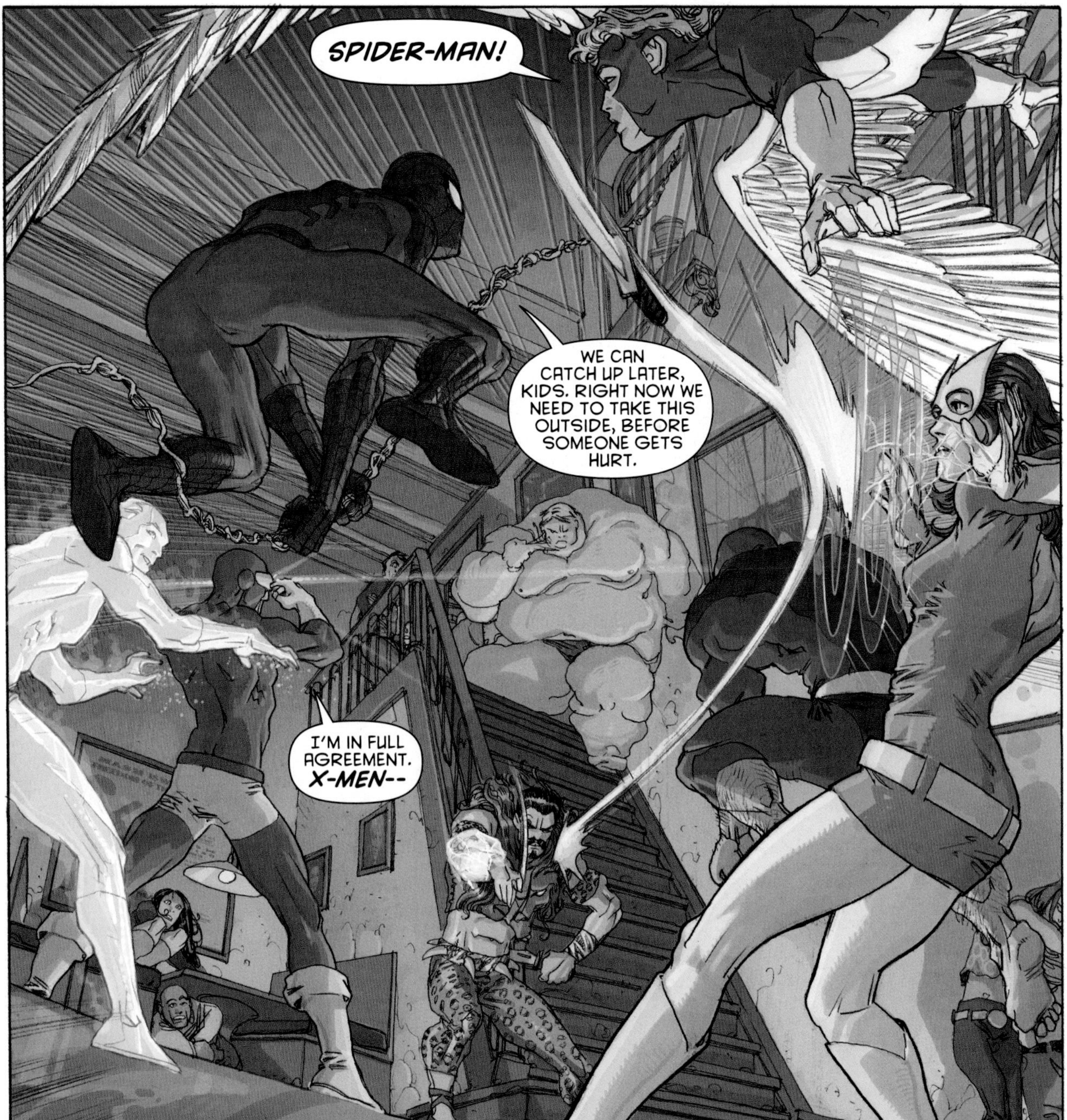
SPIDER-MAN!
WE CAN CATCH UP LATER, KIDS. RIGHT NOW WE NEED TO TAKE THIS OUTSIDE, BEFORE SOMEONE GETS HURT.
I'M IN FULL AGREEMENT. X-MEN--

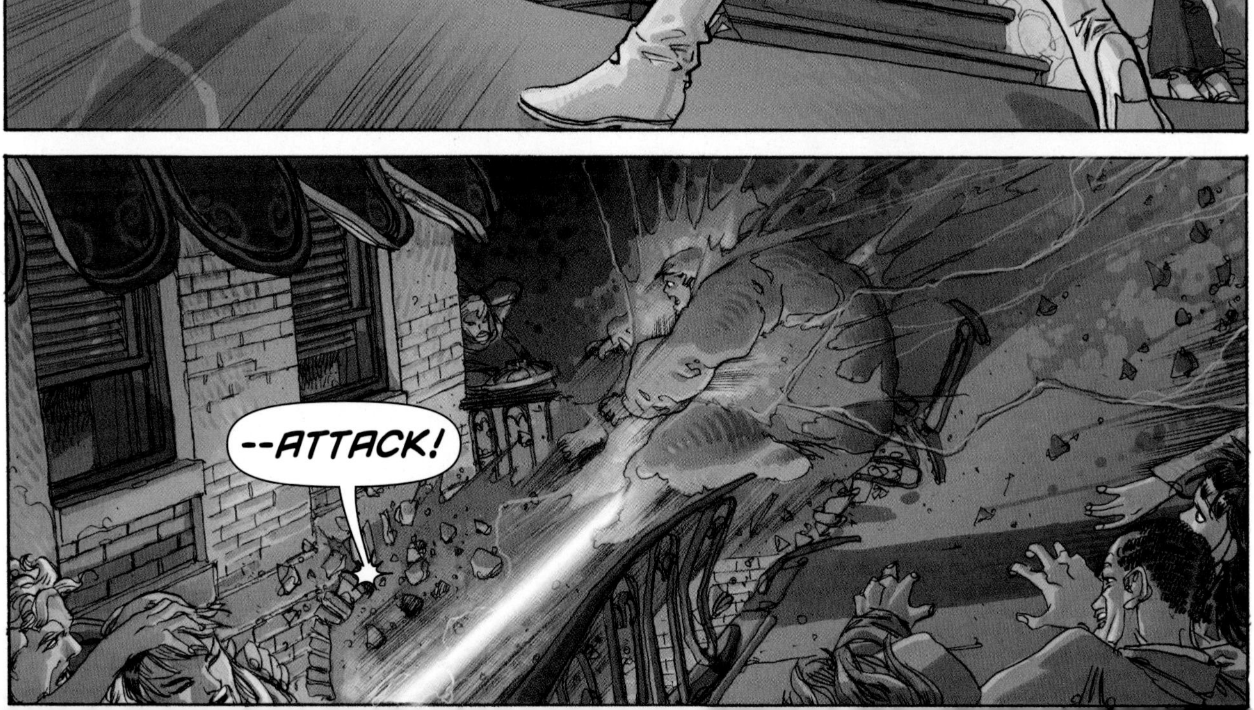
--ATTACK!

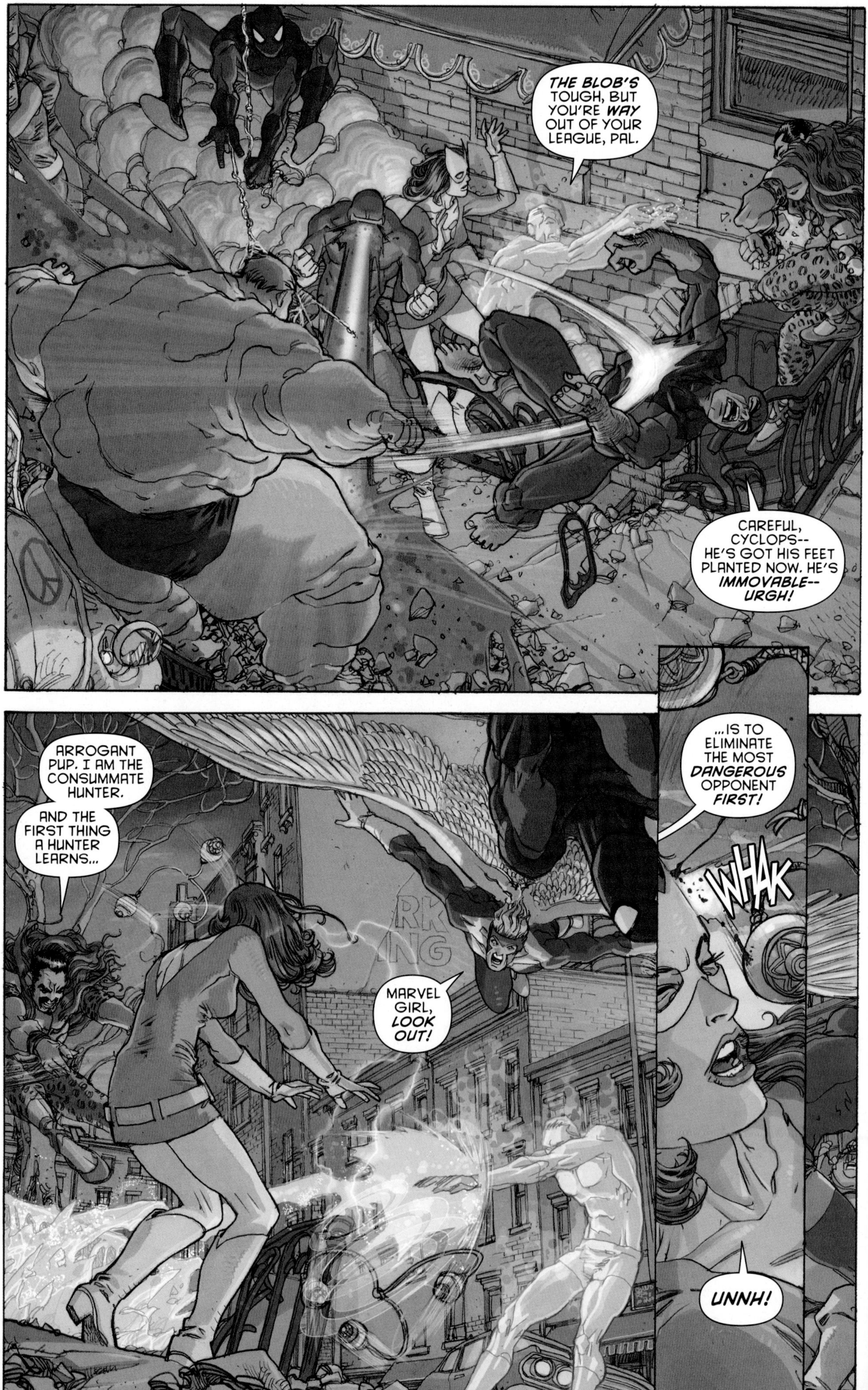
THE BLOB'S TOUGH, BUT YOU'RE WAY OUT OF YOUR LEAGUE, PAL.
CAREFUL, CYCLOPS-- HE'S GOT HIS FEET PLANTED NOW. HE'S IMMOVABLE-- URGH!
ARROGANT PUP. I AM THE CONSUMMATE HUNTER.
AND THE FIRST THING A HUNTER LEARNS...
...IS TO ELIMINATE THE MOST DANGEROUS OPPONENT FIRST!
WHAK
MARVEL GIRL, LOOK OUT!
UNNH!

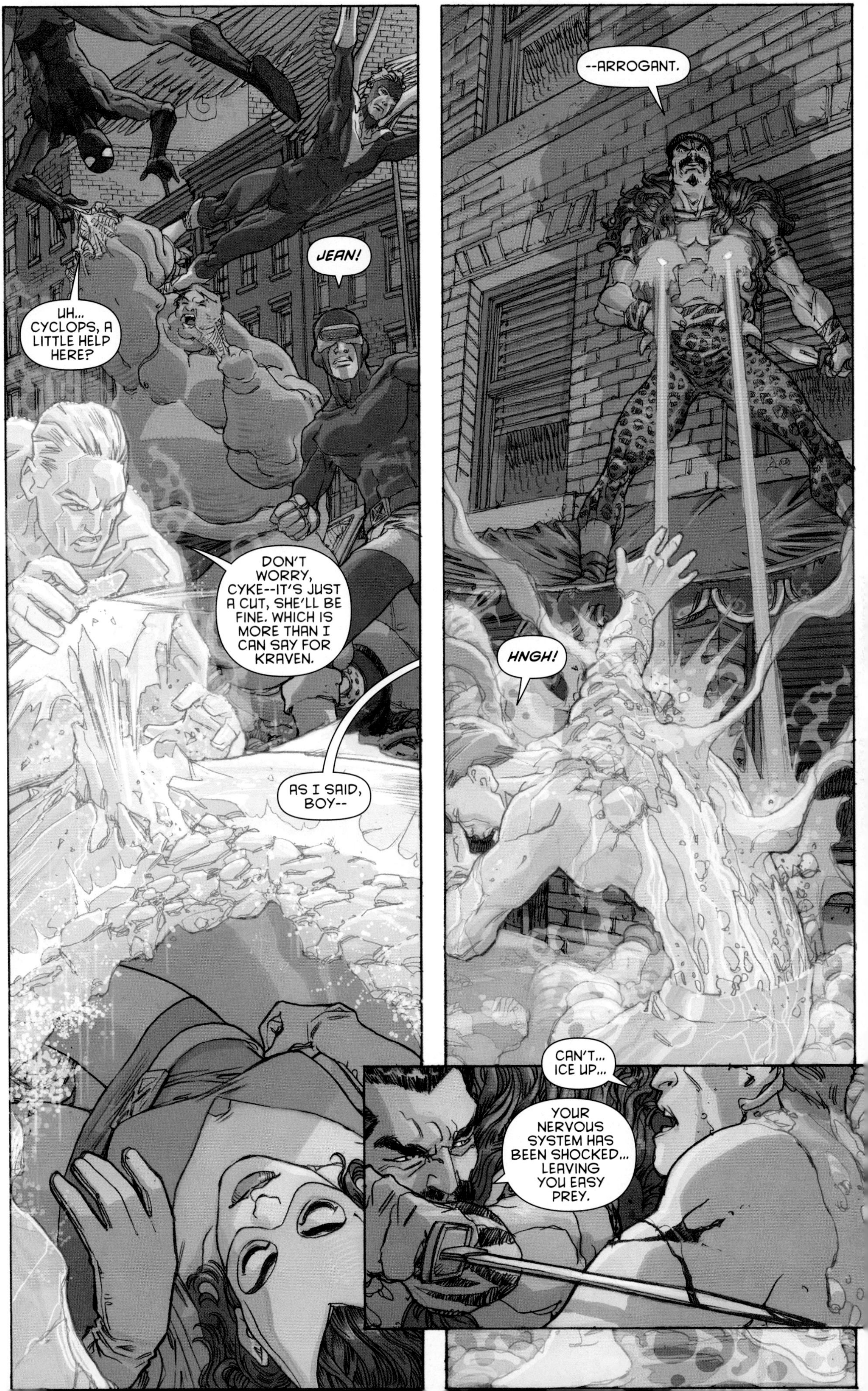
JEAN!
UH... CYCLOPS, A LITTLE HELP HERE?
DON'T WORRY, CYKE--IT'S JUST A CUT, SHE'LL BE FINE. WHICH IS MORE THAN I CAN SAY FOR KRAVEN.
AS I SAID, BOY--
--ARROGANT.
HNGH!
CAN'T... ICE UP...
YOUR NERVOUS SYSTEM HAS BEEN SHOCKED... LEAVING YOU EASY PREY.

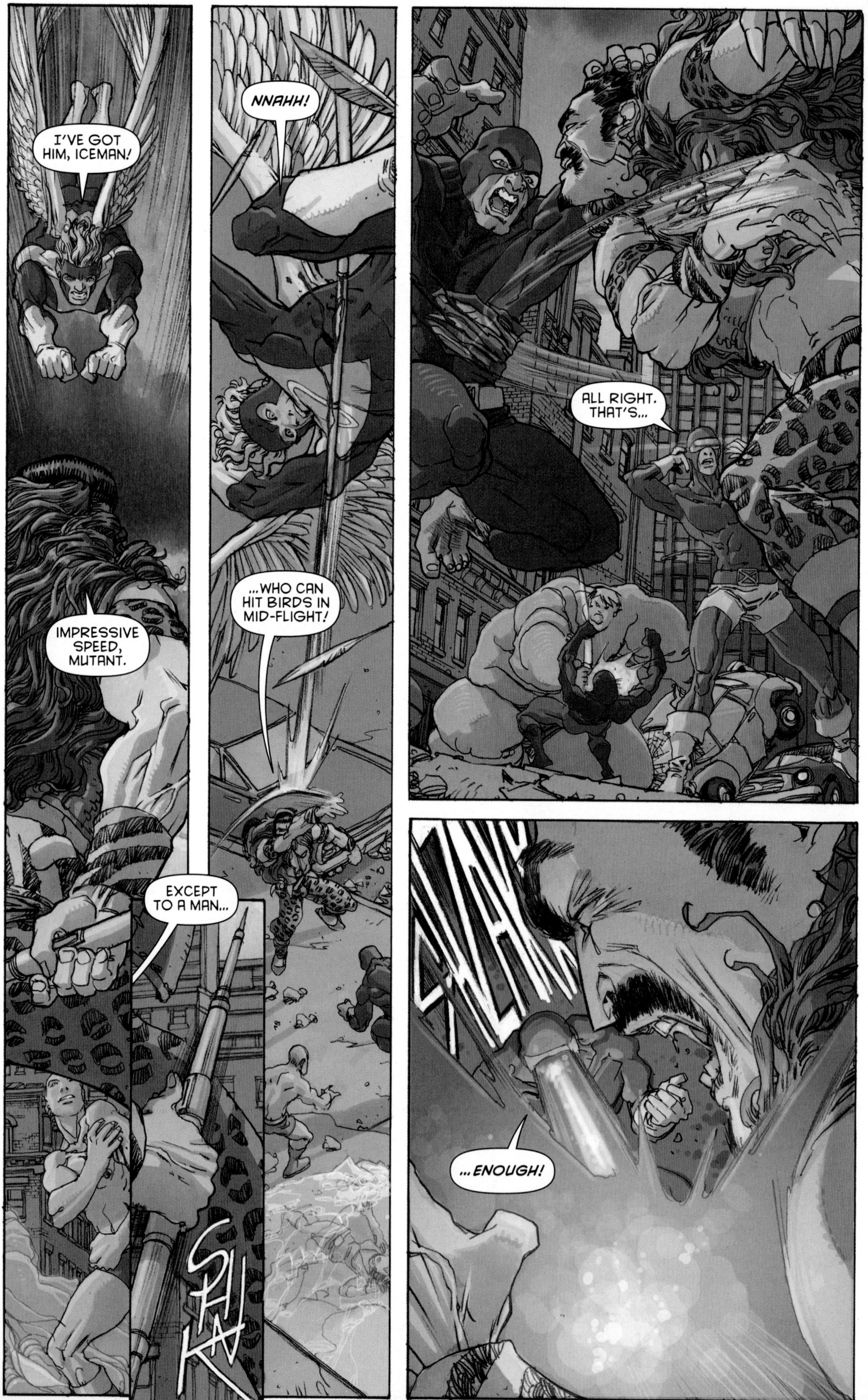
I'VE GOT HIM, ICEMAN!
IMPRESSIVE SPEED, MUTANT.
EXCEPT TO A MAN...
NNAHH!
...WHO CAN HIT BIRDS IN MID-FLIGHT!
ALL RIGHT. THAT'S...
...ENOUGH!

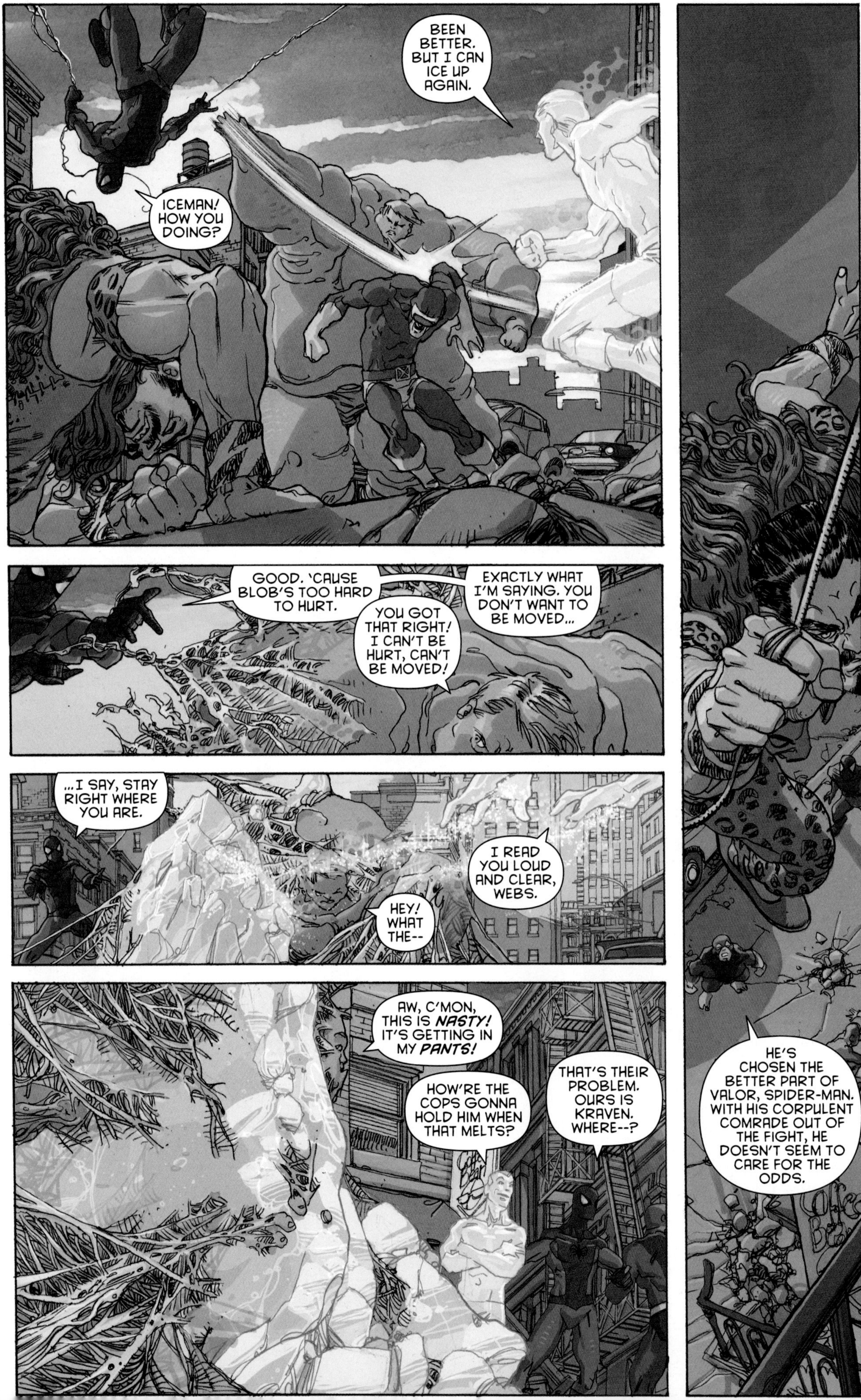
BEEN BETTER. BUT I CAN ICE UP AGAIN.
ICEMAN! HOW YOU DOING?
GOOD. 'CAUSE BLOB'S TOO HARD TO HURT.
YOU GOT THAT RIGHT! I CAN'T BE HURT, CAN'T BE MOVED!
EXACTLY WHAT I'M SAYING. YOU DON'T WANT TO BE MOVED...
...I SAY, STAY RIGHT WHERE YOU ARE.
I READ YOU LOUD AND CLEAR, WEBS.
HEY! WHAT THE--
AW, C'MON, THIS IS NASTY! IT'S GETTING IN MY PANTS!
HOW'RE THE COPS GONNA HOLD HIM WHEN THAT MELTS?
THAT'S THEIR PROBLEM. OURS IS KRAVEN. WHERE--?
HE'S CHOSEN THE BETTER PART OF VALOR, SPIDER-MAN. WITH HIS CORPULENT COMRADE OUT OF THE FIGHT, HE DOESN'T SEEM TO CARE FOR THE ODDS.

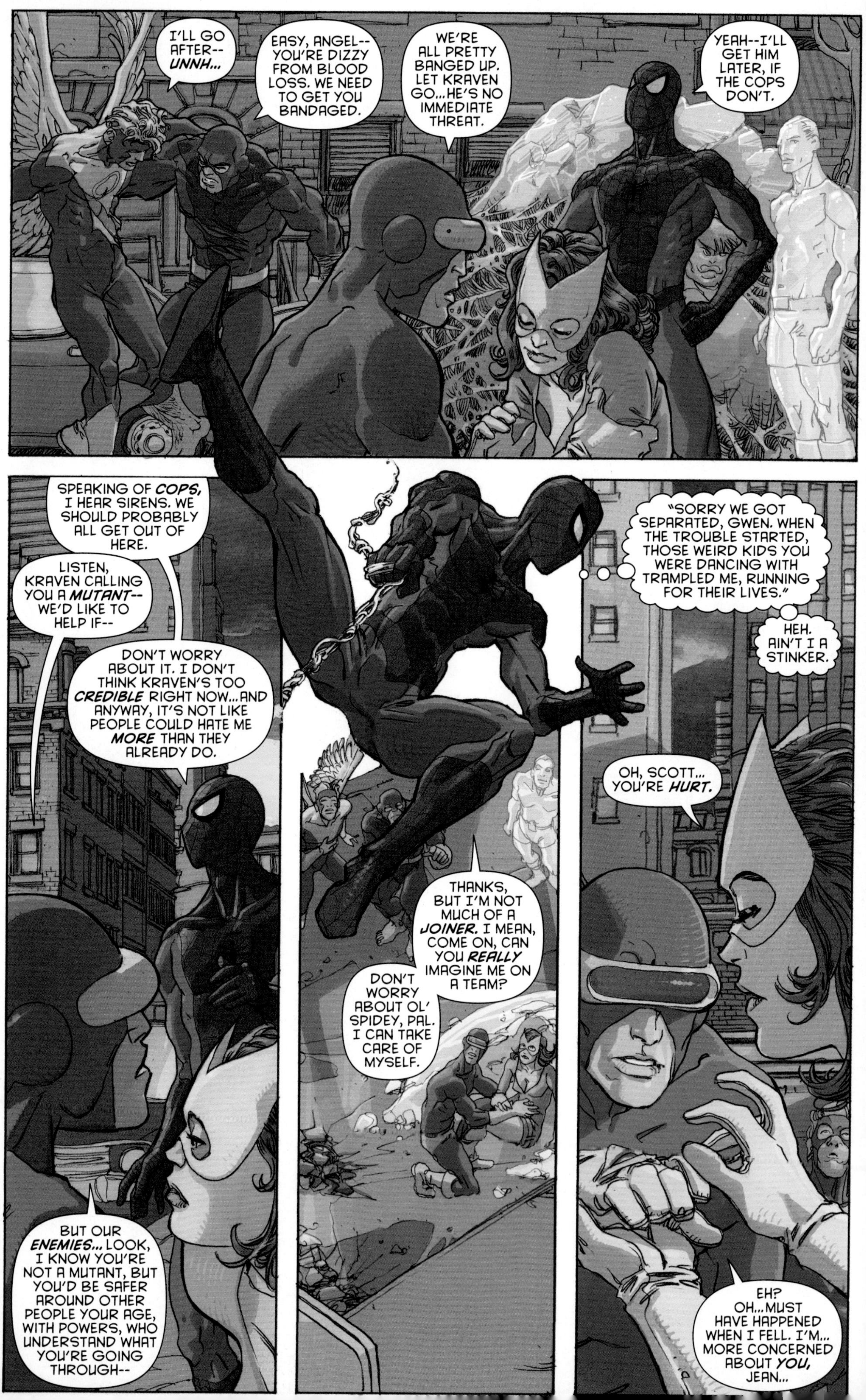

I'LL GO AFTER-- UNNH...
EASY, ANGEL-- YOU'RE DIZZY FROM BLOOD LOSS. WE NEED TO GET YOU BANDAGED.
WE'RE ALL PRETTY BANGED UP. LET KRAVEN GO... HE'S NO IMMEDIATE THREAT.
YEAH--I'LL GET HIM LATER, IF THE COPS DON'T.
SPEAKING OF COPS, I HEAR SIRENS. WE SHOULD PROBABLY ALL GET OUT OF HERE.
LISTEN, KRAVEN CALLING YOU A MUTANT-- WE'D LIKE TO HELP IF--
DON'T WORRY ABOUT IT. I DON'T THINK KRAVEN'S TOO CREDIBLE RIGHT NOW... AND ANYWAY, IT'S NOT LIKE PEOPLE COULD HATE ME MORE THAN THEY ALREADY DO.
BUT OUR ENEMIES... LOOK, I KNOW YOU'RE NOT A MUTANT, BUT YOU'D BE SAFER AROUND OTHER PEOPLE YOUR AGE, WITH POWERS, WHO UNDERSTAND WHAT YOU'RE GOING THROUGH--
THANKS, BUT I'M NOT MUCH OF A JOINER. I MEAN, COME ON, CAN YOU REALLY IMAGINE ME ON A TEAM?
DON'T WORRY ABOUT OL' SPIDEY, PAL. I CAN TAKE CARE OF MYSELF.
"SORRY WE GOT SEPARATED, GWEN. WHEN THE TROUBLE STARTED, THOSE WEIRD KIDS YOU WERE DANCING WITH TRAMPLED ME, RUNNING FOR THEIR LIVES."
HEH. AIN'T I A STINKER.
OH, SCOTT... YOU'RE HURT.
EH? OH... MUST HAVE HAPPENED WHEN I FELL. I'M... MORE CONCERNED ABOUT YOU, JEAN...

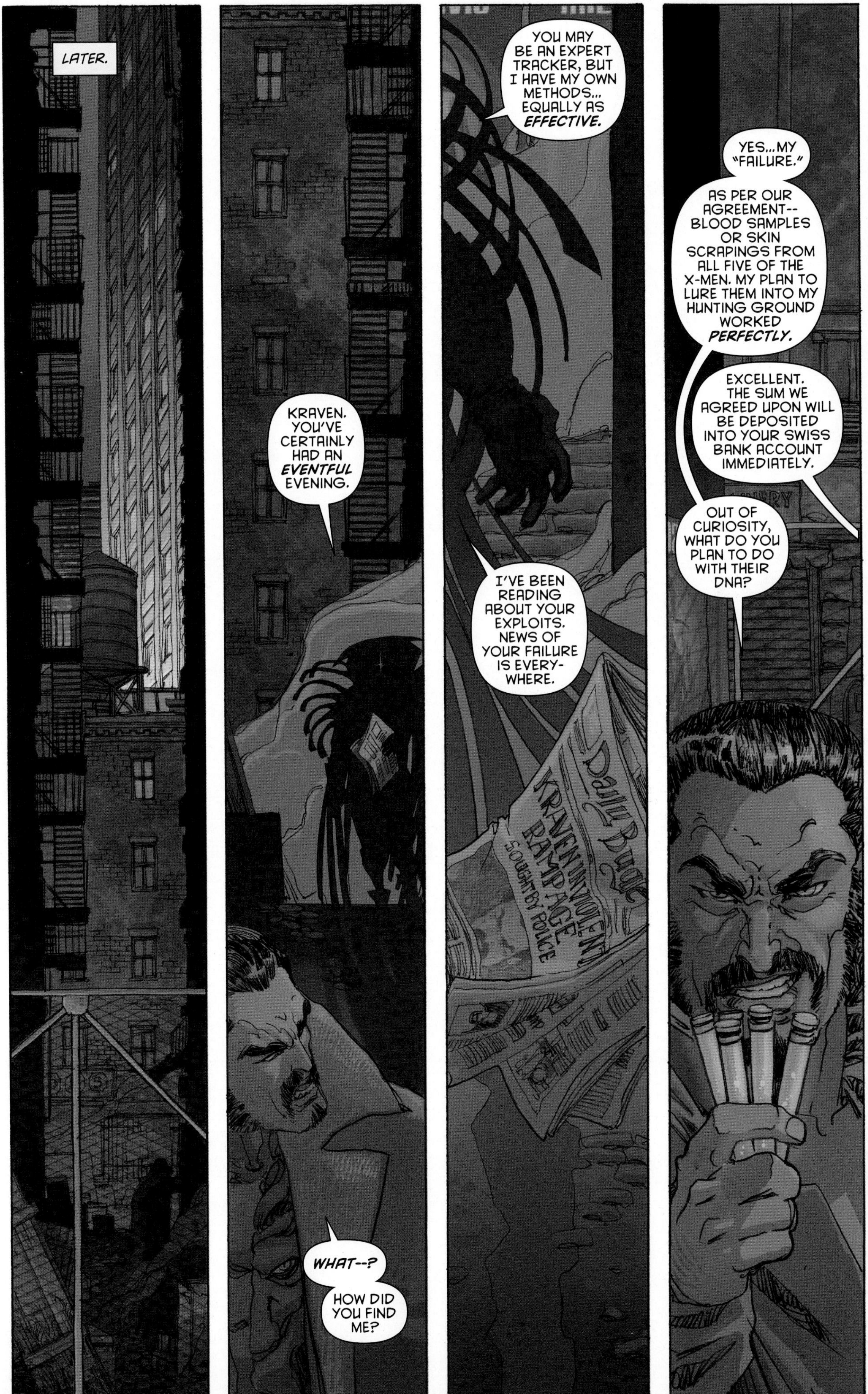
LATER.
KRAVEN. YOU'VE CERTAINLY HAD AN *EVENTFUL* EVENING.
WHAT--?
HOW DID YOU FIND ME?
YOU MAY BE AN EXPERT TRACKER, BUT I HAVE MY OWN METHODS... EQUALLY AS *EFFECTIVE.*
I'VE BEEN READING ABOUT YOUR EXPLOITS. NEWS OF YOUR FAILURE IS EVERY-WHERE.
Daily Bugle
KRAVEN IN VIOLENT RAMPAGE
SOUGHT BY POLICE
YES...MY "FAILURE."
AS PER OUR AGREEMENT-- BLOOD SAMPLES OR SKIN SCRAPINGS FROM ALL FIVE OF THE X-MEN. MY PLAN TO LURE THEM INTO MY HUNTING GROUND WORKED *PERFECTLY.*
EXCELLENT. THE SUM WE AGREED UPON WILL BE DEPOSITED INTO YOUR SWISS BANK ACCOUNT IMMEDIATELY.
OUT OF CURIOSITY, WHAT DO YOU PLAN TO DO WITH THEIR DNA?

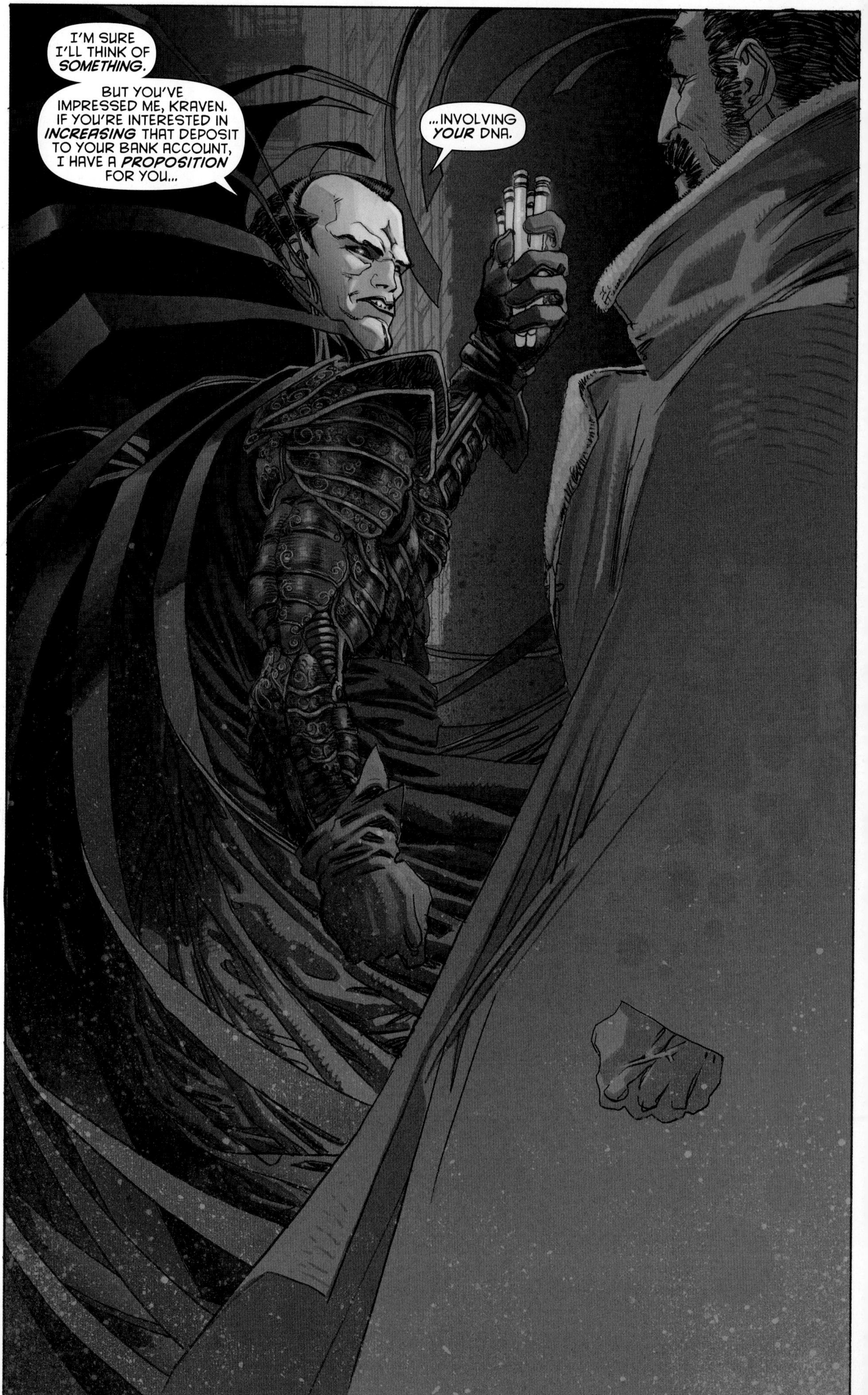
I'M SURE I'LL THINK OF *SOMETHING*.
BUT YOU'VE IMPRESSED ME, KRAVEN. IF YOU'RE INTERESTED IN *INCREASING* THAT DEPOSIT TO YOUR BANK ACCOUNT, I HAVE A *PROPOSITION* FOR YOU...
...INVOLVING *YOUR* DNA.

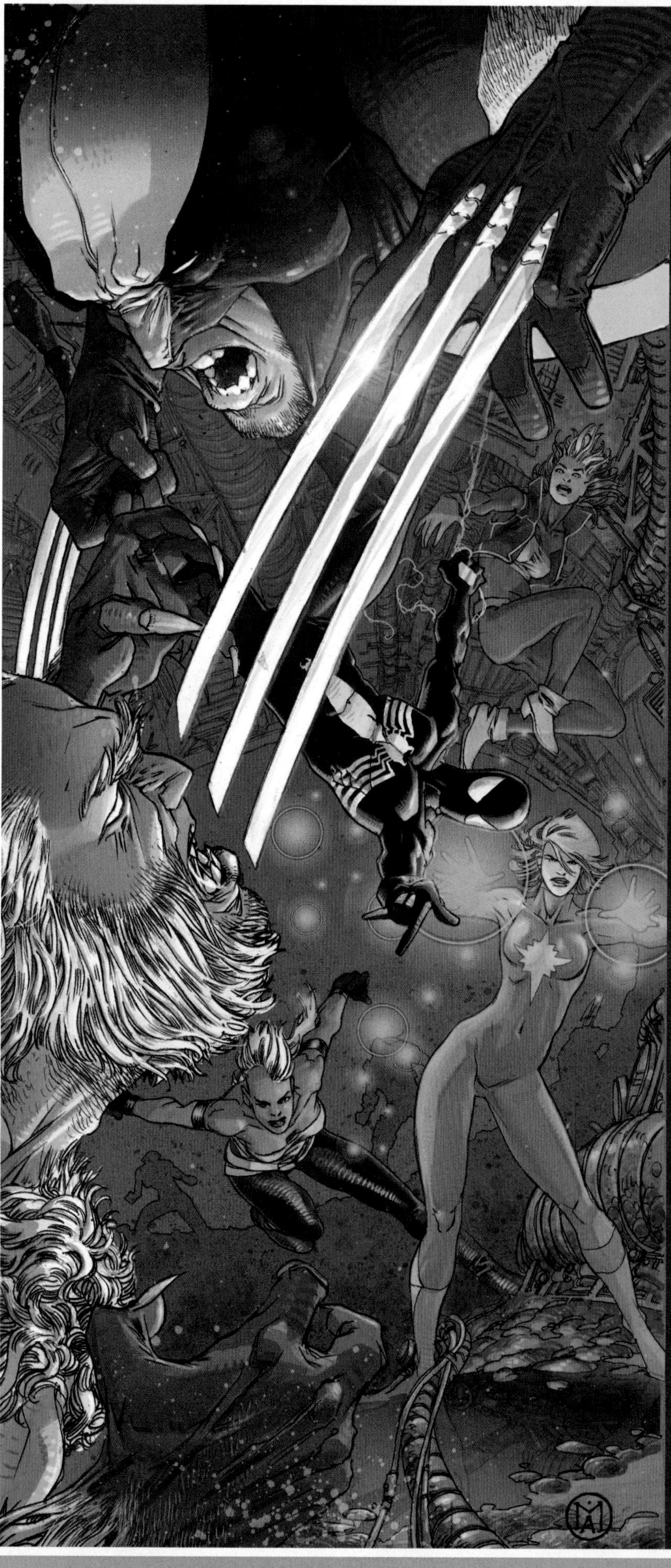

TWO

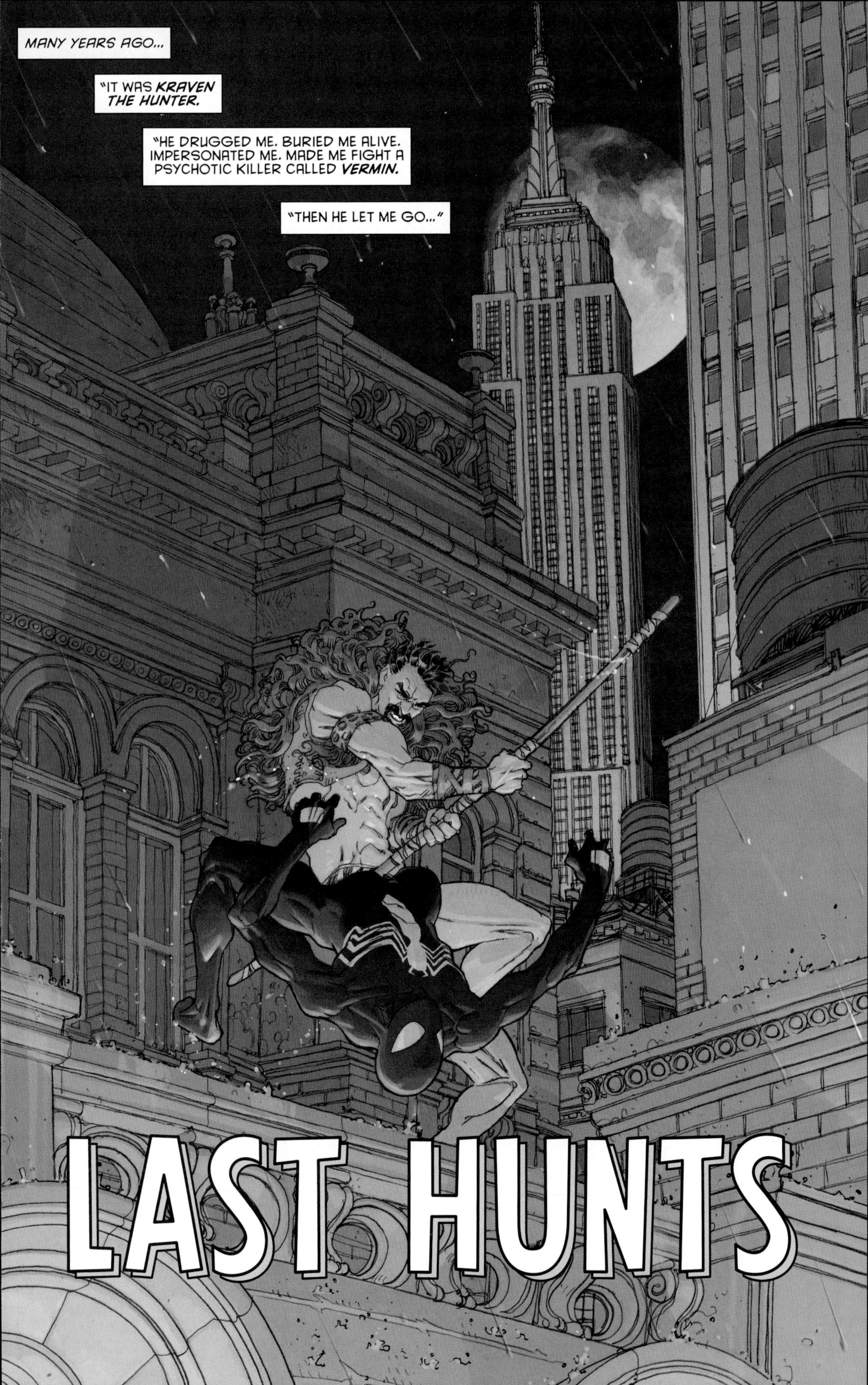
MANY YEARS AGO...
"IT WAS KRAVEN THE HUNTER.
"HE DRUGGED ME. BURIED ME ALIVE. IMPERSONATED ME. MADE ME FIGHT A PSYCHOTIC KILLER CALLED VERMIN.
"THEN HE LET ME GO..."
LAST HUNTS

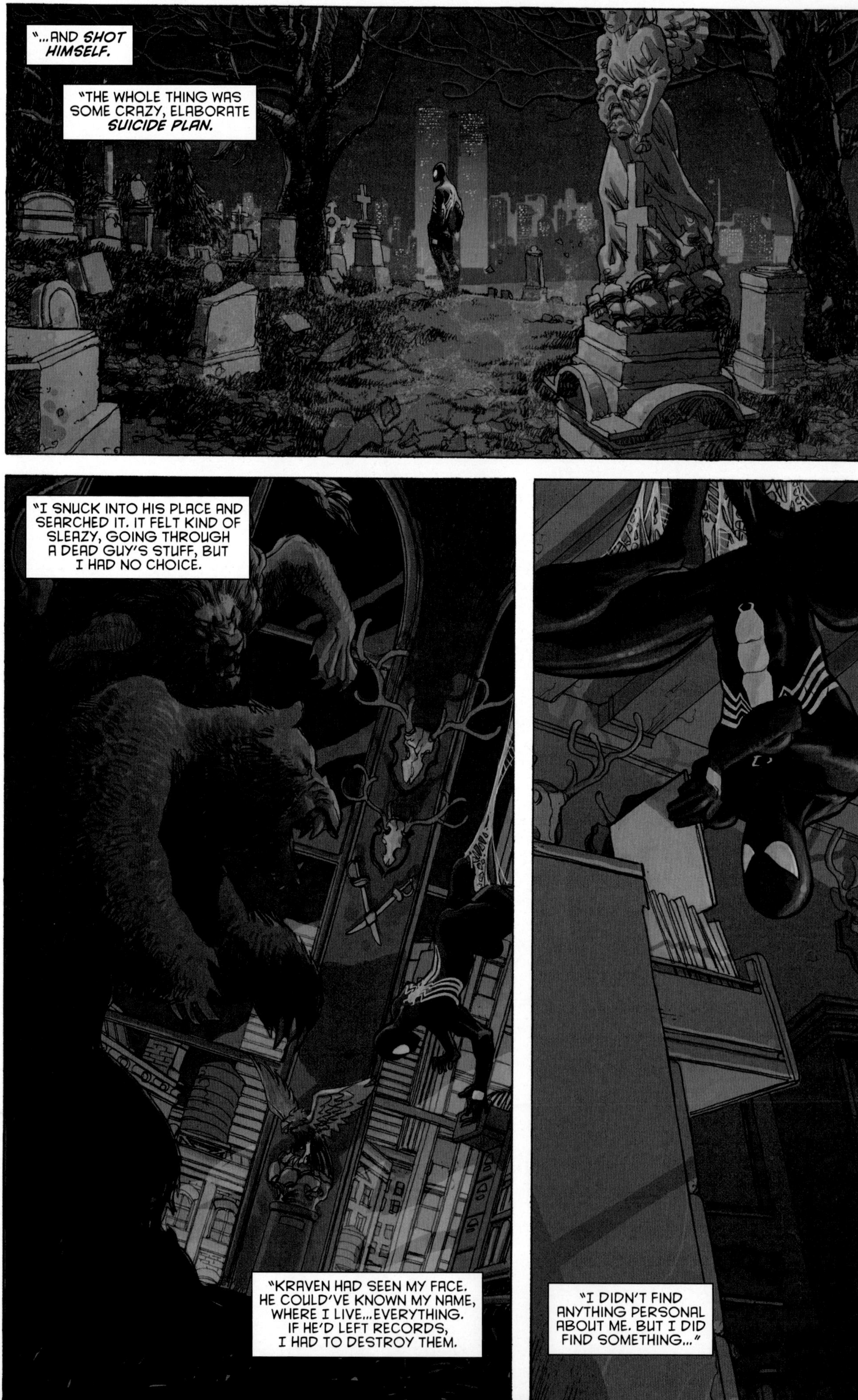
"...AND SHOT HIMSELF.
"THE WHOLE THING WAS SOME CRAZY, ELABORATE SUICIDE PLAN.
"I SNUCK INTO HIS PLACE AND SEARCHED IT. IT FELT KIND OF SLEAZY, GOING THROUGH A DEAD GUY'S STUFF, BUT I HAD NO CHOICE.
"KRAVEN HAD SEEN MY FACE. HE COULD'VE KNOWN MY NAME, WHERE I LIVE...EVERYTHING. IF HE'D LEFT RECORDS, I HAD TO DESTROY THEM.
"I DIDN'T FIND ANYTHING PERSONAL ABOUT ME. BUT I DID FIND SOMETHING..."

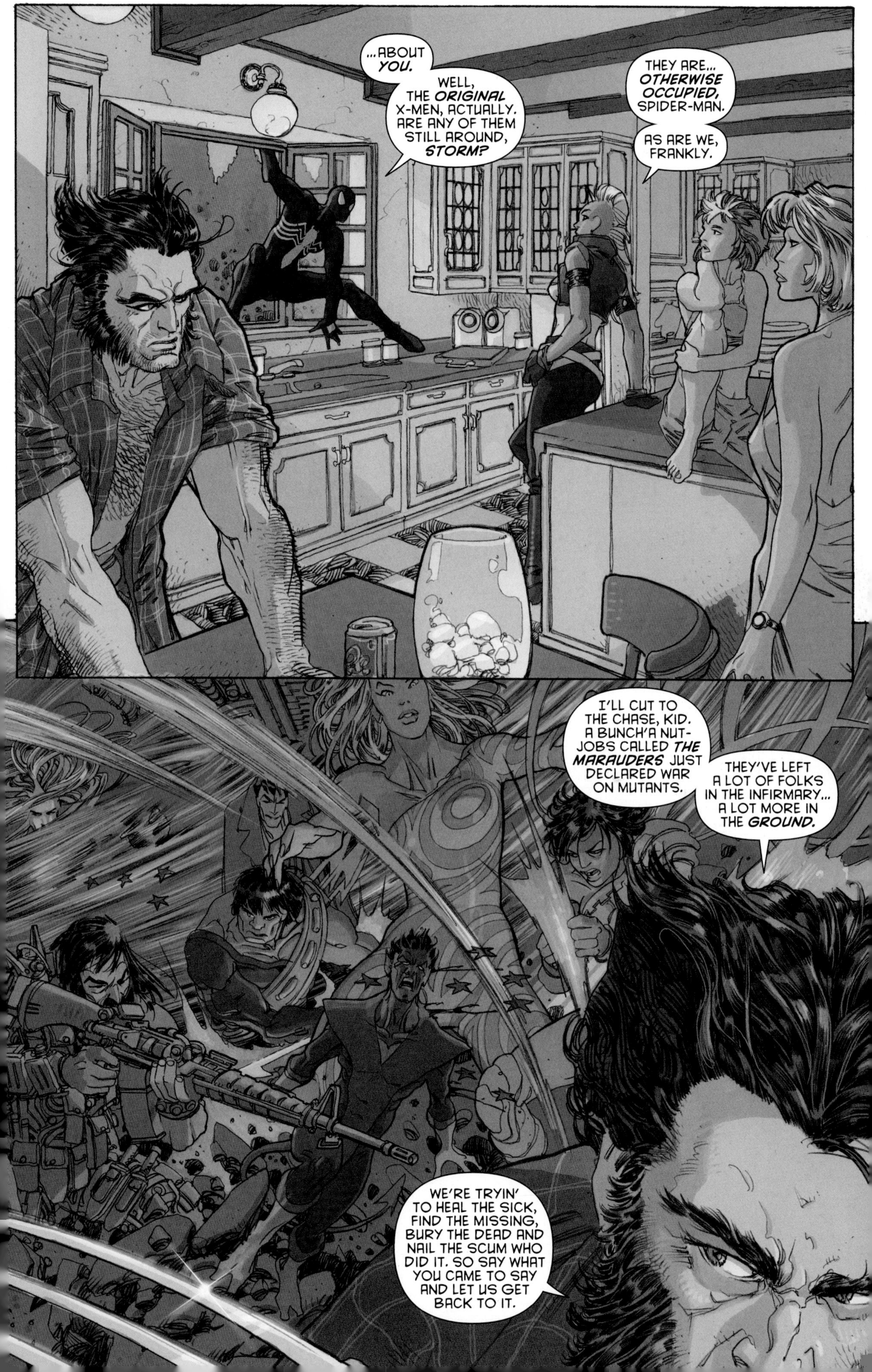
...ABOUT YOU.
WELL, THE ORIGINAL X-MEN, ACTUALLY. ARE ANY OF THEM STILL AROUND, STORM?
THEY ARE... OTHERWISE OCCUPIED, SPIDER-MAN.
AS ARE WE, FRANKLY.
I'LL CUT TO THE CHASE, KID. A BUNCH'A NUT-JOBS CALLED THE MARAUDERS JUST DECLARED WAR ON MUTANTS.
THEY'VE LEFT A LOT OF FOLKS IN THE INFIRMARY... A LOT MORE IN THE GROUND.
WE'RE TRYIN' TO HEAL THE SICK, FIND THE MISSING, BURY THE DEAD AND NAIL THE SCUM WHO DID IT. SO SAY WHAT YOU CAME TO SAY AND LET US GET BACK TO IT.

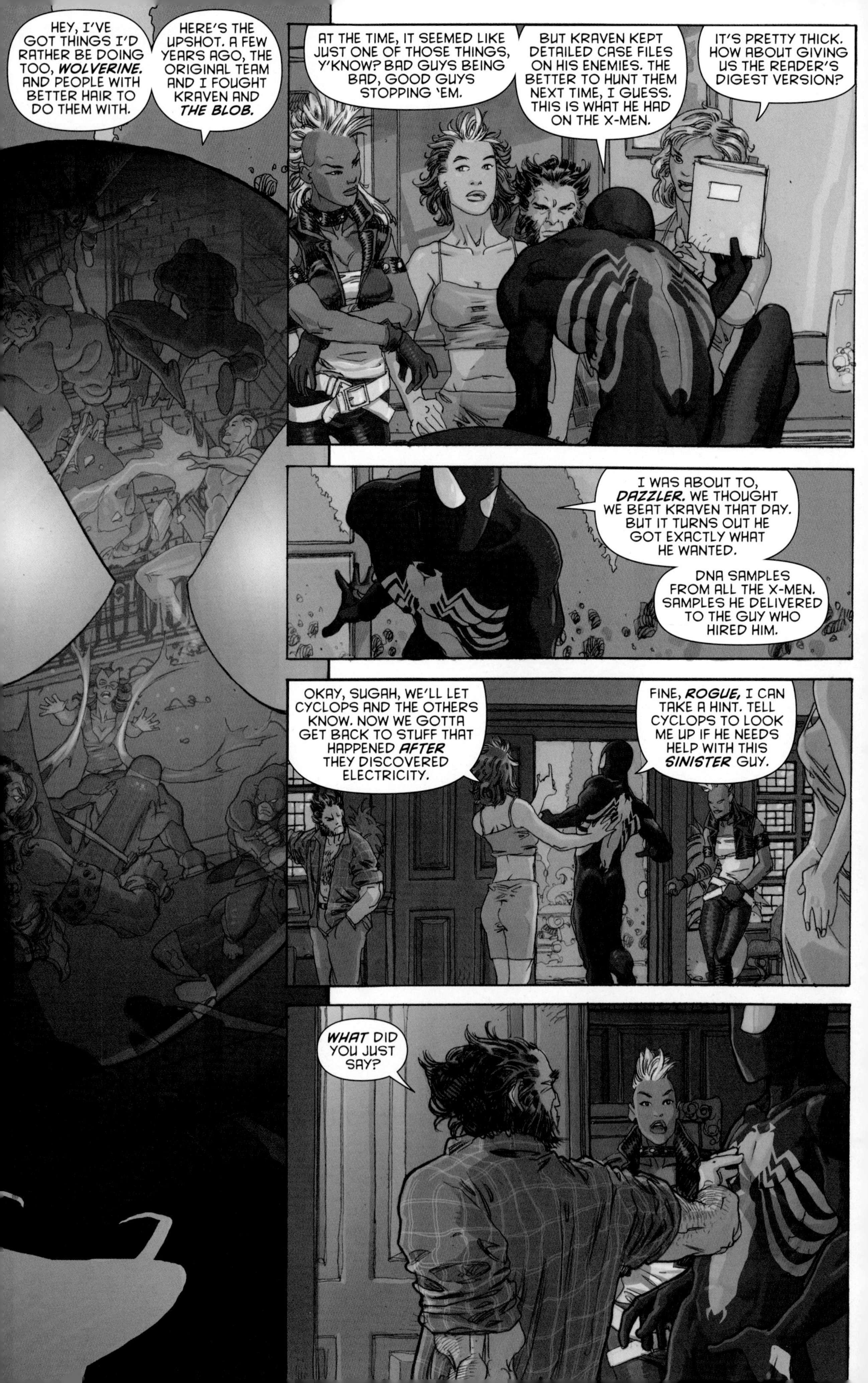
HEY, I'VE GOT THINGS I'D RATHER BE DOING TOO, WOLVERINE. AND PEOPLE WITH BETTER HAIR TO DO THEM WITH.
HERE'S THE UPSHOT. A FEW YEARS AGO, THE ORIGINAL TEAM AND I FOUGHT KRAVEN AND THE BLOB.
AT THE TIME, IT SEEMED LIKE JUST ONE OF THOSE THINGS, Y'KNOW? BAD GUYS BEING BAD, GOOD GUYS STOPPING 'EM.
BUT KRAVEN KEPT DETAILED CASE FILES ON HIS ENEMIES. THE BETTER TO HUNT THEM NEXT TIME, I GUESS. THIS IS WHAT HE HAD ON THE X-MEN.
IT'S PRETTY THICK. HOW ABOUT GIVING US THE READER'S DIGEST VERSION?
I WAS ABOUT TO, DAZZLER. WE THOUGHT WE BEAT KRAVEN THAT DAY. BUT IT TURNS OUT HE GOT EXACTLY WHAT HE WANTED.
DNA SAMPLES FROM ALL THE X-MEN. SAMPLES HE DELIVERED TO THE GUY WHO HIRED HIM.
OKAY, SUGAH, WE'LL LET CYCLOPS AND THE OTHERS KNOW. NOW WE GOTTA GET BACK TO STUFF THAT HAPPENED AFTER THEY DISCOVERED ELECTRICITY.
FINE, ROGUE, I CAN TAKE A HINT. TELL CYCLOPS TO LOOK ME UP IF HE NEEDS HELP WITH THIS SINISTER GUY.
WHAT DID YOU JUST SAY?

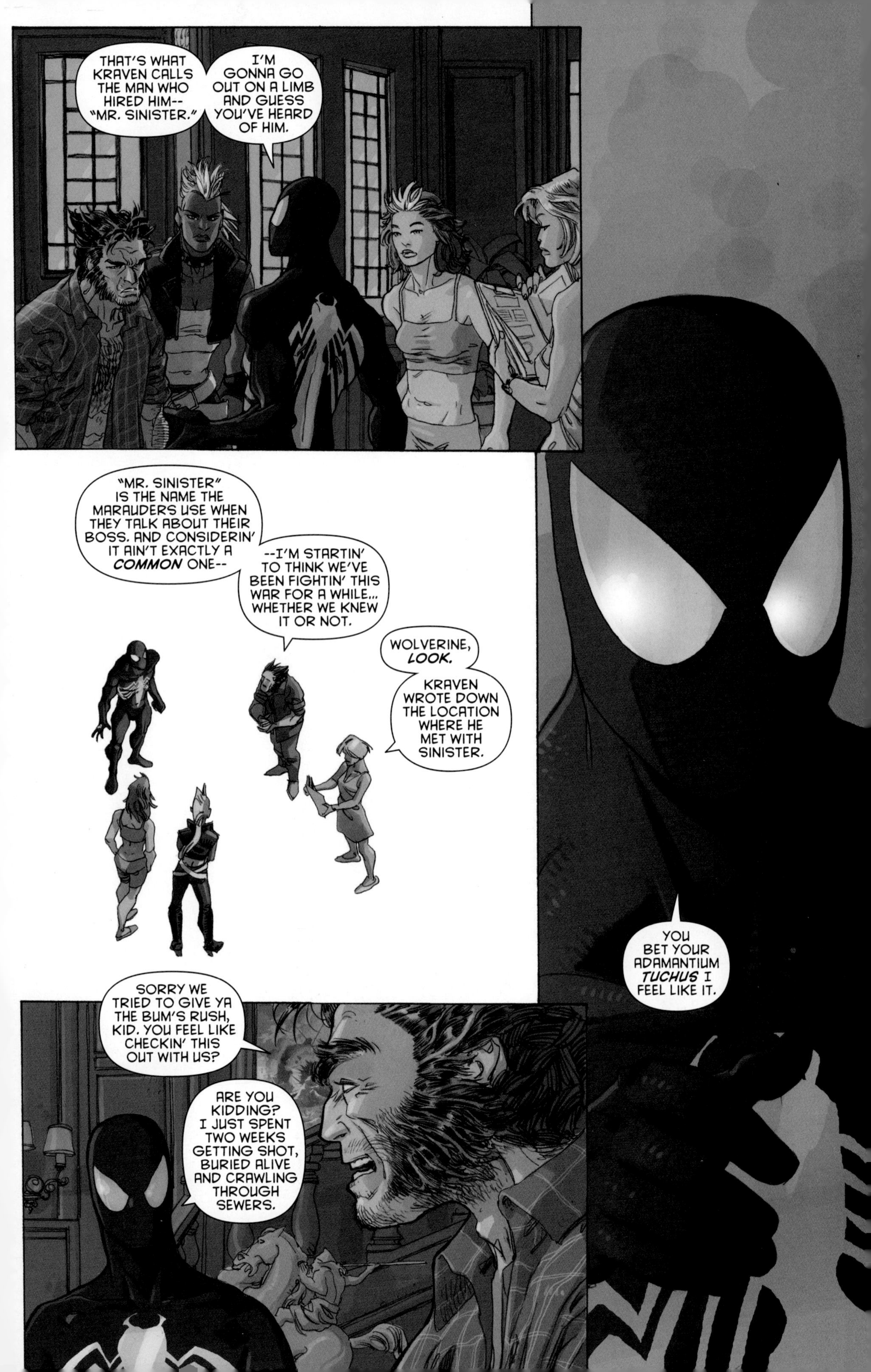
THAT'S WHAT KRAVEN CALLS THE MAN WHO HIRED HIM-- "MR. SINISTER."
I'M GONNA GO OUT ON A LIMB AND GUESS YOU'VE HEARD OF HIM.
"MR. SINISTER" IS THE NAME THE MARAUDERS USE WHEN THEY TALK ABOUT THEIR BOSS. AND CONSIDERIN' IT AIN'T EXACTLY A COMMON ONE--
--I'M STARTIN' TO THINK WE'VE BEEN FIGHTIN' THIS WAR FOR A WHILE... WHETHER WE KNEW IT OR NOT.
WOLVERINE, LOOK.
KRAVEN WROTE DOWN THE LOCATION WHERE HE MET WITH SINISTER.
SORRY WE TRIED TO GIVE YA THE BUM'S RUSH, KID. YOU FEEL LIKE CHECKIN' THIS OUT WITH US?
ARE YOU KIDDING? I JUST SPENT TWO WEEKS GETTING SHOT, BURIED ALIVE AND CRAWLING THROUGH SEWERS.
YOU BET YOUR ADAMANTIUM TUCHUS I FEEL LIKE IT.

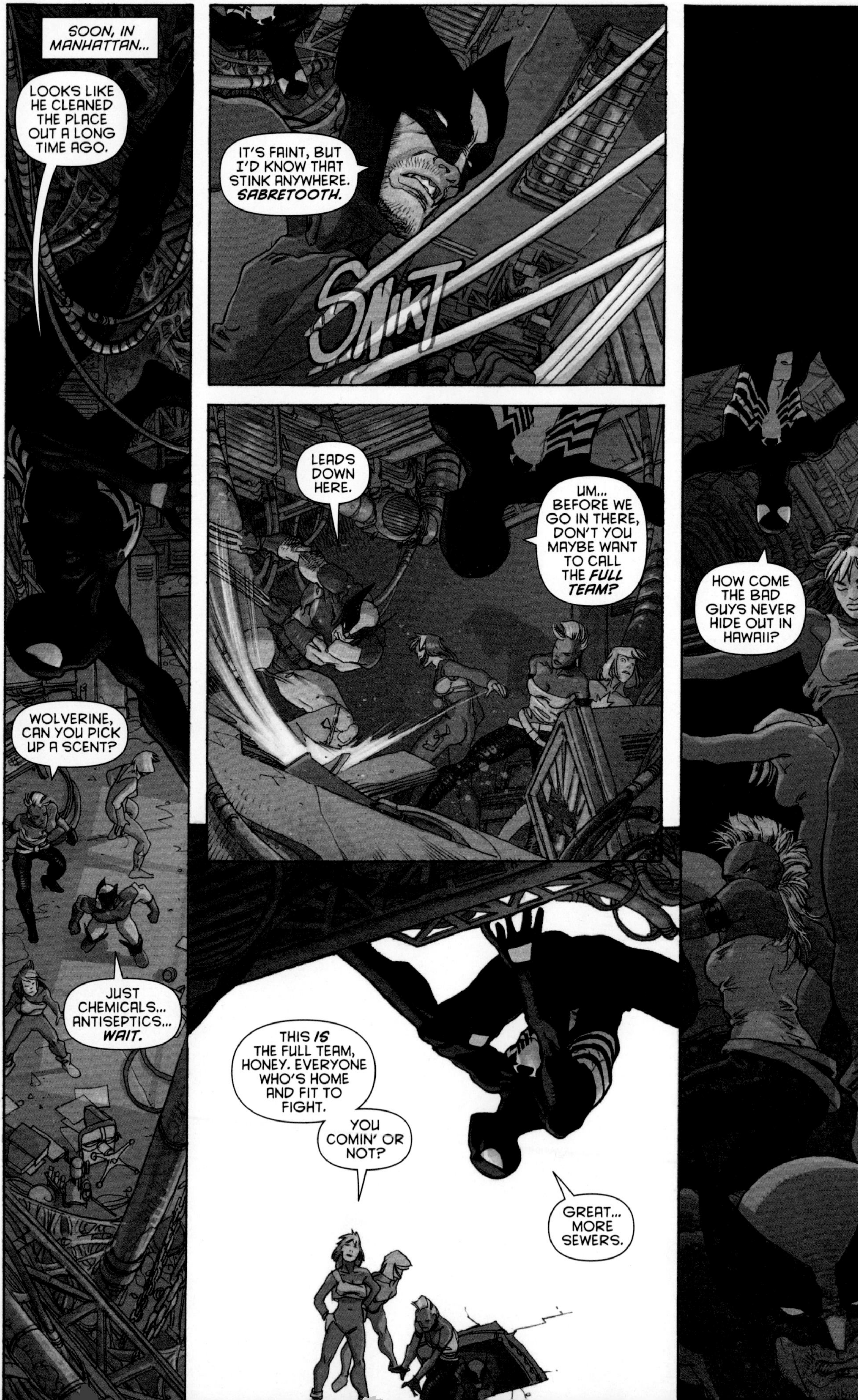
SOON, IN MANHATTAN...
LOOKS LIKE HE CLEANED THE PLACE OUT A LONG TIME AGO.
IT'S FAINT, BUT I'D KNOW THAT STINK ANYWHERE. SABRETOOTH.
SNIKT
WOLVERINE, CAN YOU PICK UP A SCENT?
JUST CHEMICALS... ANTISEPTICS... WAIT.
LEADS DOWN HERE.
UM... BEFORE WE GO IN THERE, DON'T YOU MAYBE WANT TO CALL THE FULL TEAM?
THIS IS THE FULL TEAM, HONEY. EVERYONE WHO'S HOME AND FIT TO FIGHT.
YOU COMIN' OR NOT?
GREAT... MORE SEWERS.
HOW COME THE BAD GUYS NEVER HIDE OUT IN HAWAII?

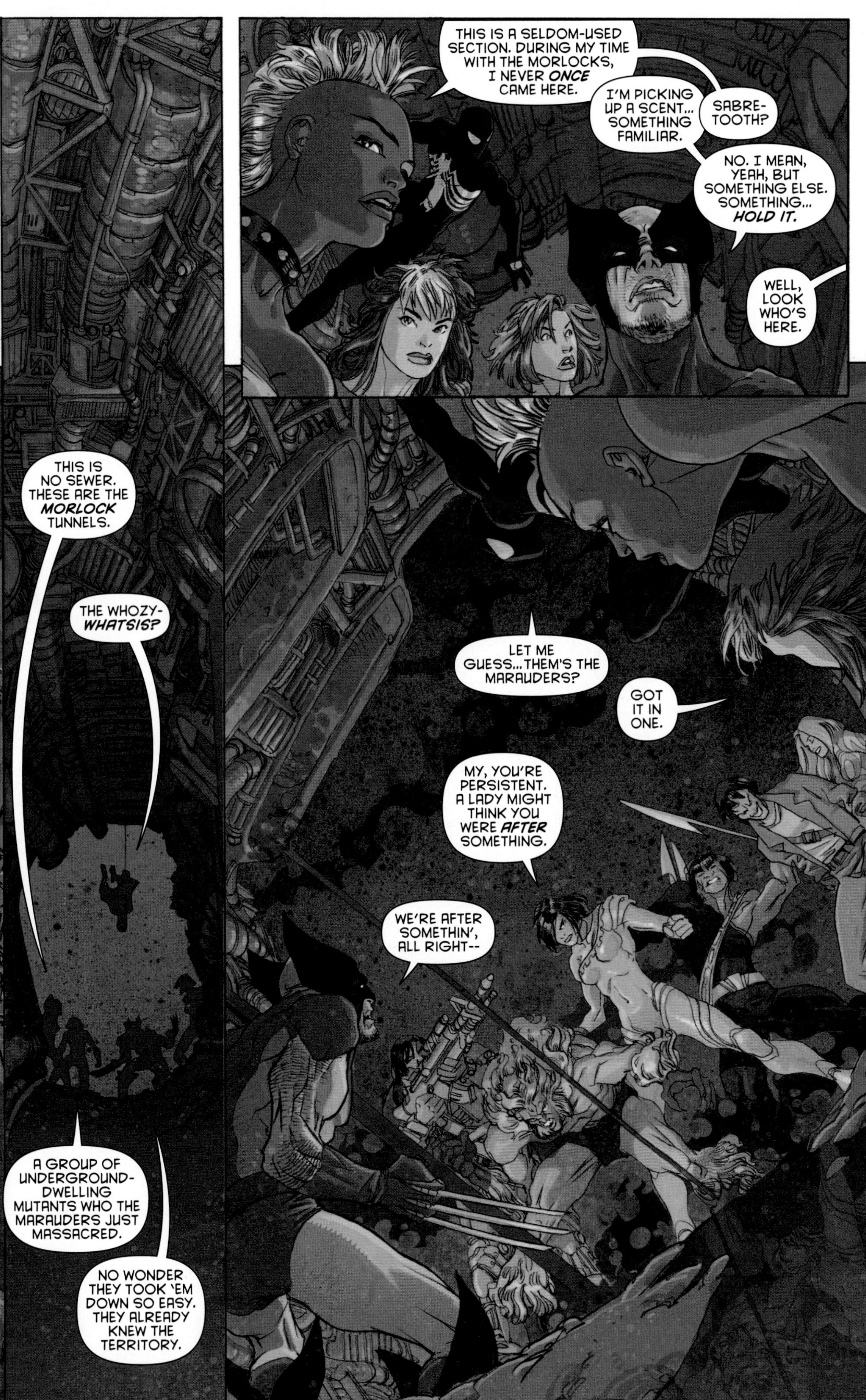
THIS IS A SELDOM-USED SECTION. DURING MY TIME WITH THE MORLOCKS, I NEVER ONCE CAME HERE.
I'M PICKING UP A SCENT... SOMETHING FAMILIAR.
SABRE-TOOTH?
NO. I MEAN, YEAH, BUT SOMETHING ELSE. SOMETHING... HOLD IT.
WELL, LOOK WHO'S HERE.
THIS IS NO SEWER. THESE ARE THE MORLOCK TUNNELS.
THE WHOZY-WHATSIS?
A GROUP OF UNDERGROUND-DWELLING MUTANTS WHO THE MARAUDERS JUST MASSACRED.
NO WONDER THEY TOOK 'EM DOWN SO EASY. THEY ALREADY KNEW THE TERRITORY.
LET ME GUESS... THEM'S THE MARAUDERS?
GOT IT IN ONE.
MY, YOU'RE PERSISTENT. A LADY MIGHT THINK YOU WERE AFTER SOMETHING.
WE'RE AFTER SOMETHIN', ALL RIGHT--

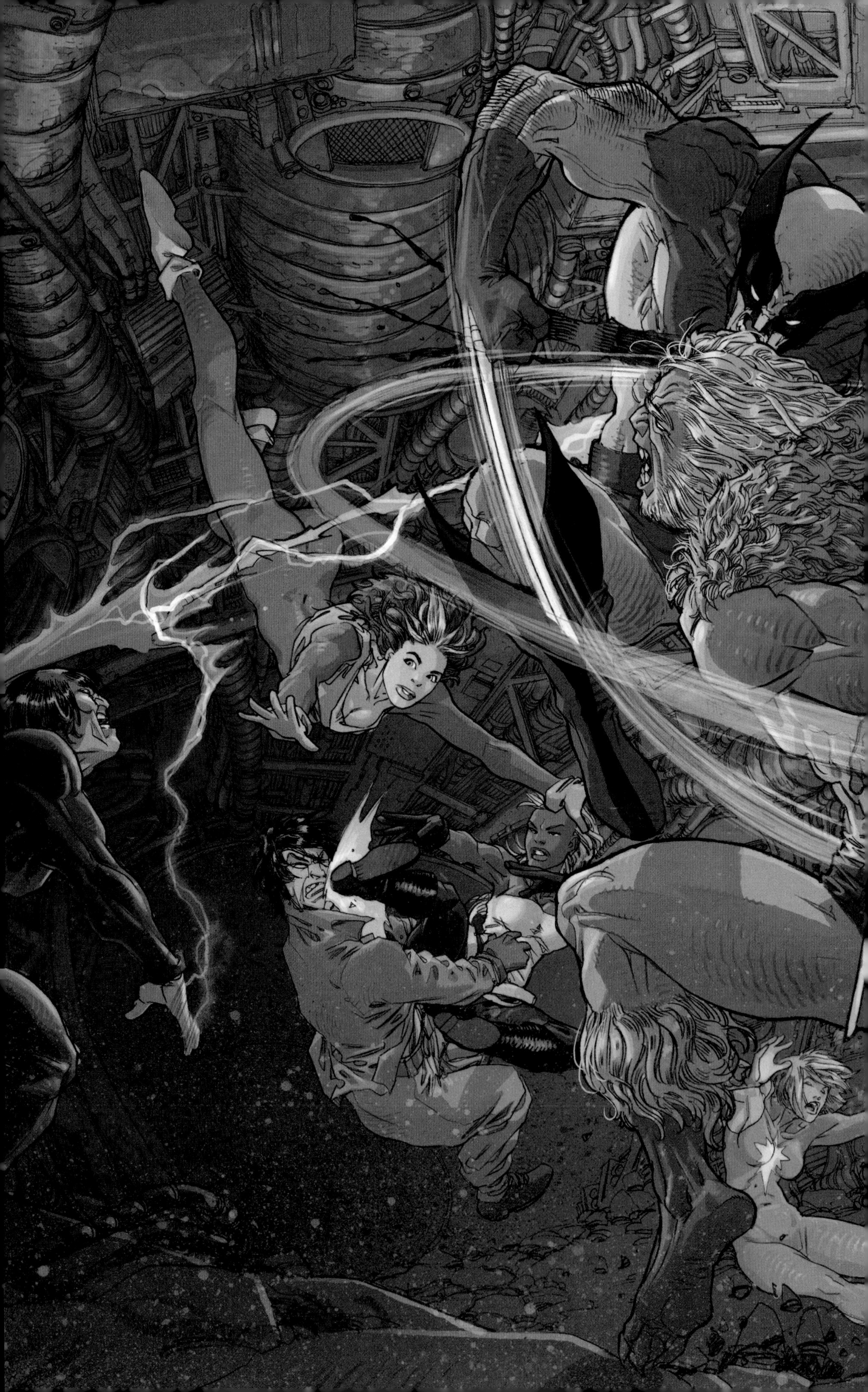

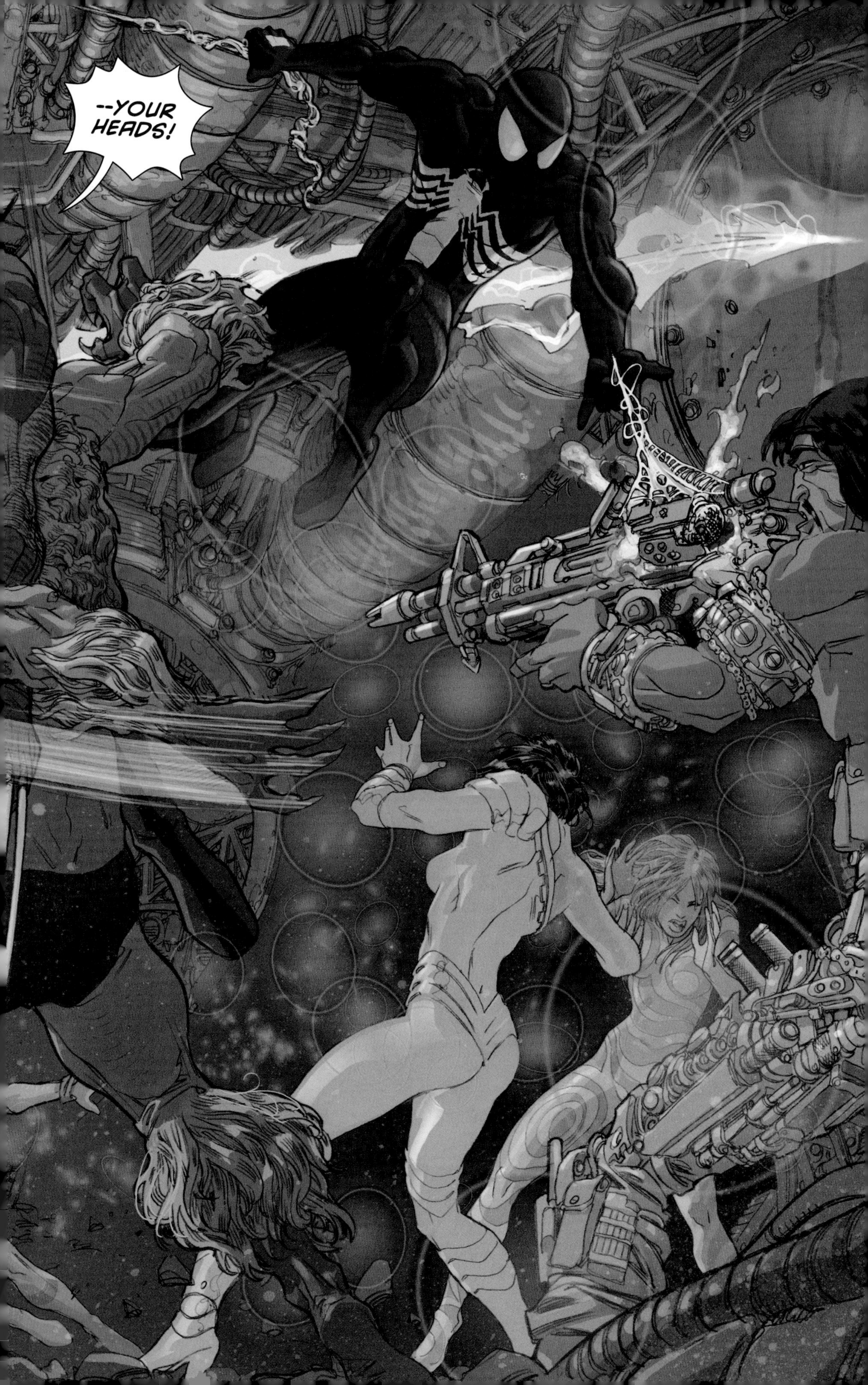
--YOUR HEADS!

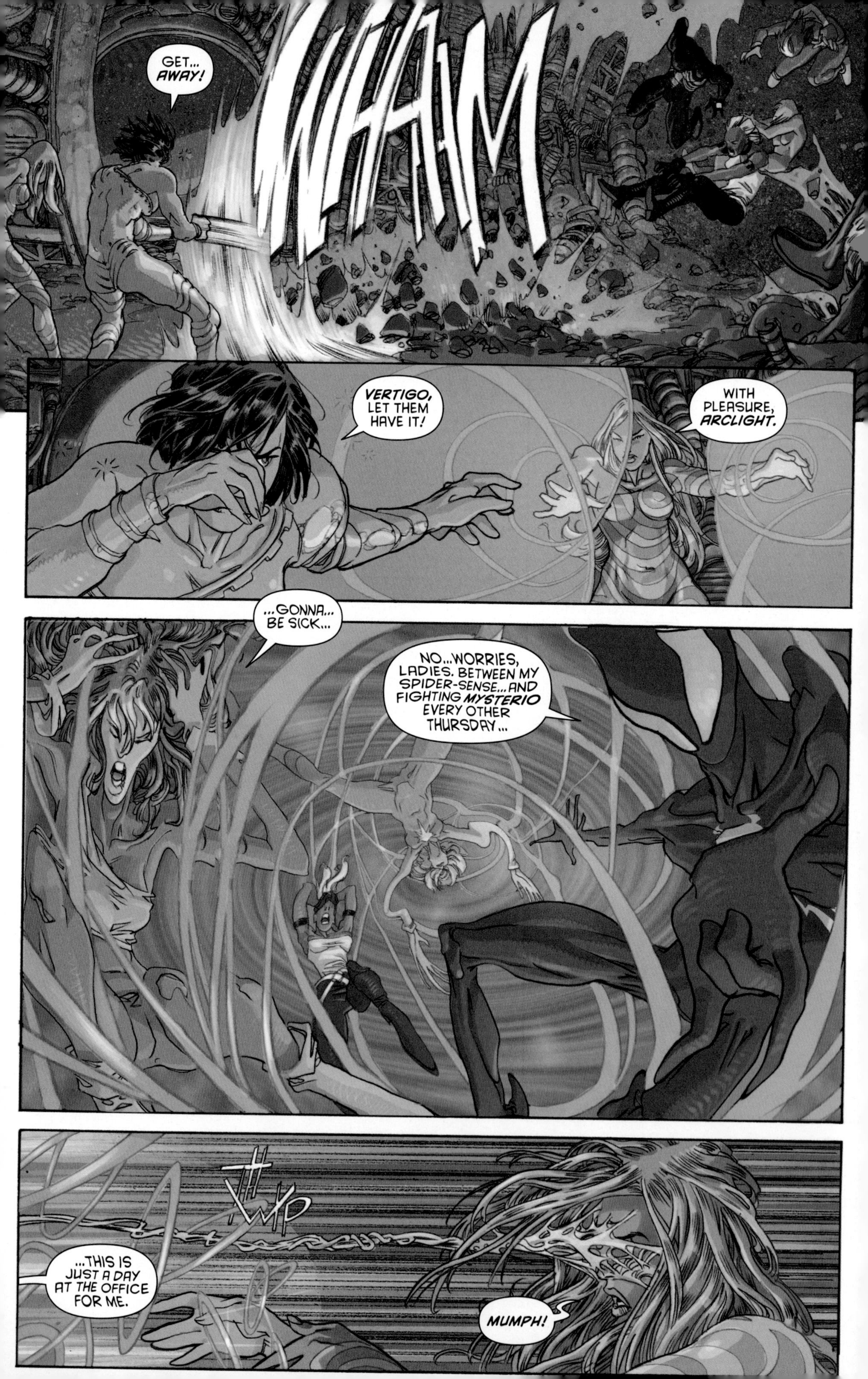
GET... AWAY!
WHAM
VERTIGO, LET THEM HAVE IT!
WITH PLEASURE, ARCLIGHT.
...GONNA... BE SICK...
NO...WORRIES, LADIES. BETWEEN MY SPIDER-SENSE...AND FIGHTING MYSTERIO EVERY OTHER THURSDAY...
THWIP
...THIS IS JUST A DAY AT THE OFFICE FOR ME.
MUMPH!

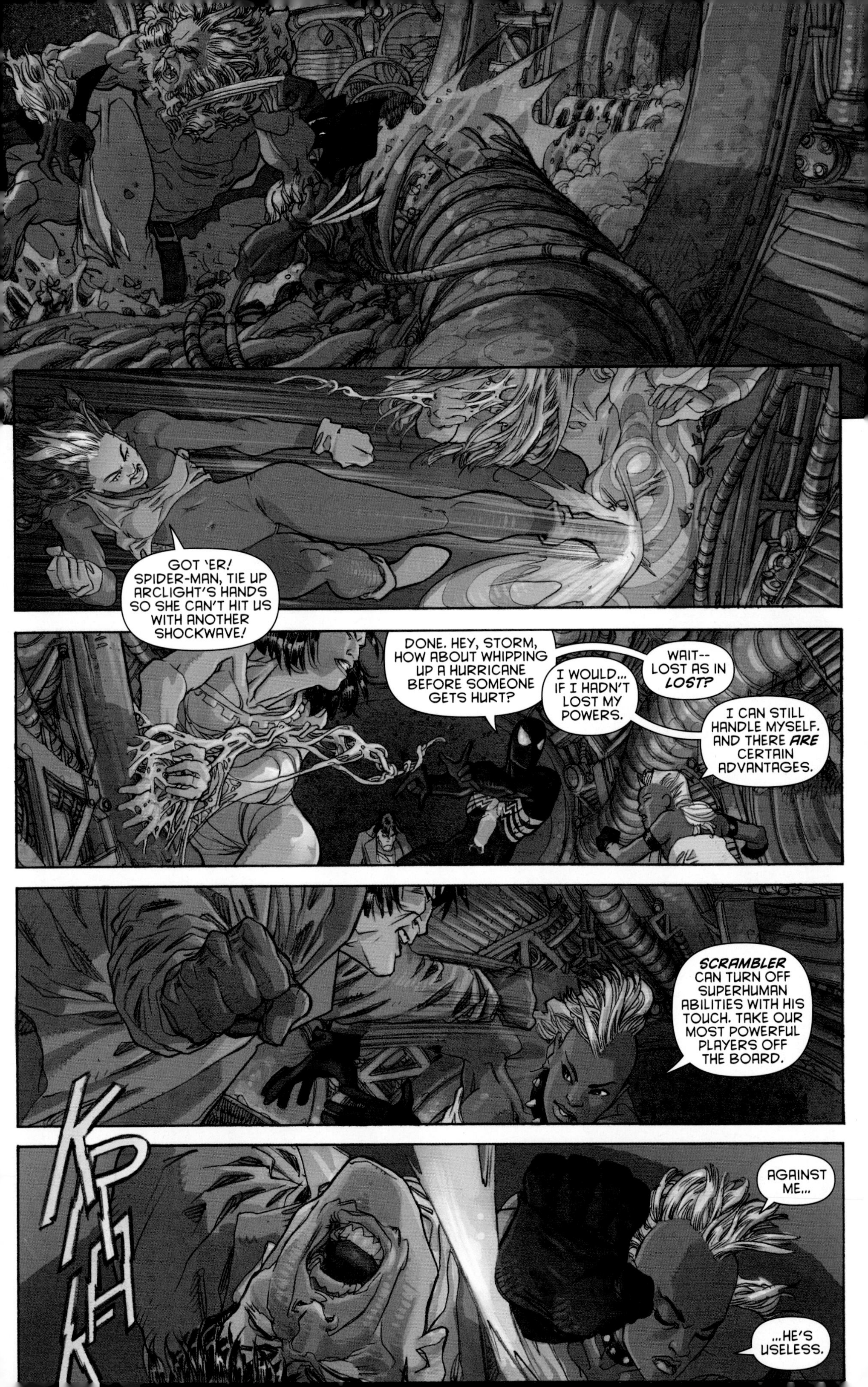
GOT 'ER! SPIDER-MAN, TIE UP ARCLIGHT'S HANDS SO SHE CAN'T HIT US WITH ANOTHER SHOCKWAVE!
DONE. HEY, STORM, HOW ABOUT WHIPPING UP A HURRICANE BEFORE SOMEONE GETS HURT?
I WOULD... IF I HADN'T LOST MY POWERS.
WAIT-- LOST AS IN *LOST?*
I CAN STILL HANDLE MYSELF. AND THERE *ARE* CERTAIN ADVANTAGES.
SCRAMBLER CAN TURN OFF SUPERHUMAN ABILITIES WITH HIS TOUCH. TAKE OUR MOST POWERFUL PLAYERS OFF THE BOARD.
KPHHK
AGAINST ME...
...HE'S USELESS.

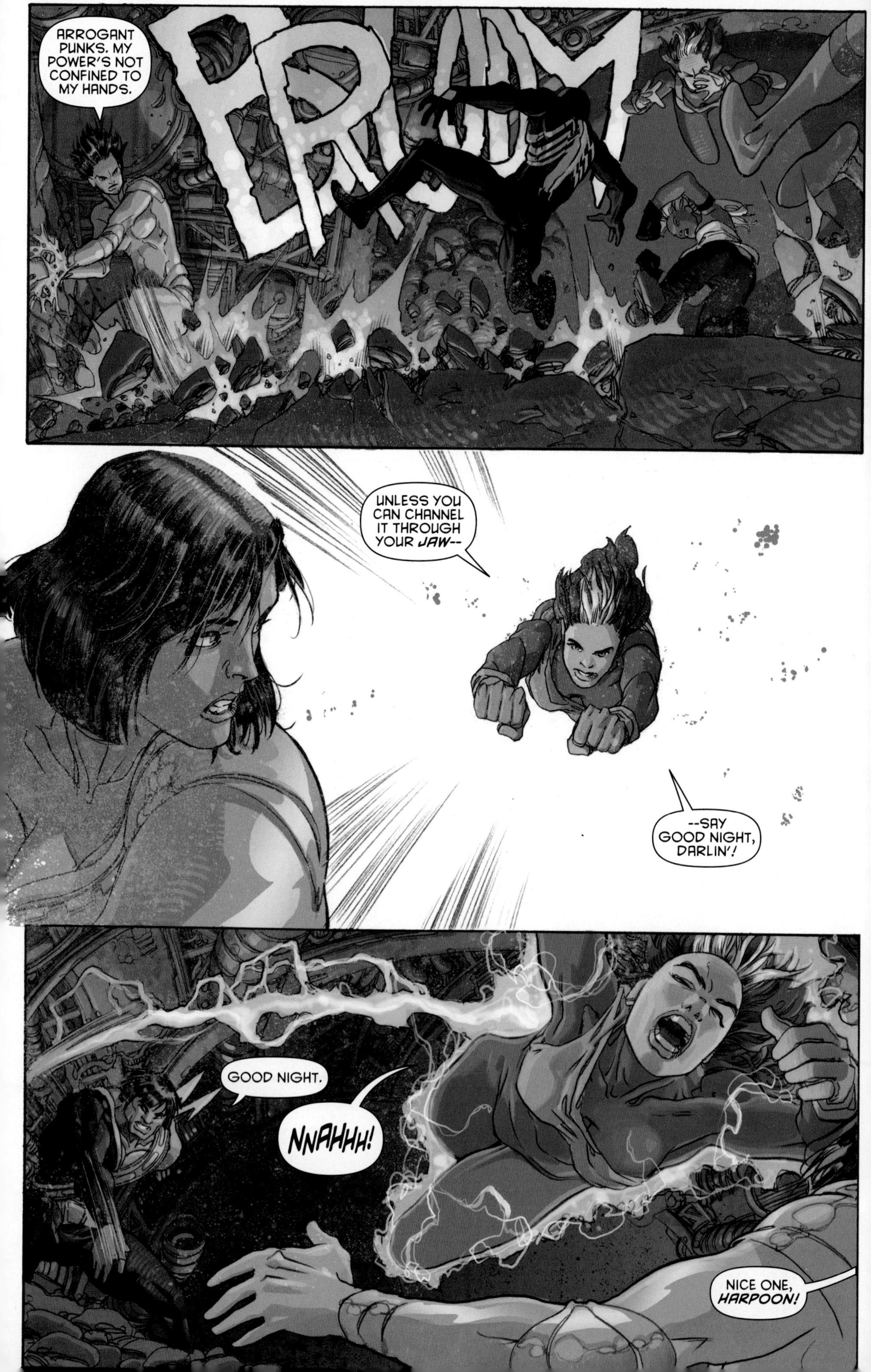
ARROGANT PUNKS. MY POWER'S NOT CONFINED TO MY HANDS.
FRAAM
UNLESS YOU CAN CHANNEL IT THROUGH YOUR *JAW*--
--SAY GOOD NIGHT, DARLIN'!
GOOD NIGHT.
NNAHHH!
NICE ONE, *HARPOON!*

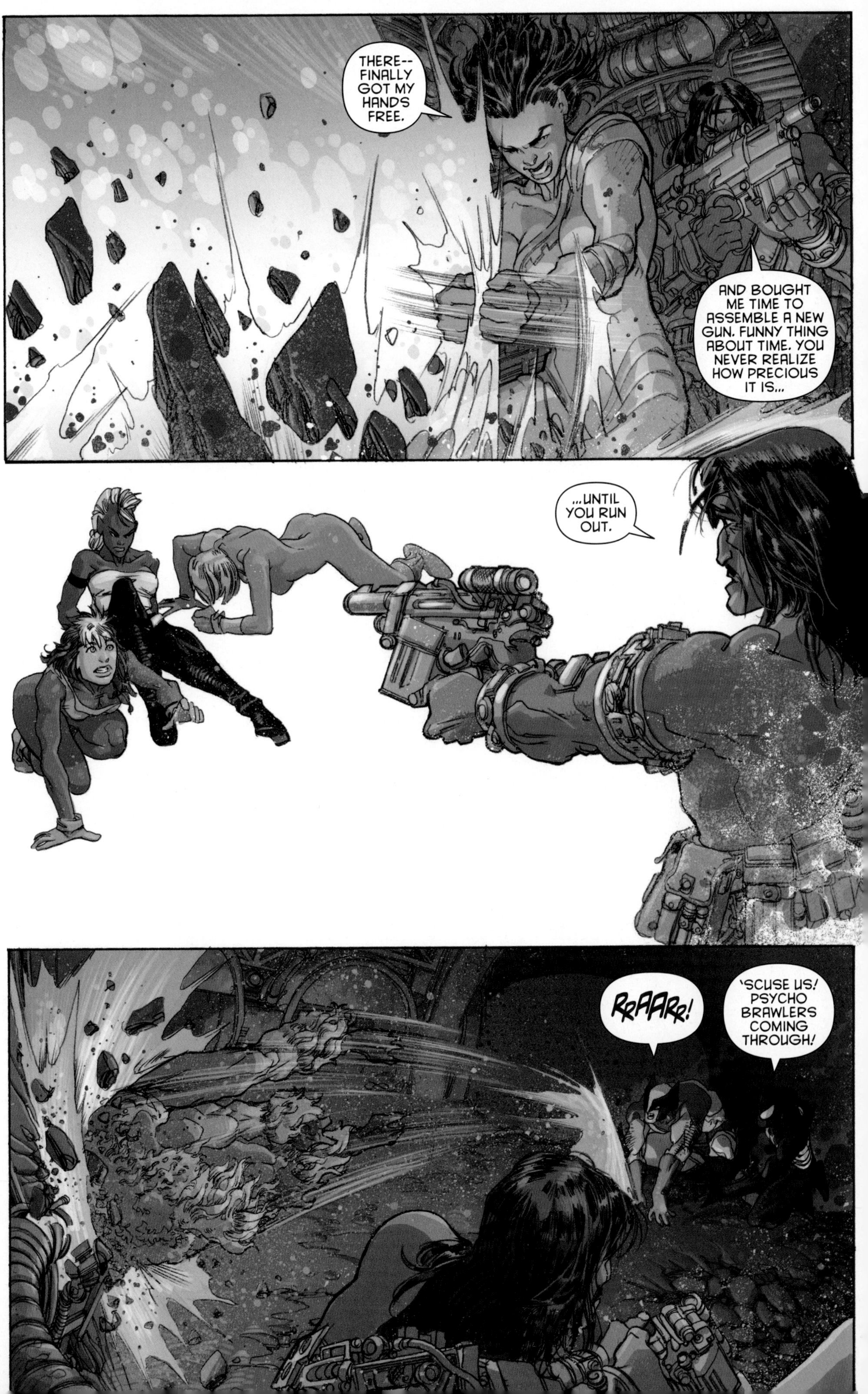
THERE-- FINALLY GOT MY HANDS FREE.
AND BOUGHT ME TIME TO ASSEMBLE A NEW GUN. FUNNY THING ABOUT TIME. YOU NEVER REALIZE HOW PRECIOUS IT IS...
...UNTIL YOU RUN OUT.
RRAARR!
'SCUSE US! PSYCHO BRAWLERS COMING THROUGH!

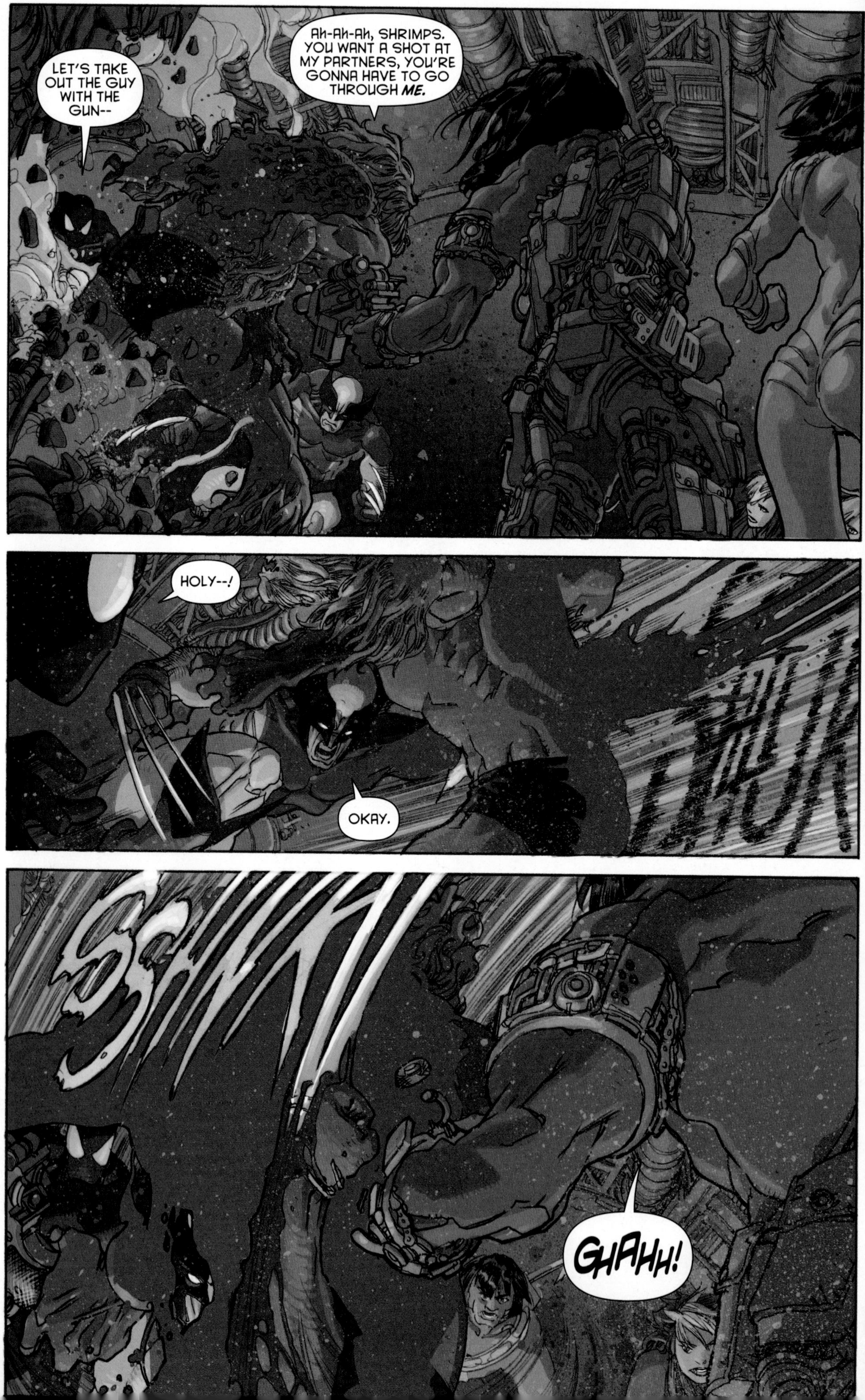
LET'S TAKE OUT THE GUY WITH THE GUN--
AH-AH-AH, SHRIMPS. YOU WANT A SHOT AT MY PARTNERS, YOU'RE GONNA HAVE TO GO THROUGH *ME.*
HOLY--!
OKAY.
GHAHH!

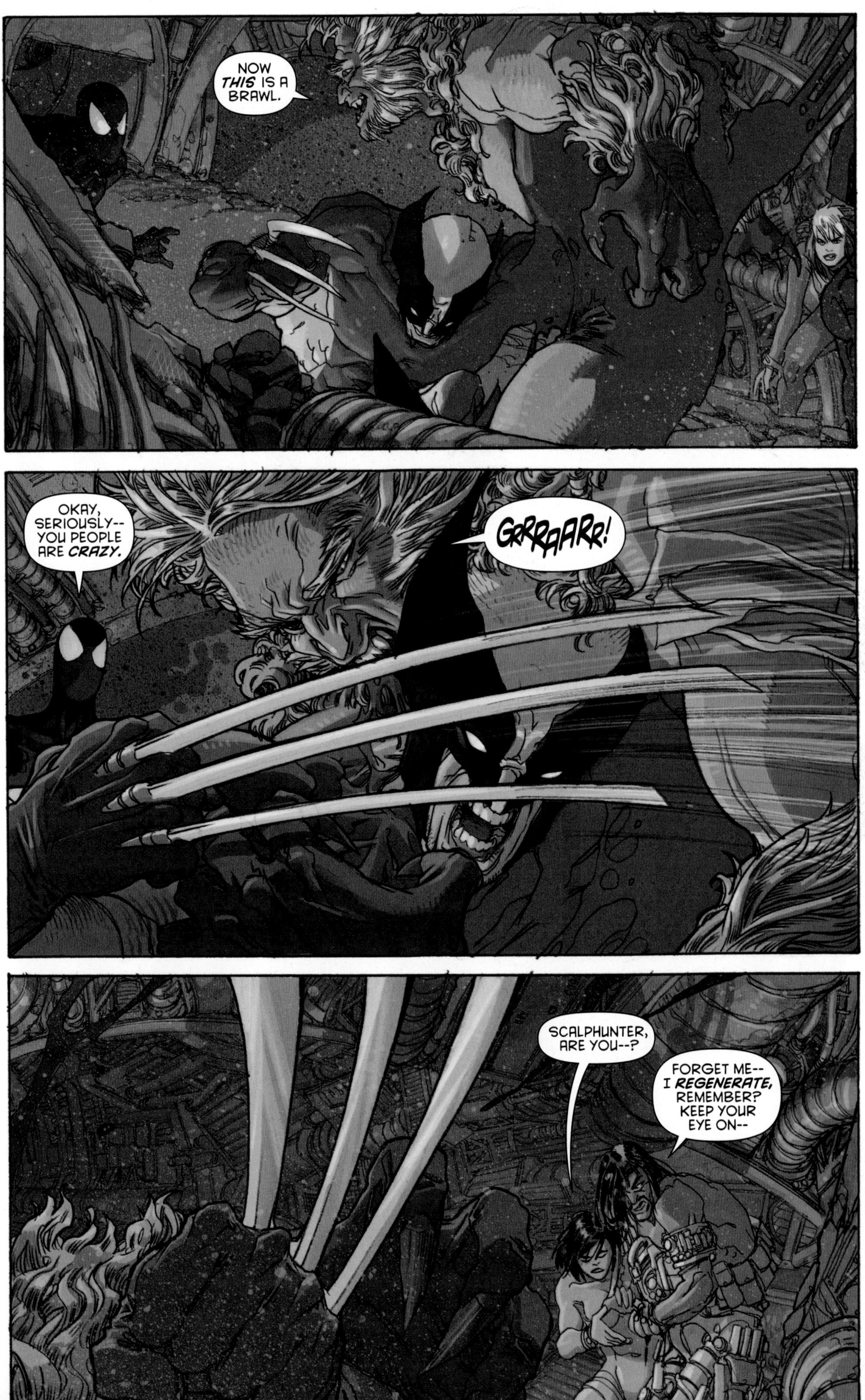
NOW THIS IS A BRAWL.
OKAY, SERIOUSLY-- YOU PEOPLE ARE CRAZY.
GRRRAAARR!
SCALPHUNTER, ARE YOU--?
FORGET ME-- I REGENERATE, REMEMBER? KEEP YOUR EYE ON--

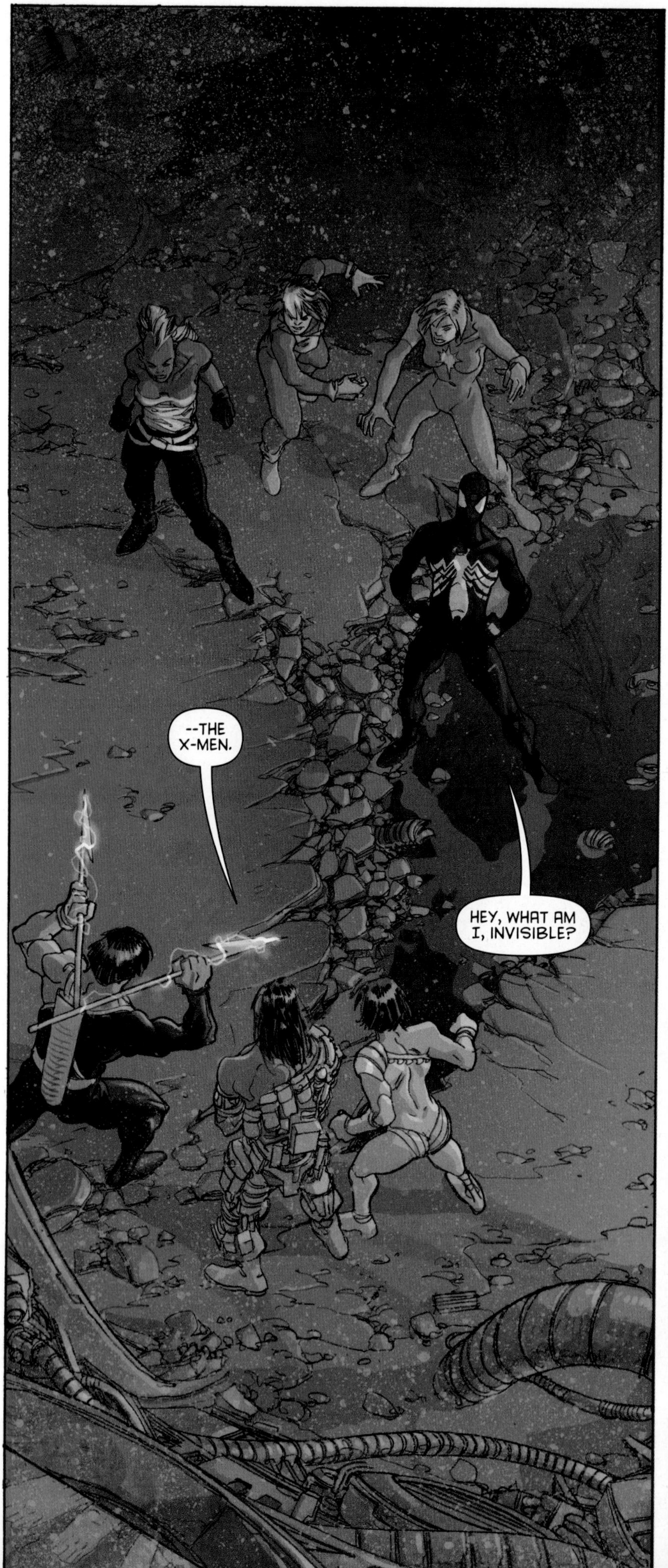
--THE X-MEN.
HEY, WHAT AM I, INVISIBLE?

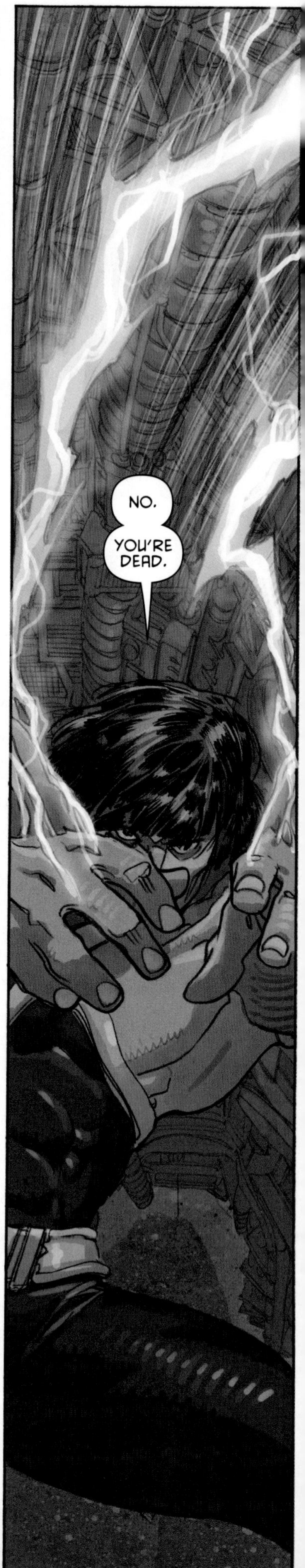
NO.
YOU'RE DEAD.

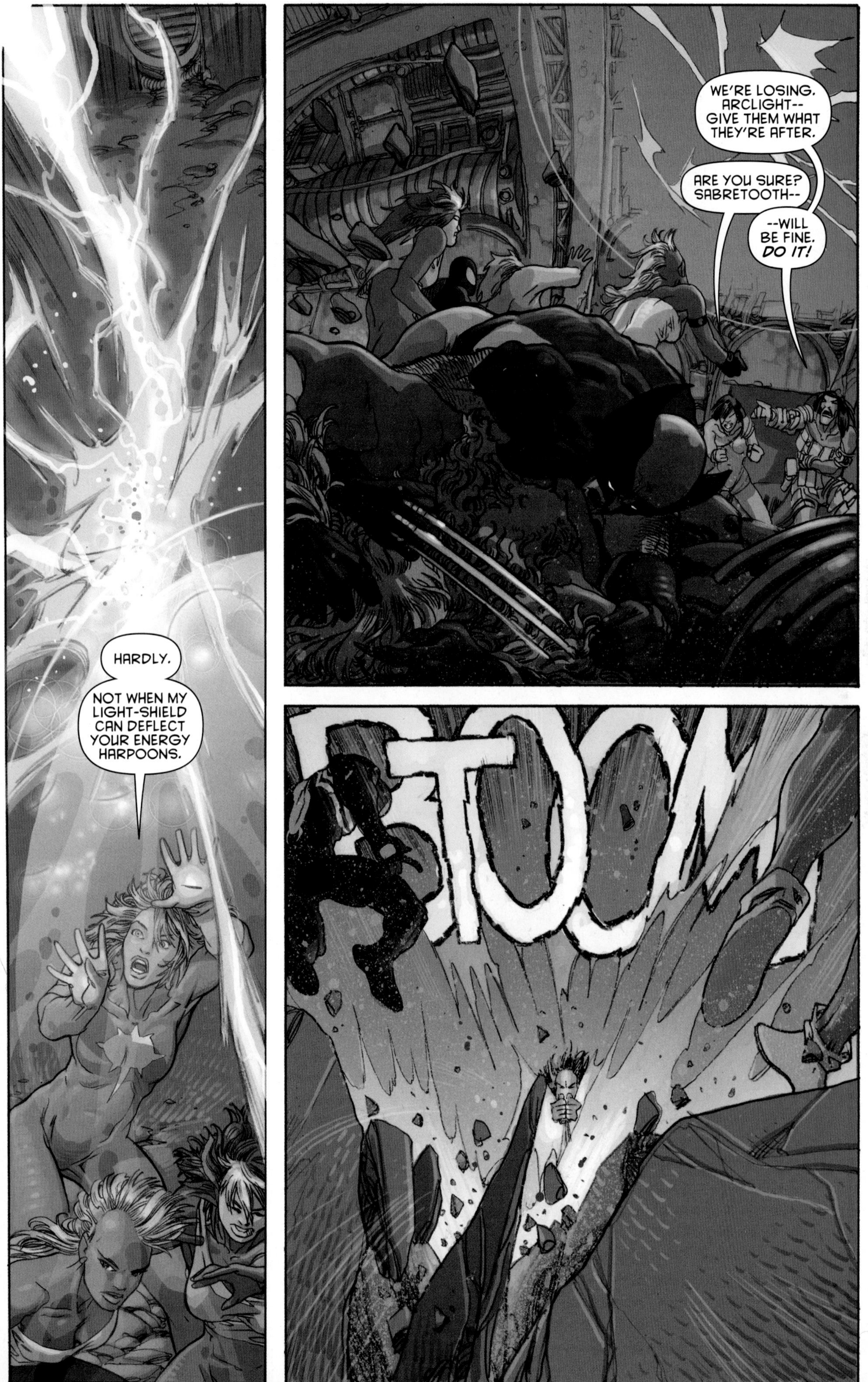
HARDLY.
NOT WHEN MY LIGHT-SHIELD CAN DEFLECT YOUR ENERGY HARPOONS.
WE'RE LOSING. ARCLIGHT-- GIVE THEM WHAT THEY'RE AFTER.
ARE YOU SURE? SABRETOOTH--
--WILL BE FINE. DO IT!

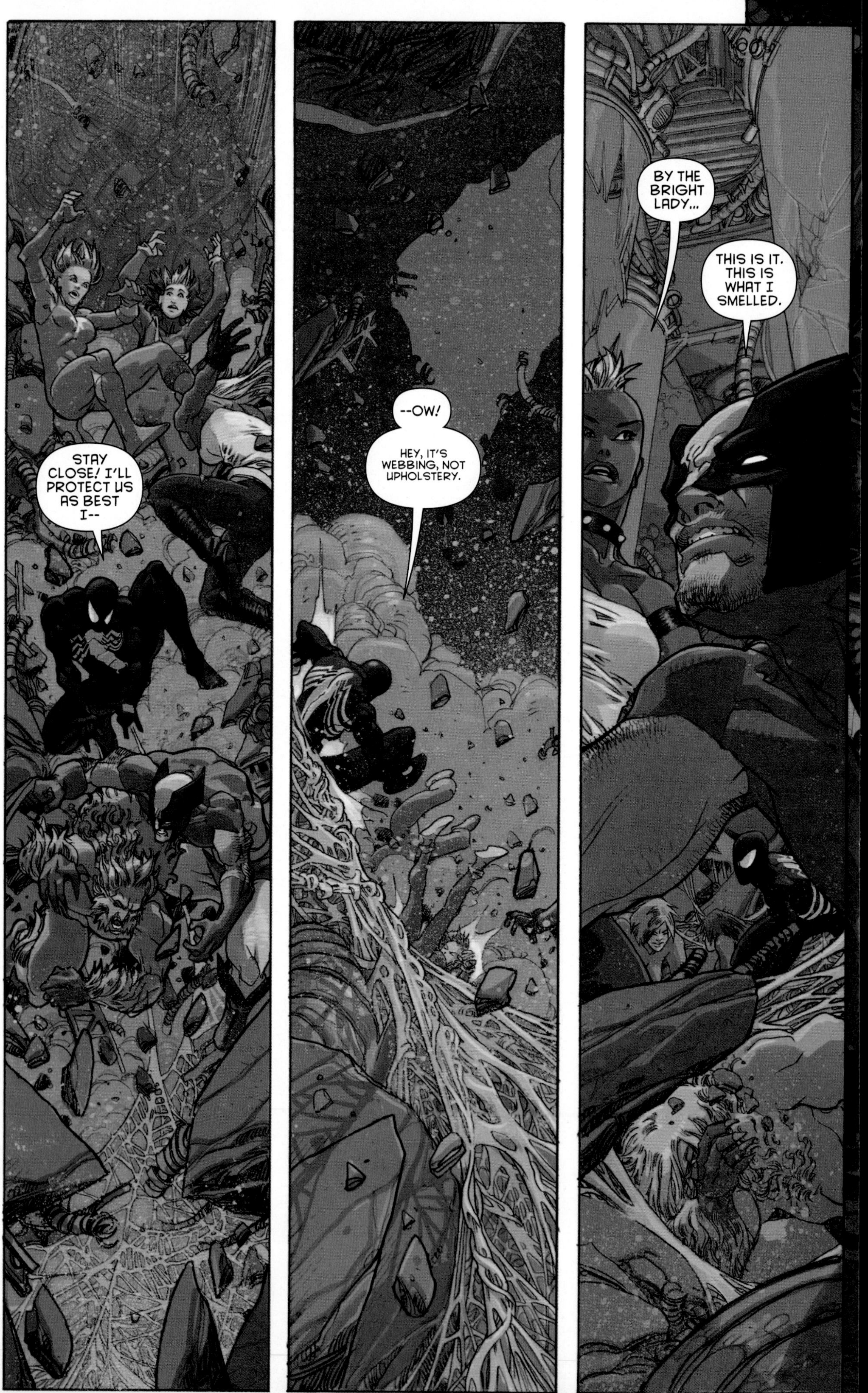
STAY CLOSE! I'LL PROTECT US AS BEST I--
--OW!
HEY, IT'S WEBBING, NOT UPHOLSTERY.
BY THE BRIGHT LADY...
THIS IS IT. THIS IS WHAT I SMELLED.

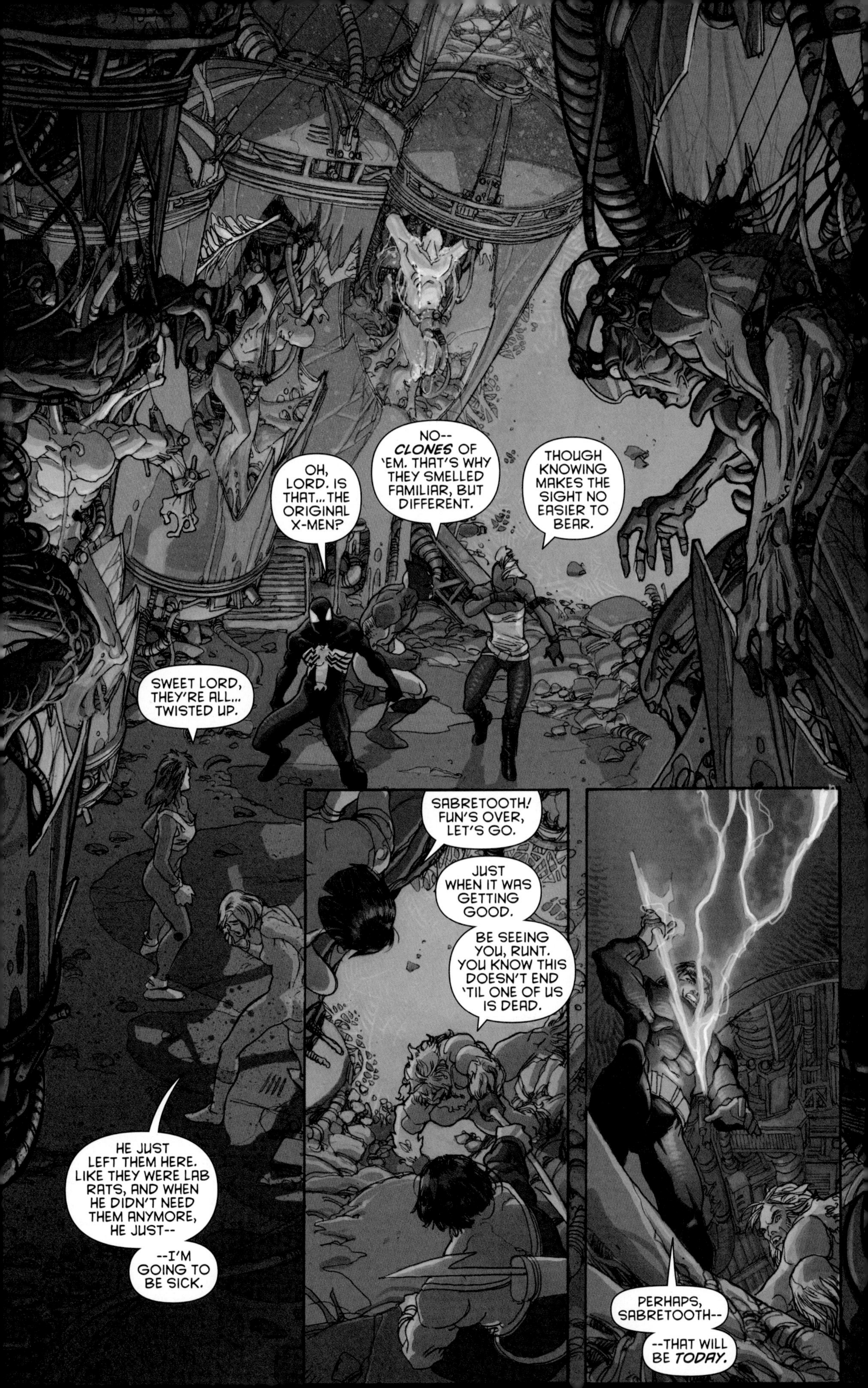
OH, LORD. IS THAT... THE ORIGINAL X-MEN?
NO-- *CLONES* OF 'EM. THAT'S WHY THEY SMELLED FAMILIAR, BUT DIFFERENT.
THOUGH KNOWING MAKES THE SIGHT NO EASIER TO BEAR.
SWEET LORD, THEY'RE ALL... TWISTED UP.
HE JUST LEFT THEM HERE. LIKE THEY WERE LAB RATS, AND WHEN HE DIDN'T NEED THEM ANYMORE, HE JUST--
--I'M GOING TO BE SICK.
SABRETOOTH! FUN'S OVER, LET'S GO.
JUST WHEN IT WAS GETTING GOOD.
BE SEEING YOU, RUNT. YOU KNOW THIS DOESN'T END 'TIL ONE OF US IS DEAD.
PERHAPS, SABRETOOTH--
--THAT WILL BE *TODAY.*

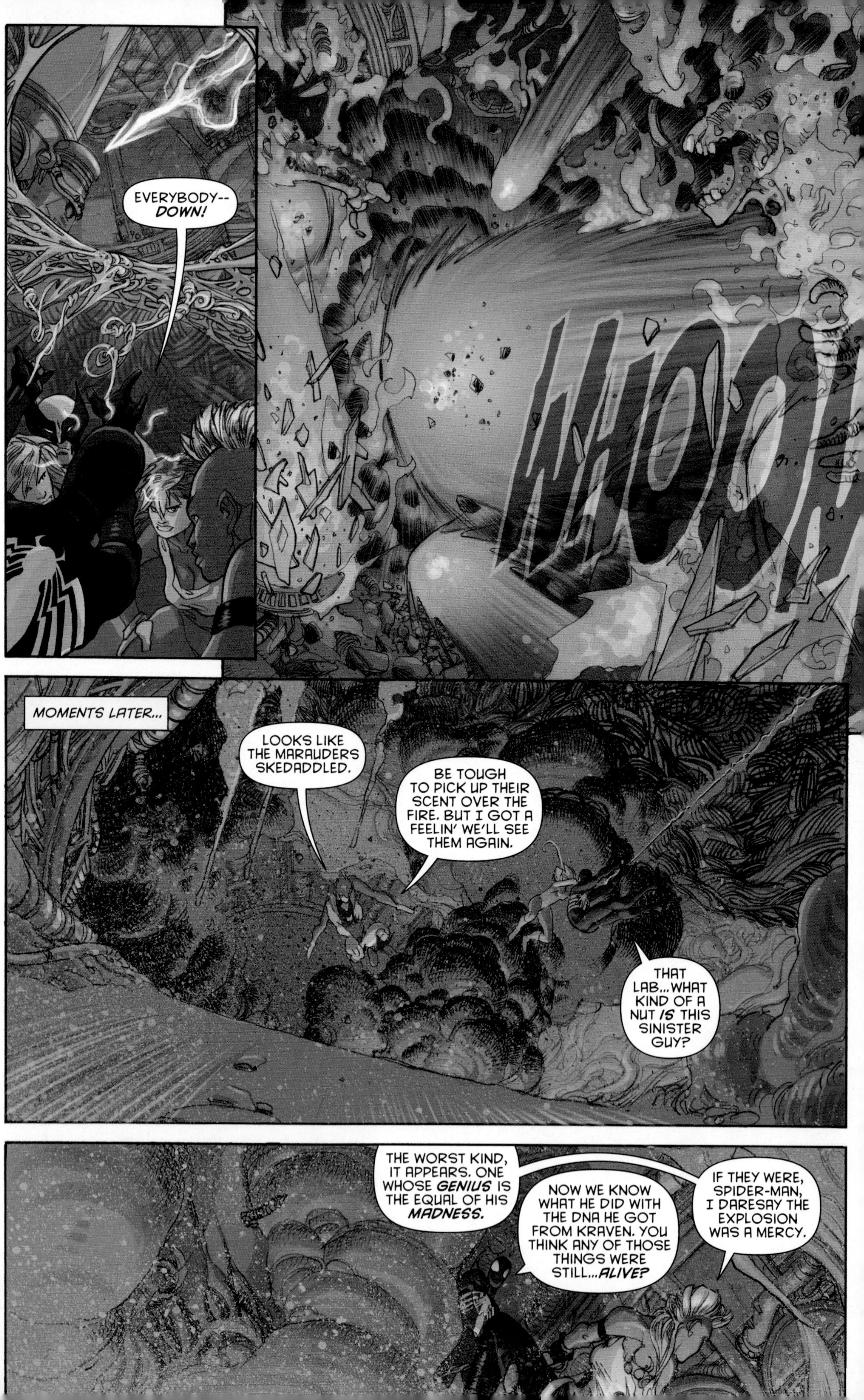
EVERYBODY-- DOWN!
WHOOM
MOMENTS LATER...
LOOKS LIKE THE MARAUDERS SKEDADDLED.
BE TOUGH TO PICK UP THEIR SCENT OVER THE FIRE. BUT I GOT A FEELIN' WE'LL SEE THEM AGAIN.
THAT LAB...WHAT KIND OF A NUT IS THIS SINISTER GUY?
THE WORST KIND, IT APPEARS. ONE WHOSE GENIUS IS THE EQUAL OF HIS MADNESS.
NOW WE KNOW WHAT HE DID WITH THE DNA HE GOT FROM KRAVEN. YOU THINK ANY OF THOSE THINGS WERE STILL...ALIVE?
IF THEY WERE, SPIDER-MAN, I DARESAY THE EXPLOSION WAS A MERCY.

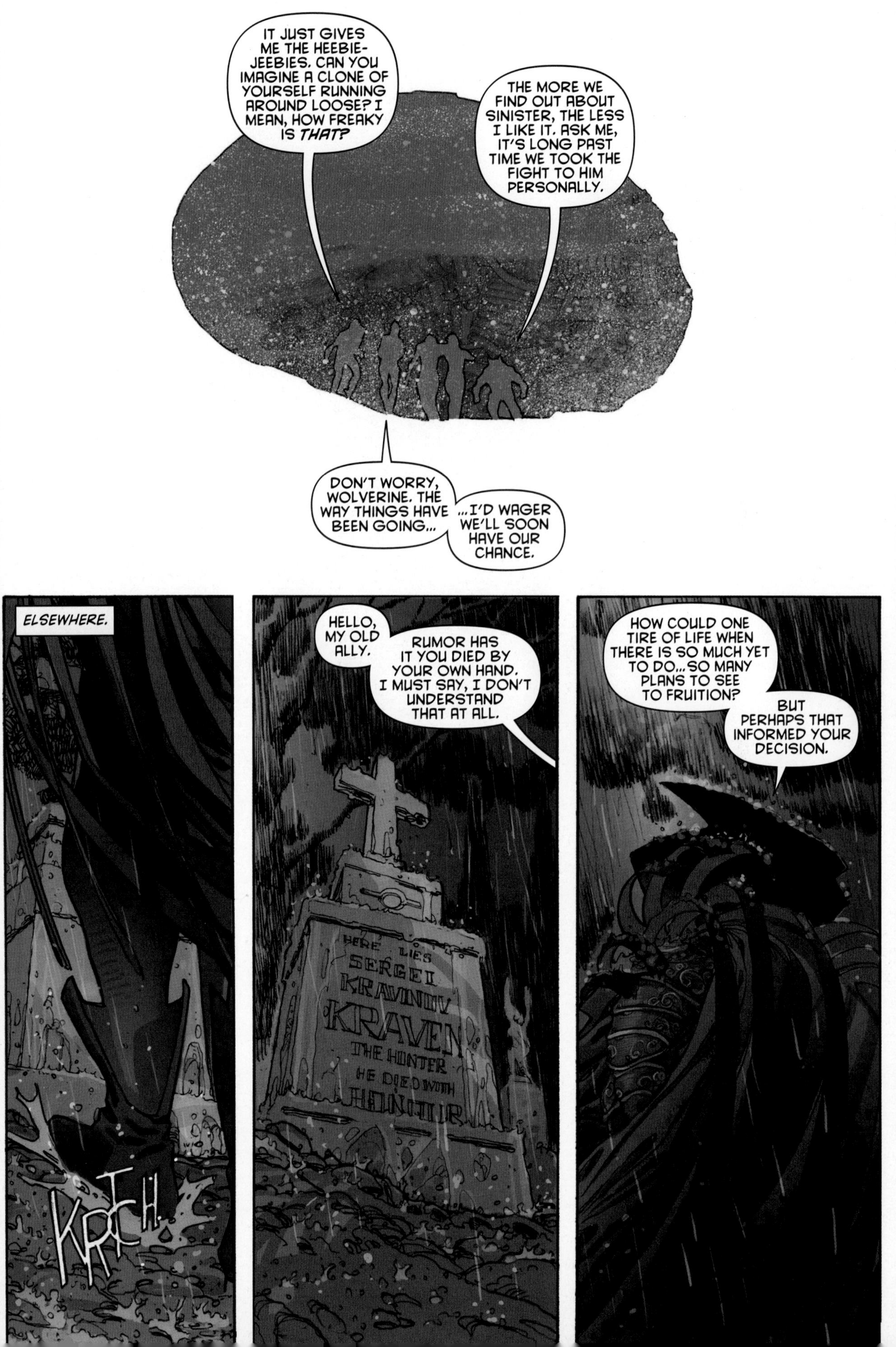

IT JUST GIVES ME THE HEEBIE-JEEBIES. CAN YOU IMAGINE A CLONE OF YOURSELF RUNNING AROUND LOOSE? I MEAN, HOW FREAKY IS *THAT?*
THE MORE WE FIND OUT ABOUT SINISTER, THE LESS I LIKE IT. ASK ME, IT'S LONG PAST TIME WE TOOK THE FIGHT TO HIM PERSONALLY.
DON'T WORRY, WOLVERINE. THE WAY THINGS HAVE BEEN GOING...
...I'D WAGER WE'LL SOON HAVE OUR CHANCE.
ELSEWHERE.
HELLO, MY OLD ALLY.
RUMOR HAS IT YOU DIED BY YOUR OWN HAND. I MUST SAY, I DON'T UNDERSTAND THAT AT ALL.
HERE LIES SERGEI KRAVINOV KRAVEN THE HUNTER HE DIED WITH HONOUR
HOW COULD ONE TIRE OF LIFE WHEN THERE IS SO MUCH YET TO DO... SO MANY PLANS TO SEE TO FRUITION?
BUT PERHAPS THAT INFORMED YOUR DECISION.

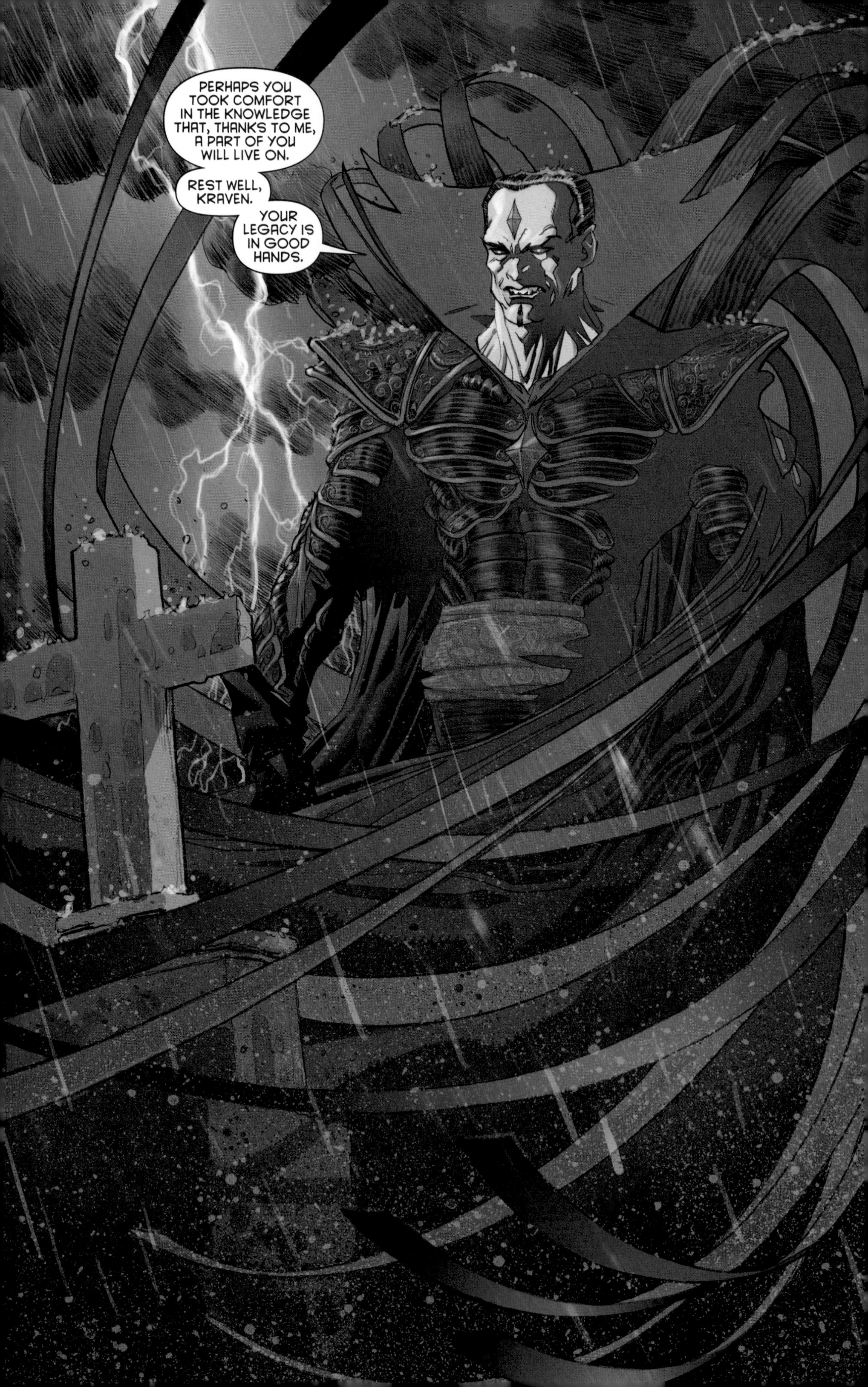
PERHAPS YOU TOOK COMFORT IN THE KNOWLEDGE THAT, THANKS TO ME, A PART OF YOU WILL LIVE ON.
REST WELL, KRAVEN.
YOUR LEGACY IS IN GOOD HANDS.

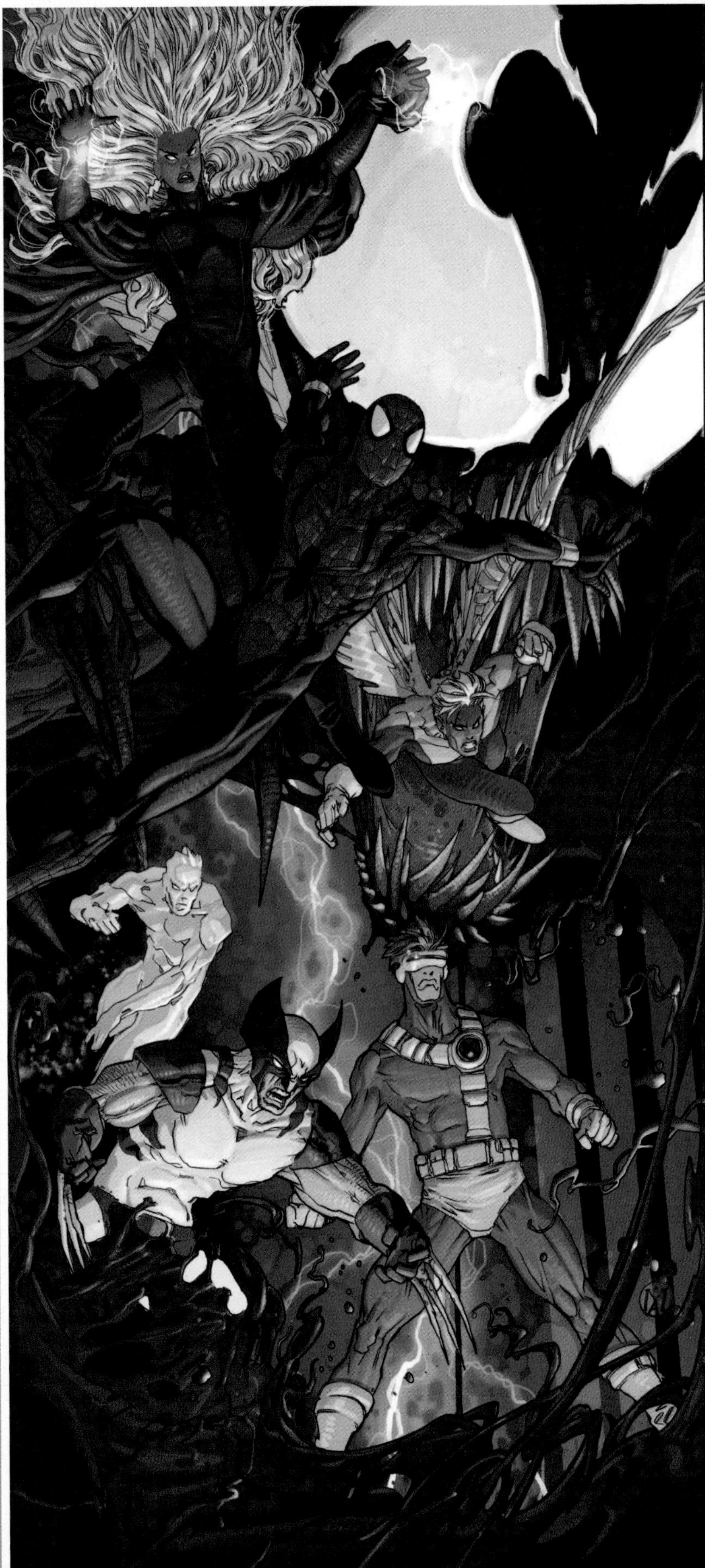

THREE

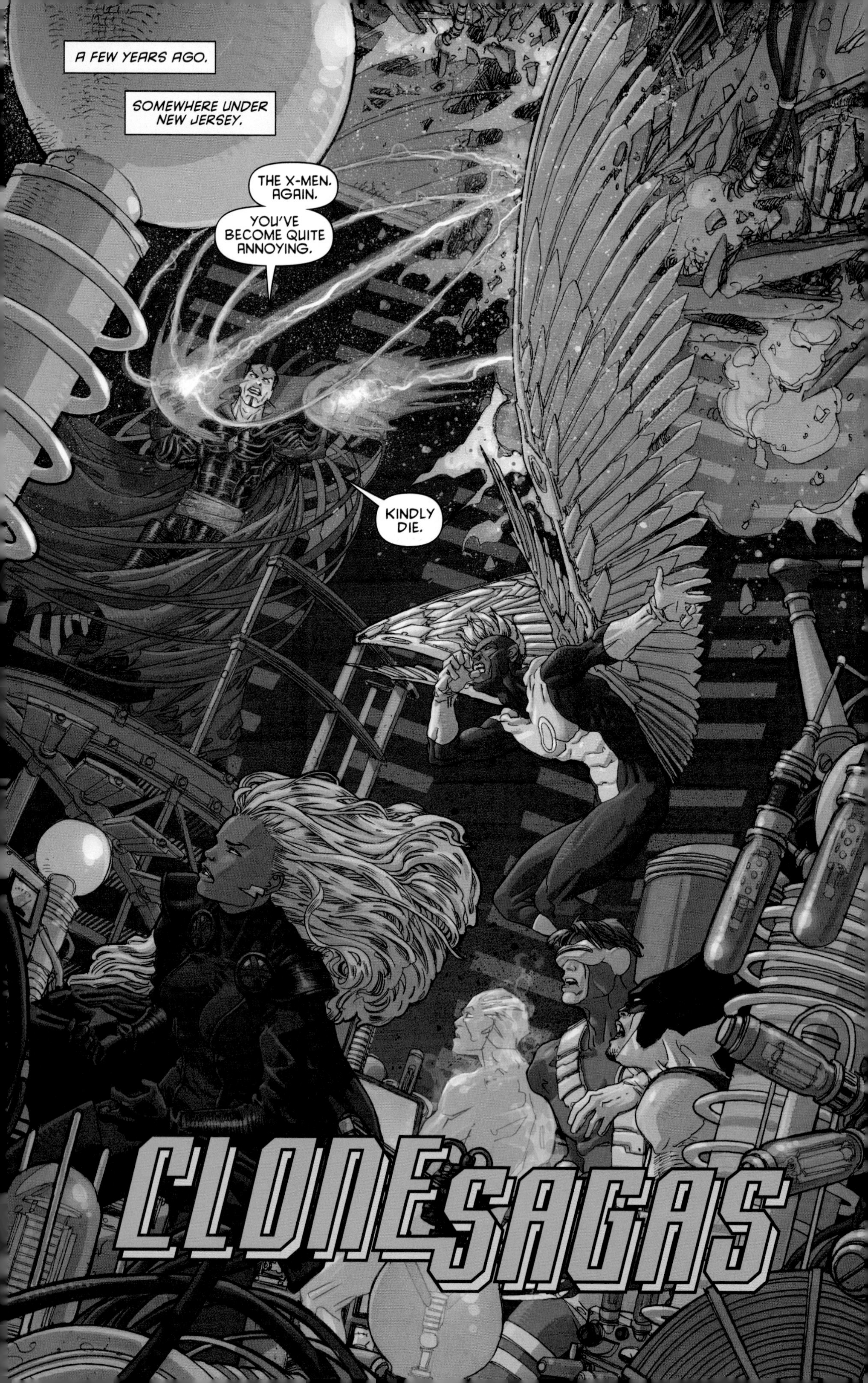
A FEW YEARS AGO.
SOMEWHERE UNDER NEW JERSEY.
THE X-MEN. AGAIN.
YOU'VE BECOME QUITE ANNOYING.
KINDLY DIE.
CLONE SAGAS

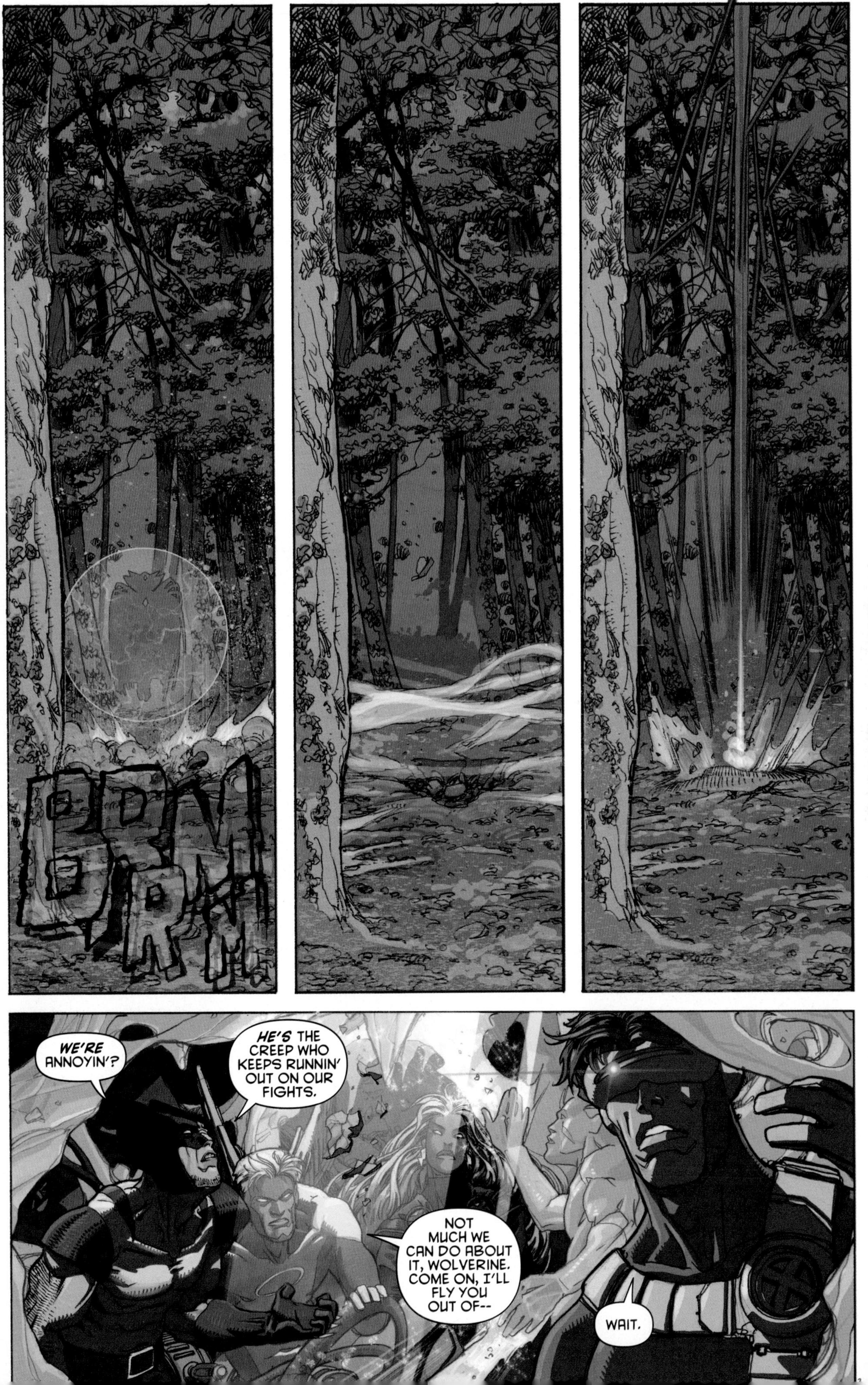
BOOM
BOOM
WE'RE ANNOYIN'?
HE'S THE CREEP WHO KEEPS RUNNIN' OUT ON OUR FIGHTS.
NOT MUCH WE CAN DO ABOUT IT, WOLVERINE. COME ON, I'LL FLY YOU OUT OF--
WAIT.

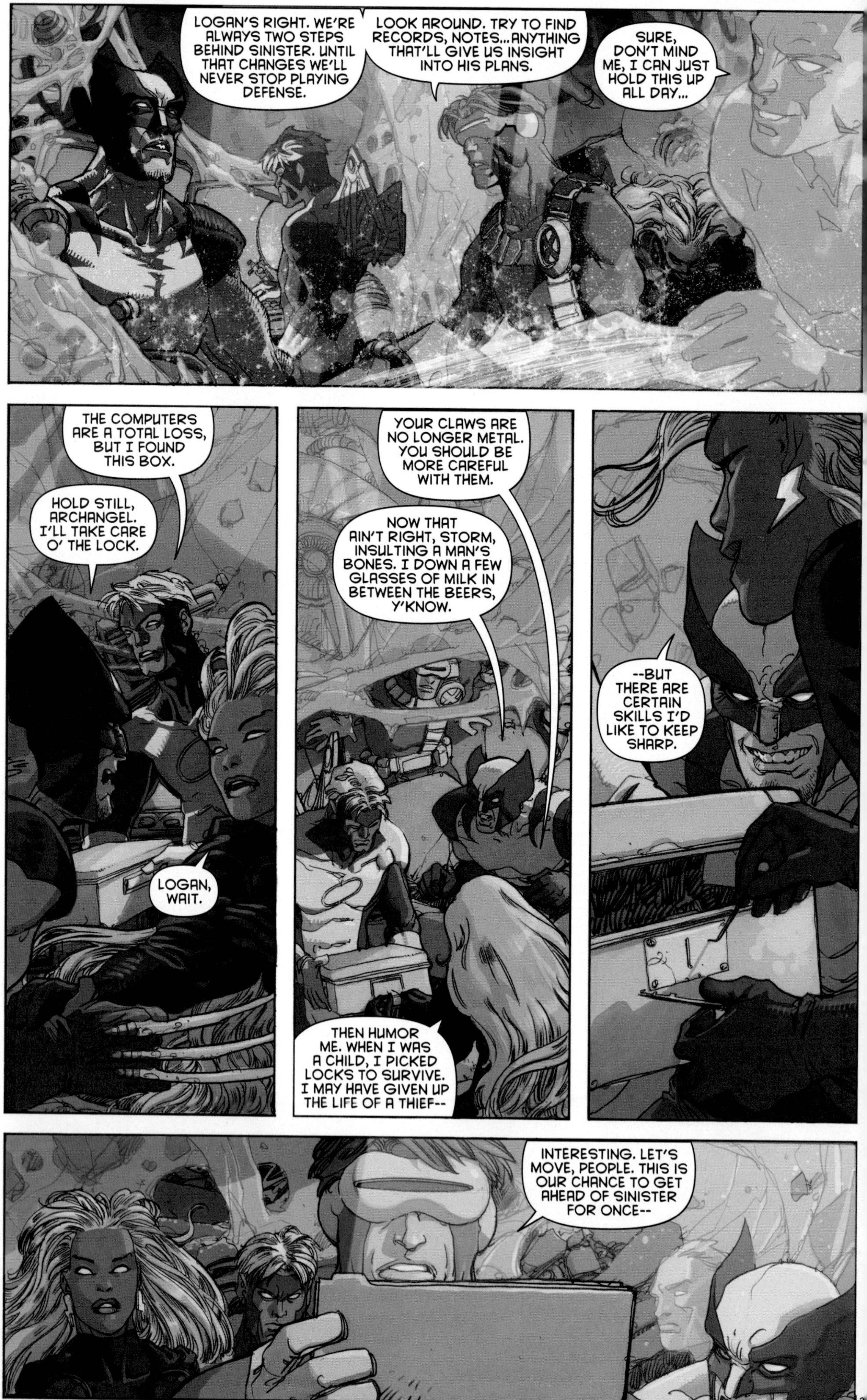
LOGAN'S RIGHT. WE'RE ALWAYS TWO STEPS BEHIND SINISTER. UNTIL THAT CHANGES WE'LL NEVER STOP PLAYING DEFENSE.
LOOK AROUND. TRY TO FIND RECORDS, NOTES... ANYTHING THAT'LL GIVE US INSIGHT INTO HIS PLANS.
SURE, DON'T MIND ME, I CAN JUST HOLD THIS UP ALL DAY...
THE COMPUTERS ARE A TOTAL LOSS, BUT I FOUND THIS BOX.
HOLD STILL, ARCHANGEL. I'LL TAKE CARE O' THE LOCK.
LOGAN, WAIT.
YOUR CLAWS ARE NO LONGER METAL. YOU SHOULD BE MORE CAREFUL WITH THEM.
NOW THAT AIN'T RIGHT, STORM, INSULTING A MAN'S BONES. I DOWN A FEW GLASSES OF MILK IN BETWEEN THE BEERS, Y'KNOW.
THEN HUMOR ME. WHEN I WAS A CHILD, I PICKED LOCKS TO SURVIVE. I MAY HAVE GIVEN UP THE LIFE OF A THIEF--
--BUT THERE ARE CERTAIN SKILLS I'D LIKE TO KEEP SHARP.
INTERESTING. LET'S MOVE, PEOPLE. THIS IS OUR CHANCE TO GET AHEAD OF SINISTER FOR ONCE--

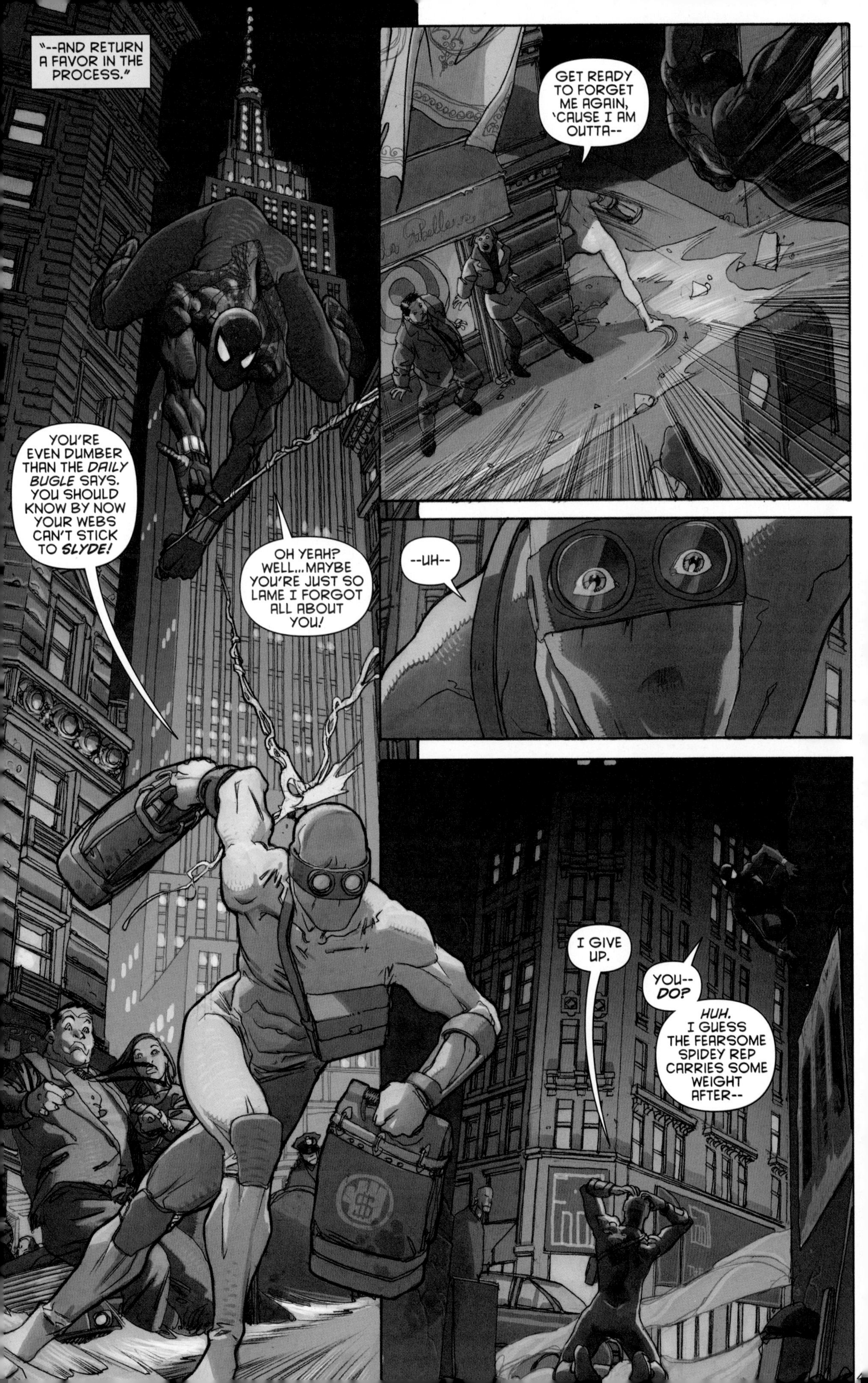
"--AND RETURN A FAVOR IN THE PROCESS."
YOU'RE EVEN DUMBER THAN THE *DAILY BUGLE* SAYS. YOU SHOULD KNOW BY NOW YOUR WEBS CAN'T STICK TO ***SLYDE!***
OH YEAH? WELL...MAYBE YOU'RE JUST SO LAME I FORGOT ALL ABOUT YOU!
GET READY TO FORGET ME AGAIN, 'CAUSE I AM OUTTA--
--UH--
I GIVE UP.
YOU-- ***DO?***
HUH. I GUESS THE FEARSOME SPIDEY REP CARRIES SOME WEIGHT AFTER--

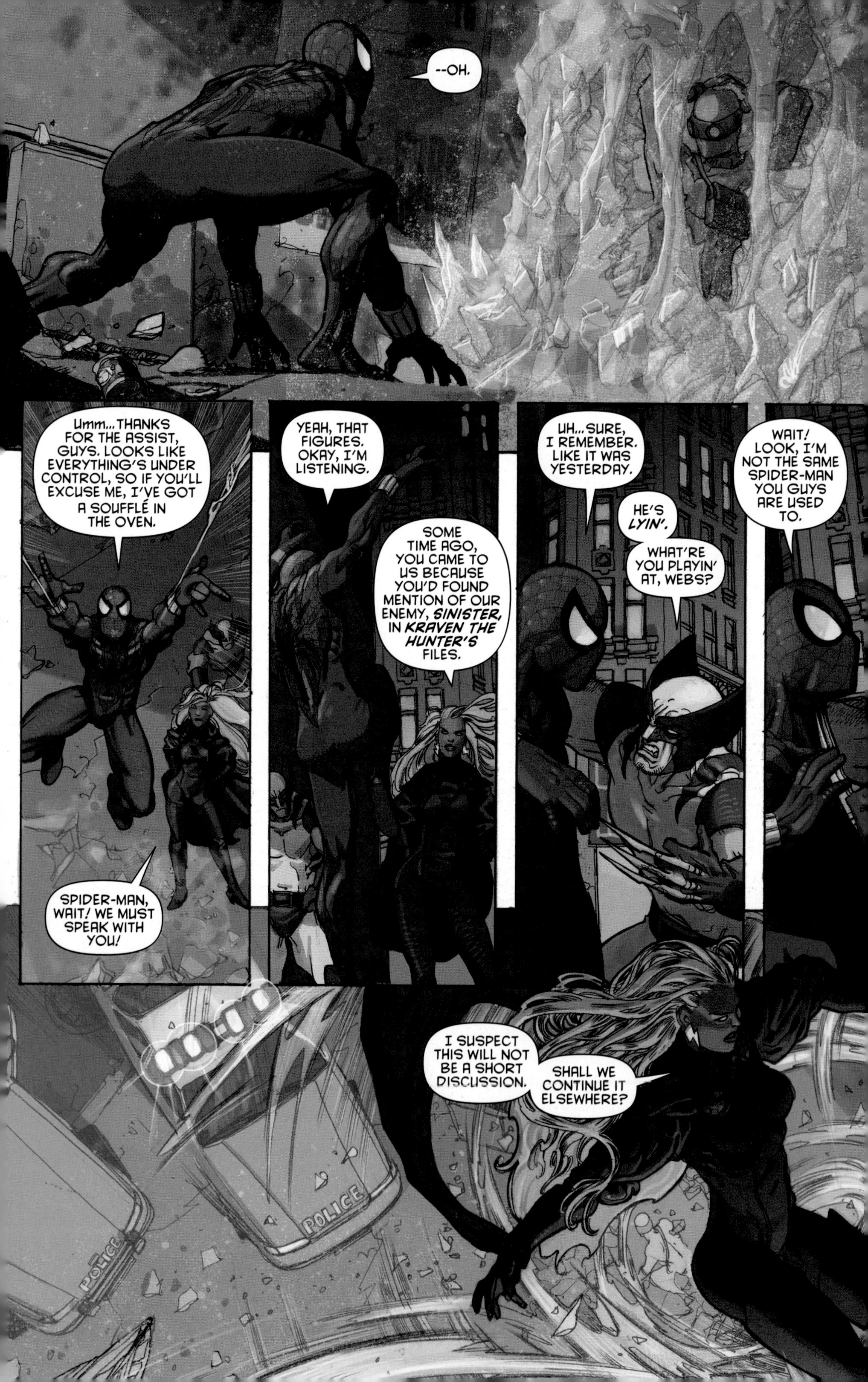
--OH.
Umm... THANKS FOR THE ASSIST, GUYS. LOOKS LIKE EVERYTHING'S UNDER CONTROL, SO IF YOU'LL EXCUSE ME, I'VE GOT A SOUFFLÉ IN THE OVEN.
SPIDER-MAN, WAIT! WE MUST SPEAK WITH YOU!
YEAH, THAT FIGURES. OKAY, I'M LISTENING.
SOME TIME AGO, YOU CAME TO US BECAUSE YOU'D FOUND MENTION OF OUR ENEMY, SINISTER, IN KRAVEN THE HUNTER'S FILES.
UH... SURE, I REMEMBER. LIKE IT WAS YESTERDAY.
HE'S LYIN'.
WHAT'RE YOU PLAYIN' AT, WEBS?
WAIT! LOOK, I'M NOT THE SAME SPIDER-MAN YOU GUYS ARE USED TO.
I SUSPECT THIS WILL NOT BE A SHORT DISCUSSION.
SHALL WE CONTINUE IT ELSEWHERE?
POLICE
POLICE

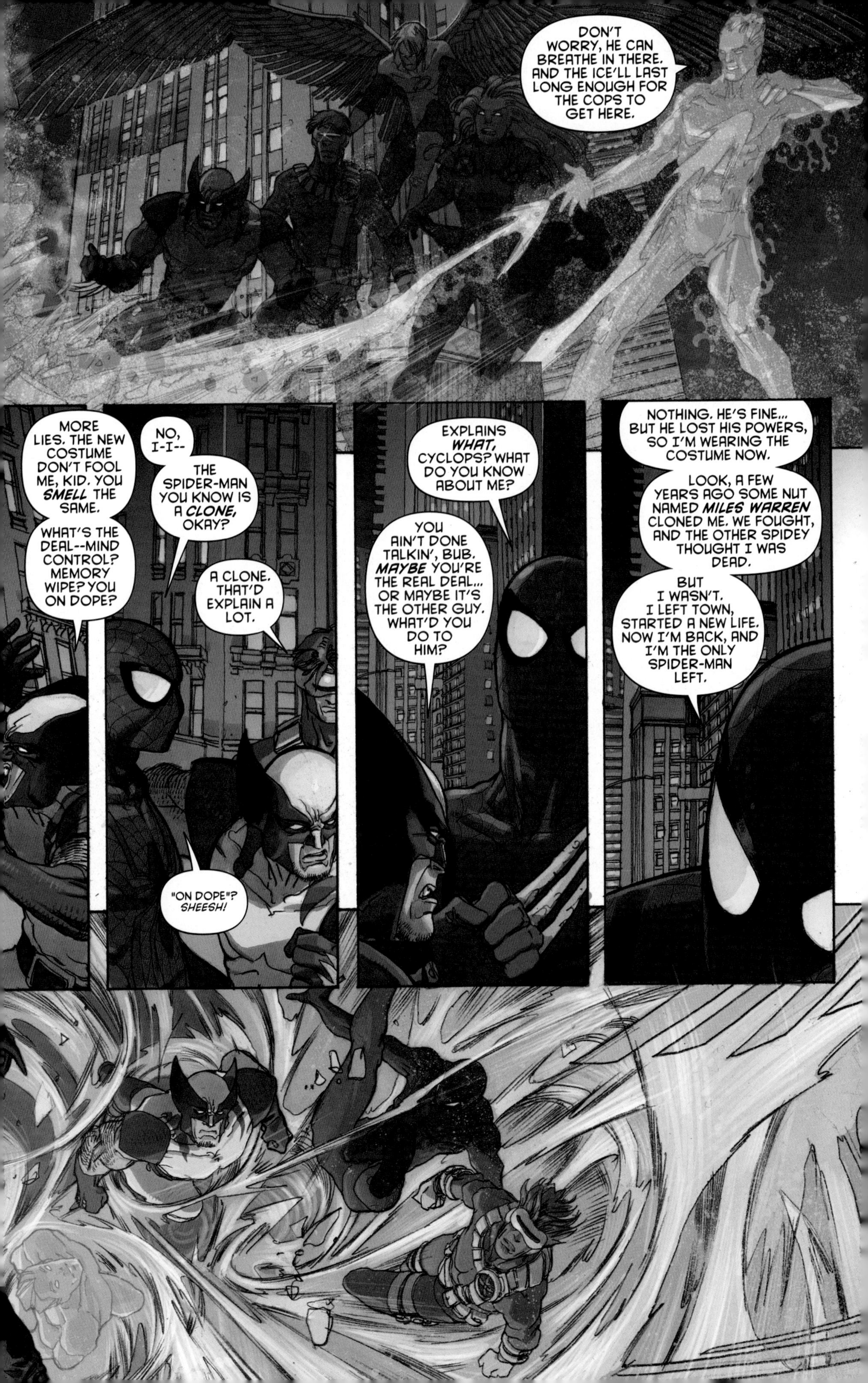
DON'T WORRY, HE CAN BREATHE IN THERE. AND THE ICE'LL LAST LONG ENOUGH FOR THE COPS TO GET HERE.
MORE LIES. THE NEW COSTUME DON'T FOOL ME, KID. YOU *SMELL* THE SAME.
WHAT'S THE DEAL--MIND CONTROL? MEMORY WIPE? YOU ON DOPE?
NO, I-I--
THE SPIDER-MAN YOU KNOW IS A *CLONE,* OKAY?
A CLONE. THAT'D EXPLAIN A LOT.
"ON DOPE"? *SHEESH!*
EXPLAINS *WHAT,* CYCLOPS? WHAT DO YOU KNOW ABOUT ME?
YOU AIN'T DONE TALKIN', BUB. *MAYBE* YOU'RE THE REAL DEAL... OR MAYBE IT'S THE OTHER GUY. WHAT'D YOU DO TO HIM?
NOTHING. HE'S FINE... BUT HE LOST HIS POWERS, SO I'M WEARING THE COSTUME NOW.
LOOK, A FEW YEARS AGO SOME NUT NAMED *MILES WARREN* CLONED ME. WE FOUGHT, AND THE OTHER SPIDEY THOUGHT I WAS DEAD.
BUT I WASN'T. I LEFT TOWN, STARTED A NEW LIFE. NOW I'M BACK, AND I'M THE ONLY SPIDER-MAN LEFT.

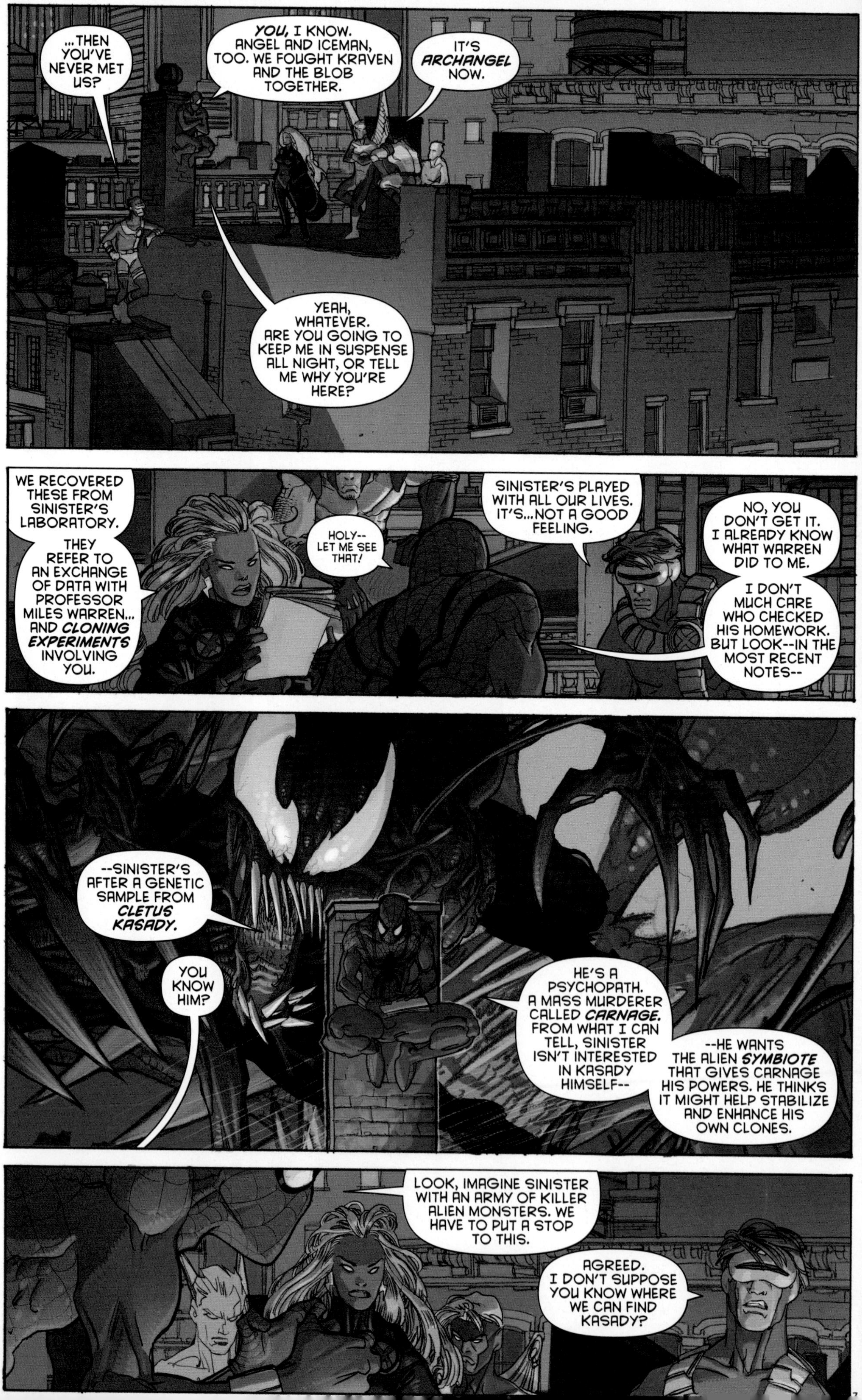
...THEN YOU'VE NEVER MET US?
YOU, I KNOW. ANGEL AND ICEMAN, TOO. WE FOUGHT KRAVEN AND THE BLOB TOGETHER.
IT'S ARCHANGEL NOW.
YEAH, WHATEVER. ARE YOU GOING TO KEEP ME IN SUSPENSE ALL NIGHT, OR TELL ME WHY YOU'RE HERE?
WE RECOVERED THESE FROM SINISTER'S LABORATORY.
THEY REFER TO AN EXCHANGE OF DATA WITH PROFESSOR MILES WARREN... AND CLONING EXPERIMENTS INVOLVING YOU.
HOLY-- LET ME SEE THAT!
SINISTER'S PLAYED WITH ALL OUR LIVES. IT'S...NOT A GOOD FEELING.
NO, YOU DON'T GET IT. I ALREADY KNOW WHAT WARREN DID TO ME.
I DON'T MUCH CARE WHO CHECKED HIS HOMEWORK. BUT LOOK--IN THE MOST RECENT NOTES--
--SINISTER'S AFTER A GENETIC SAMPLE FROM CLETUS KASADY.
YOU KNOW HIM?
HE'S A PSYCHOPATH. A MASS MURDERER CALLED CARNAGE. FROM WHAT I CAN TELL, SINISTER ISN'T INTERESTED IN KASADY HIMSELF--
--HE WANTS THE ALIEN SYMBIOTE THAT GIVES CARNAGE HIS POWERS. HE THINKS IT MIGHT HELP STABILIZE AND ENHANCE HIS OWN CLONES.
LOOK, IMAGINE SINISTER WITH AN ARMY OF KILLER ALIEN MONSTERS. WE HAVE TO PUT A STOP TO THIS.
AGREED. I DON'T SUPPOSE YOU KNOW WHERE WE CAN FIND KASADY?

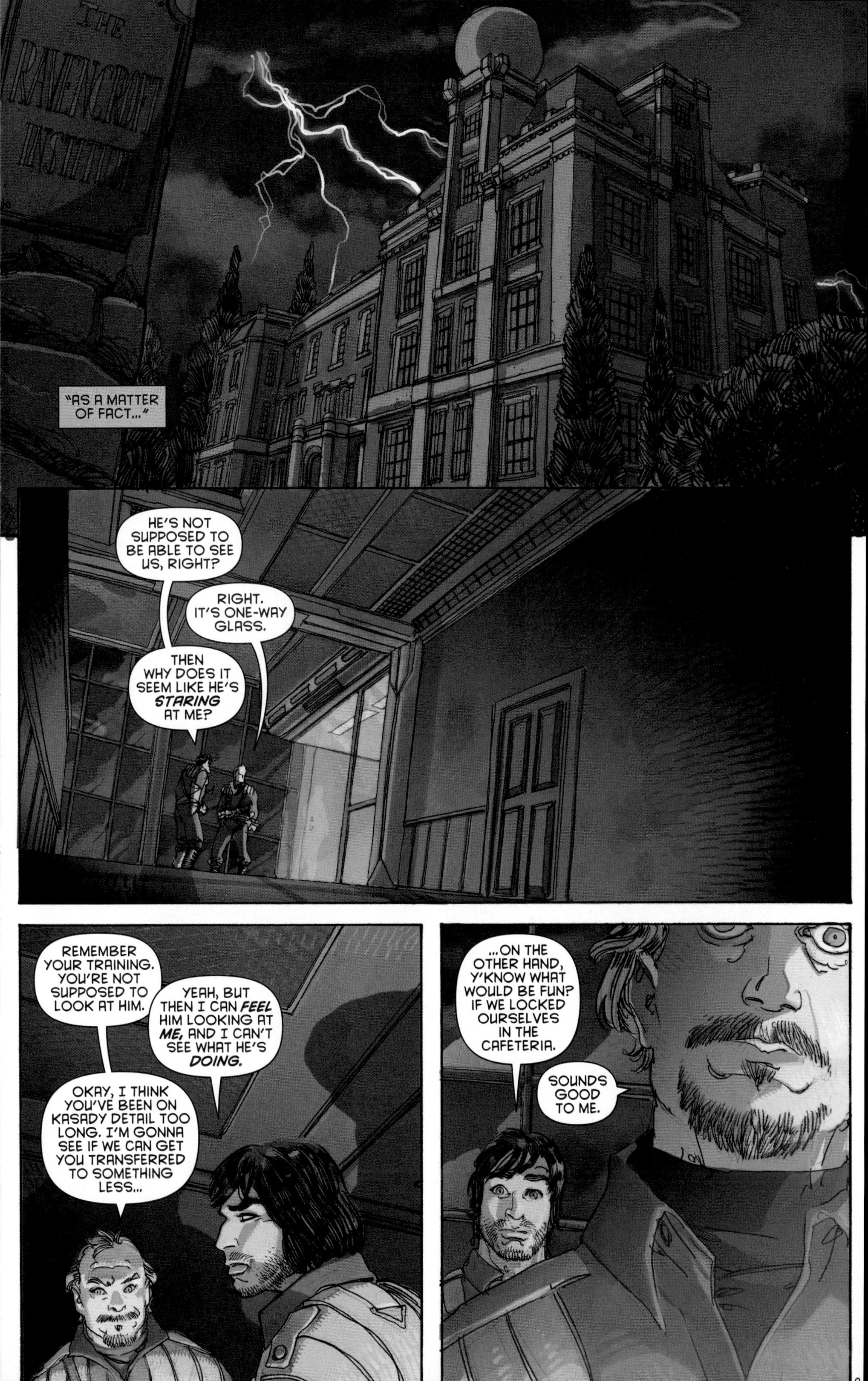
THE RAVENCROFT INSTITUTE
"AS A MATTER OF FACT..."
HE'S NOT SUPPOSED TO BE ABLE TO SEE US, RIGHT?
RIGHT. IT'S ONE-WAY GLASS.
THEN WHY DOES IT SEEM LIKE HE'S *STARING* AT ME?
REMEMBER YOUR TRAINING. YOU'RE NOT SUPPOSED TO LOOK AT HIM.
YEAH, BUT THEN I CAN *FEEL* HIM LOOKING AT *ME,* AND I CAN'T SEE WHAT HE'S *DOING.*
OKAY, I THINK YOU'VE BEEN ON KASADY DETAIL TOO LONG. I'M GONNA SEE IF WE CAN GET YOU TRANSFERRED TO SOMETHING LESS...
...ON THE OTHER HAND, Y'KNOW WHAT WOULD BE FUN? IF WE LOCKED OURSELVES IN THE CAFETERIA.
SOUNDS GOOD TO ME.

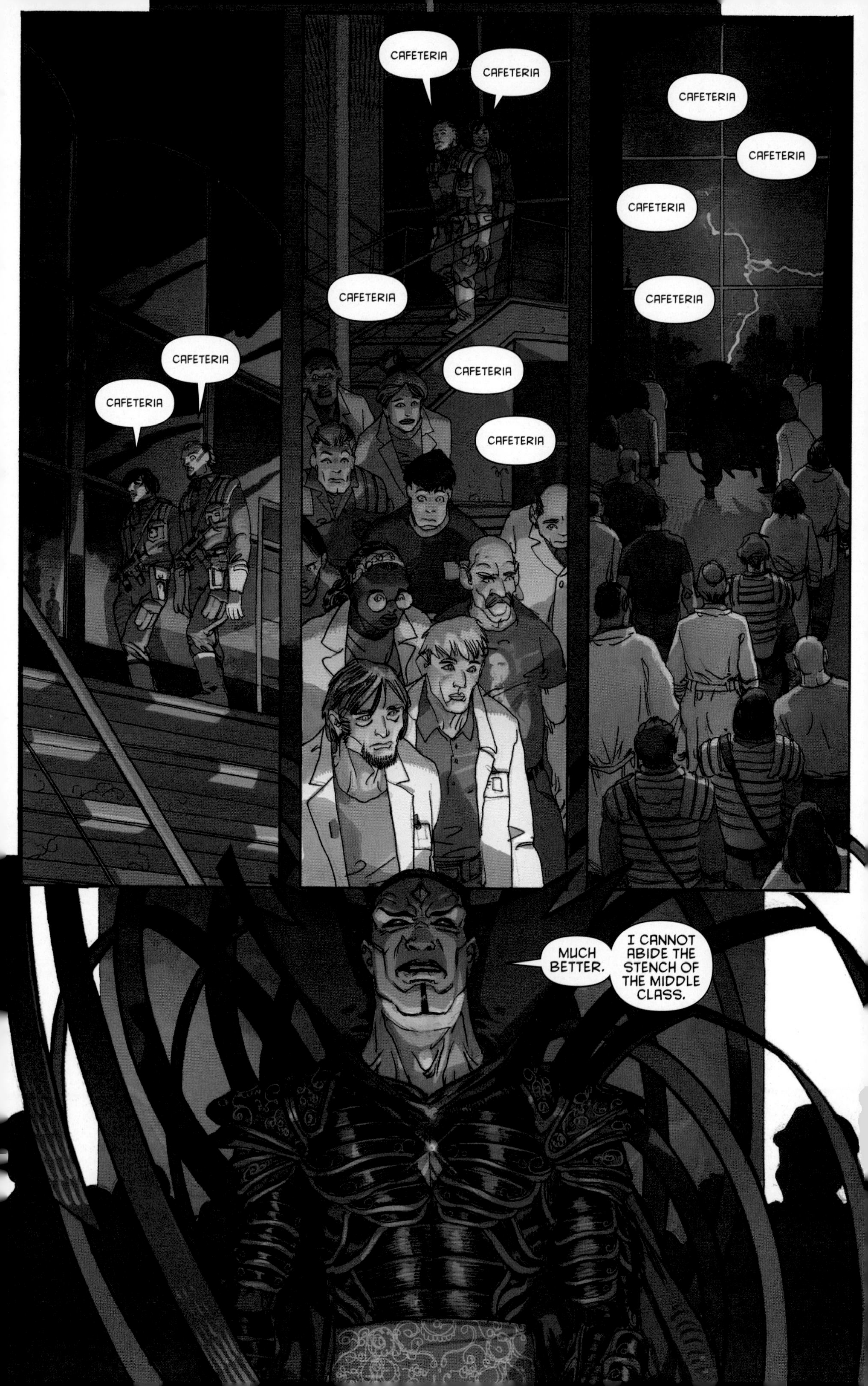
CAFETERIA
CAFETERIA
CAFETERIA
CAFETERIA
CAFETERIA
CAFETERIA
CAFETERIA
CAFETERIA
CAFETERIA
CAFETERIA
CAFETERIA
MUCH BETTER.
I CANNOT ABIDE THE STENCH OF THE MIDDLE CLASS.

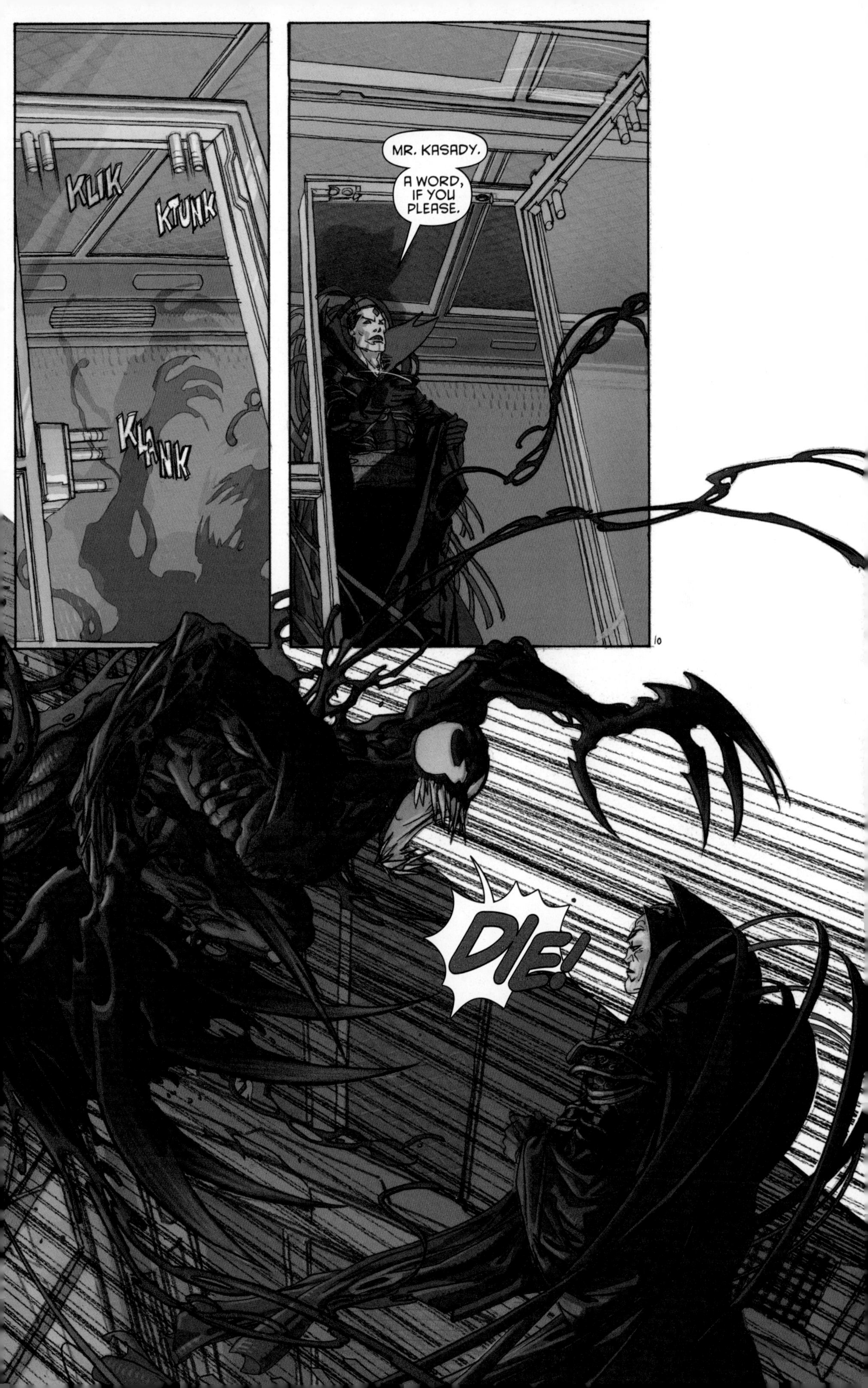
KLIK
KTUNK
KLANK
MR. KASADY.
A WORD, IF YOU PLEASE.
DIE!

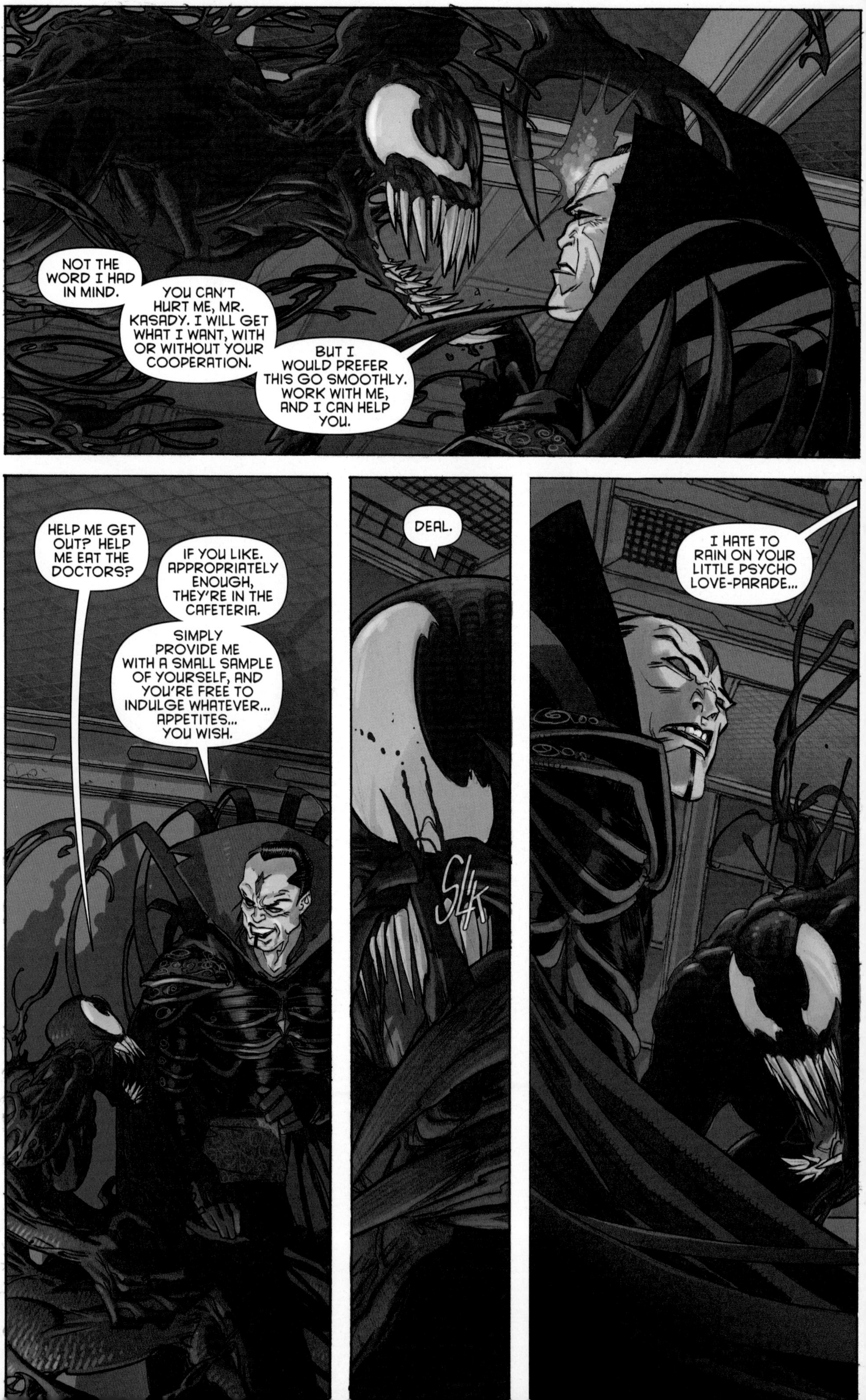
NOT THE WORD I HAD IN MIND.
YOU CAN'T HURT ME, MR. KASADY. I WILL GET WHAT I WANT, WITH OR WITHOUT YOUR COOPERATION.
BUT I WOULD PREFER THIS GO SMOOTHLY. WORK WITH ME, AND I CAN HELP YOU.
HELP ME GET OUT? HELP ME EAT THE DOCTORS?
IF YOU LIKE. APPROPRIATELY ENOUGH, THEY'RE IN THE CAFETERIA.
SIMPLY PROVIDE ME WITH A SMALL SAMPLE OF YOURSELF, AND YOU'RE FREE TO INDULGE WHATEVER... APPETITES... YOU WISH.
DEAL.
SLIK
I HATE TO RAIN ON YOUR LITTLE PSYCHO LOVE-PARADE...

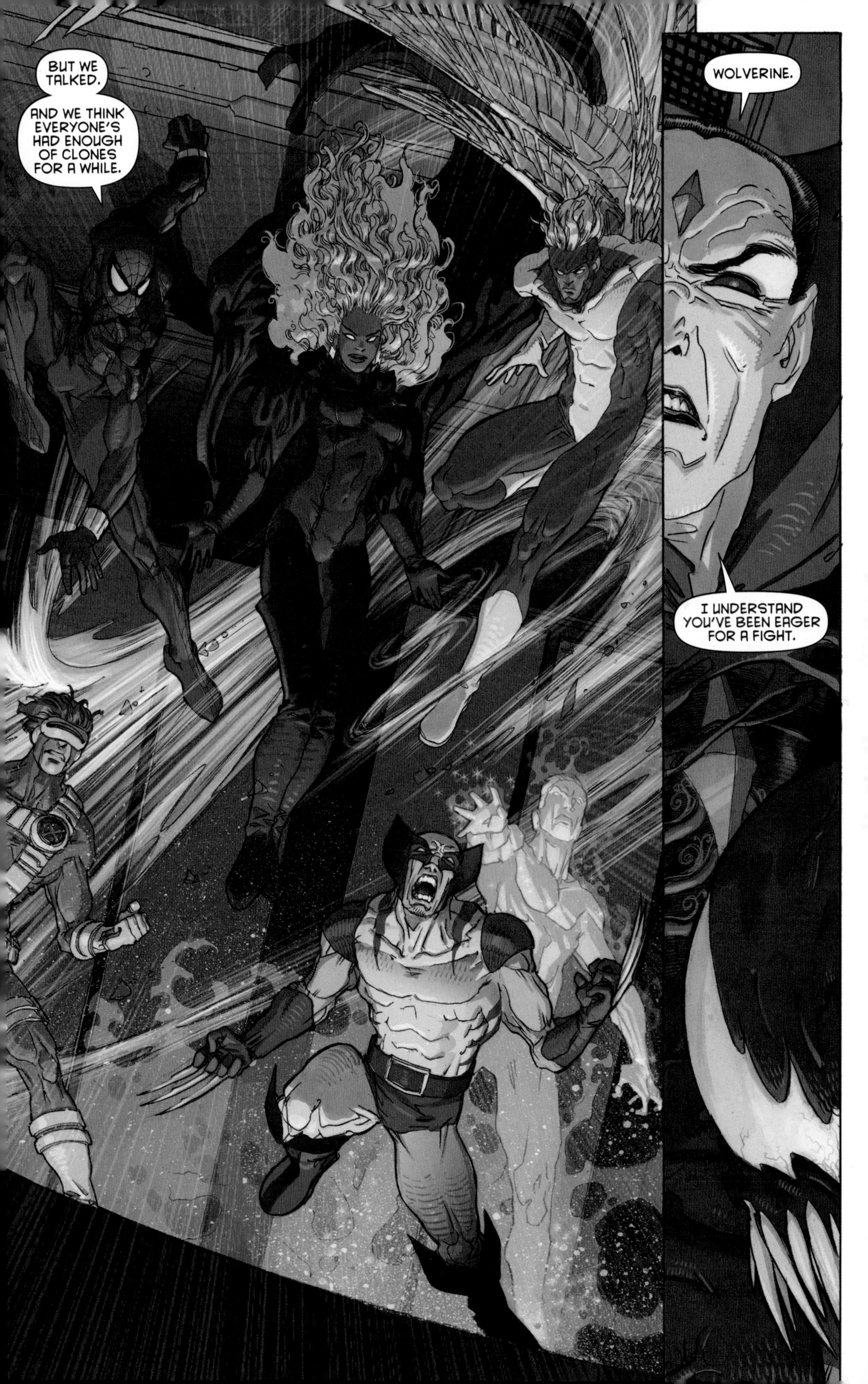
BUT WE TALKED.
AND WE THINK EVERYONE'S HAD ENOUGH OF CLONES FOR A WHILE.
WOLVERINE.
I UNDERSTAND YOU'VE BEEN EAGER FOR A FIGHT.

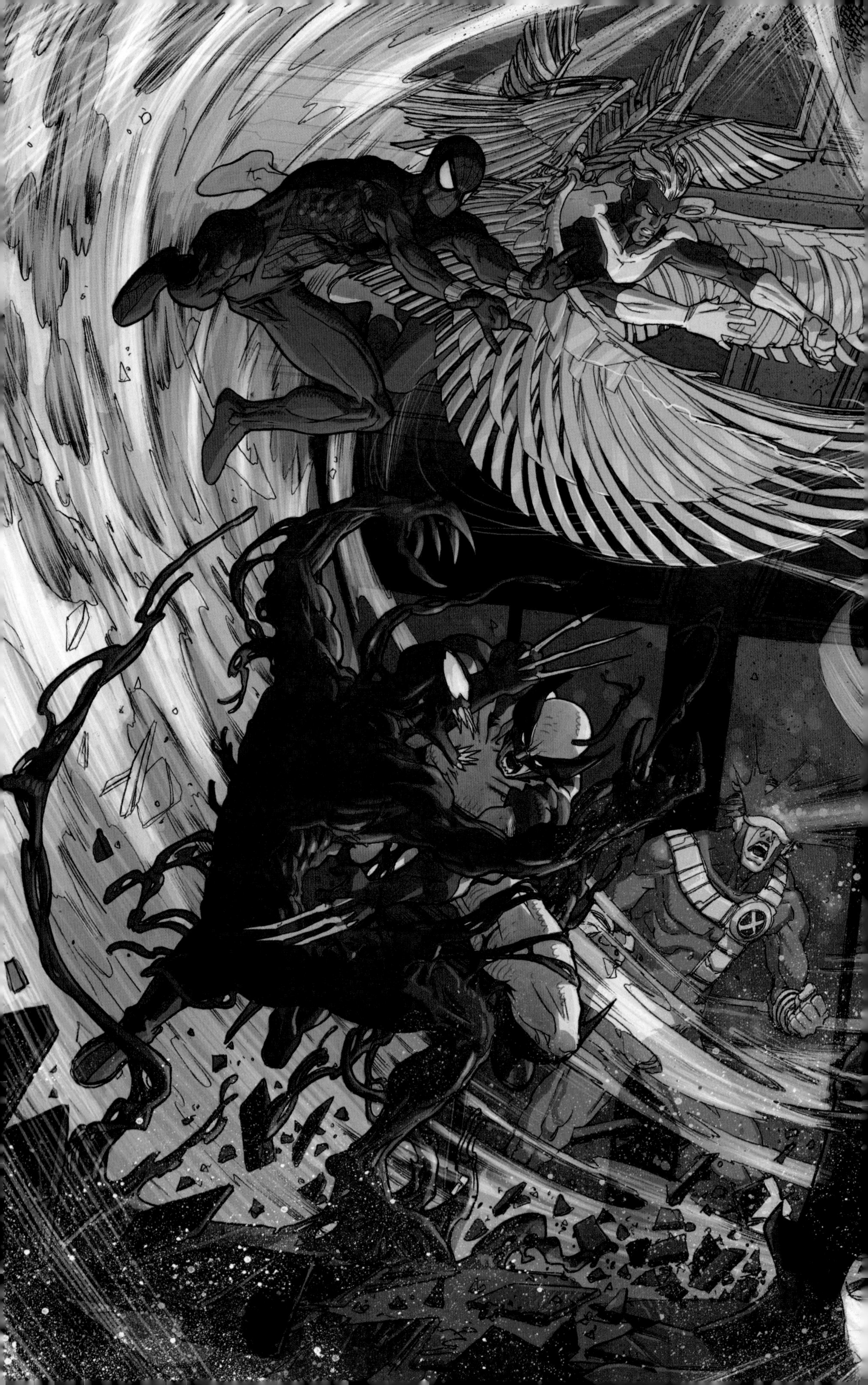

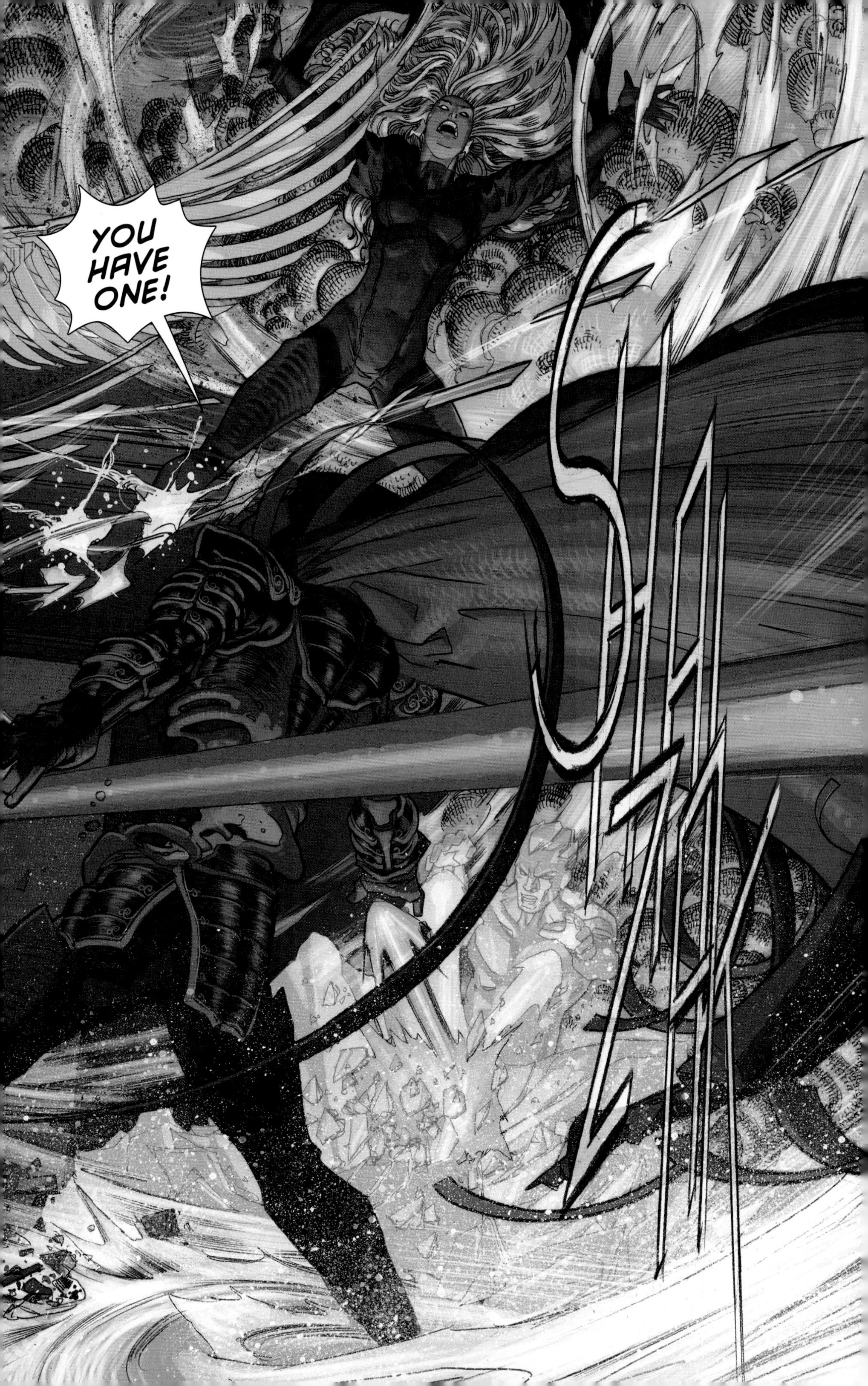
YOU HAVE ONE!

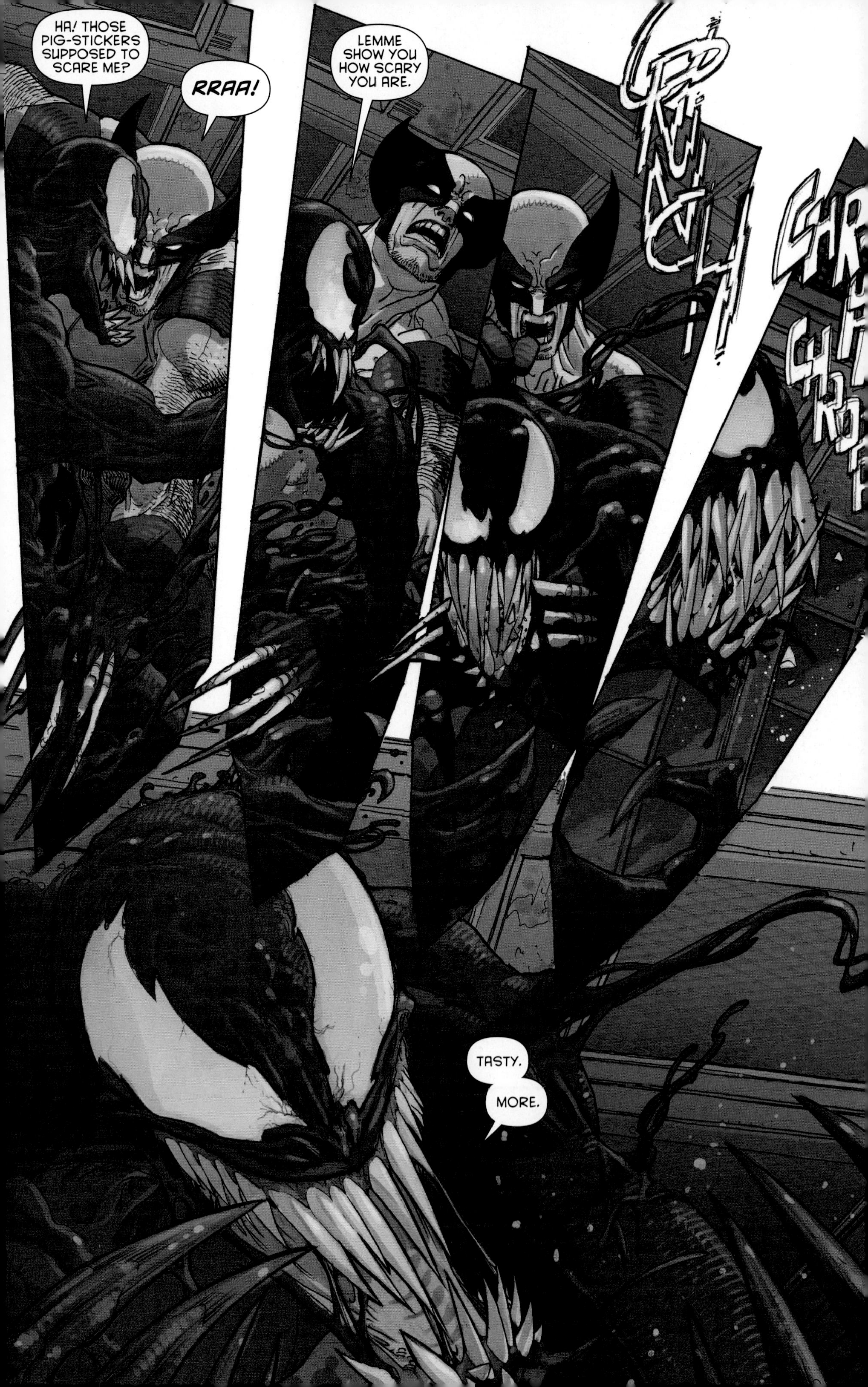

HA! THOSE PIG-STICKERS SUPPOSED TO SCARE ME?
RRAA!
LEMME SHOW YOU HOW SCARY YOU ARE.
CRUNCH
TASTY.
MORE.

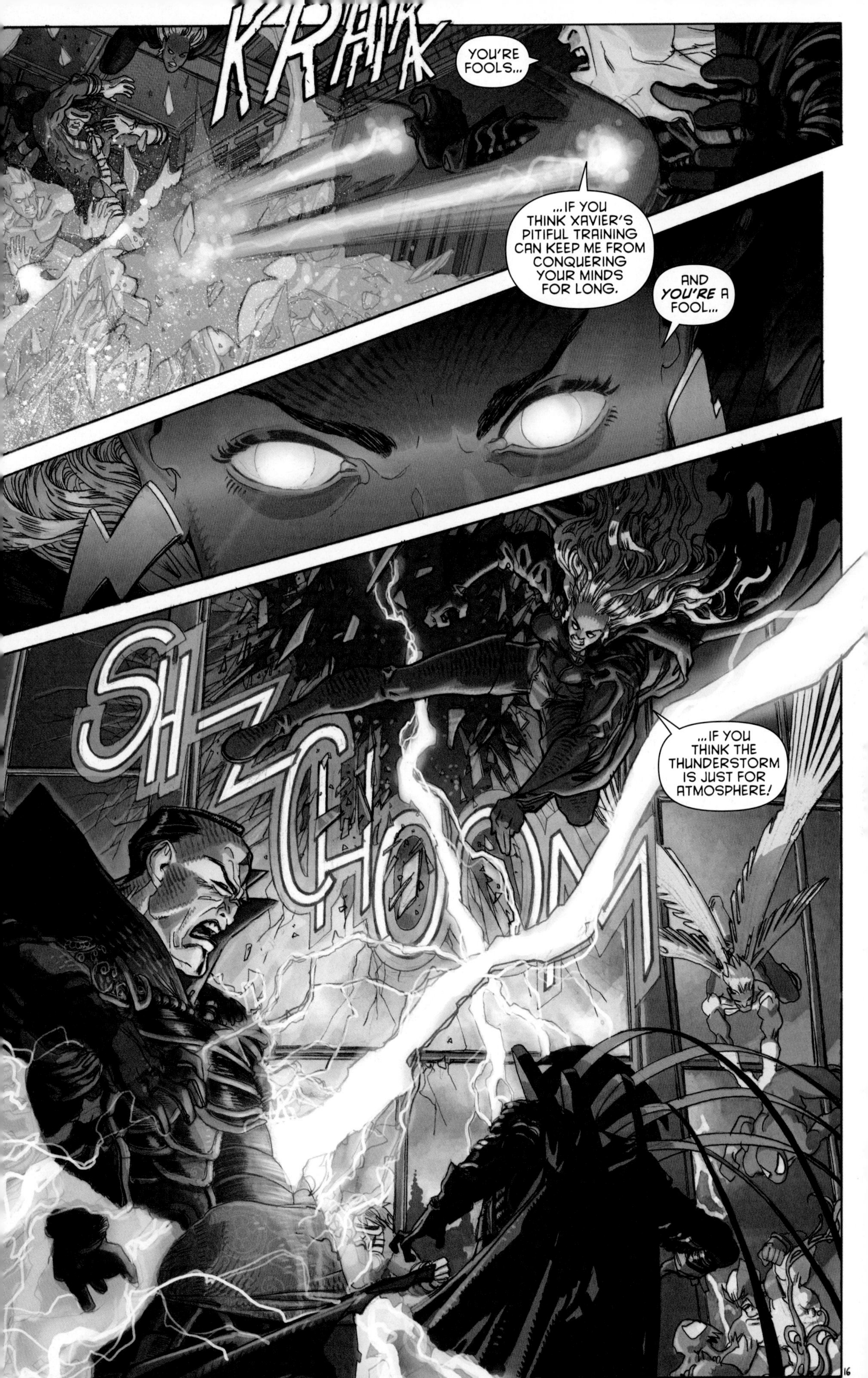
KRAAK
YOU'RE FOOLS...
...IF YOU THINK XAVIER'S PITIFUL TRAINING CAN KEEP ME FROM CONQUERING YOUR MINDS FOR LONG.
AND YOU'RE A FOOL...
SH-CHOOM
...IF YOU THINK THE THUNDERSTORM IS JUST FOR ATMOSPHERE!

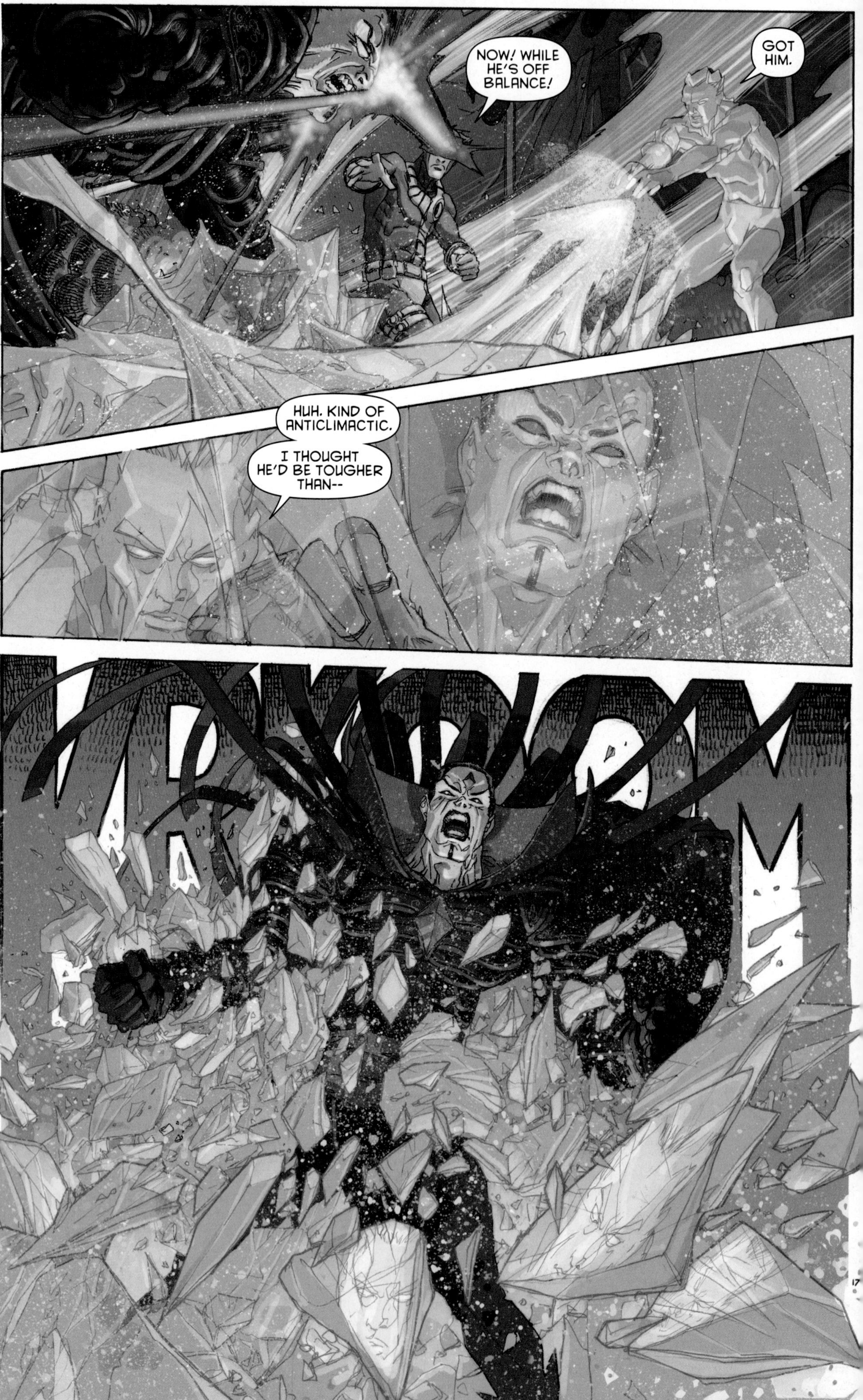
NOW! WHILE HE'S OFF BALANCE!
GOT HIM.
HUH. KIND OF ANTICLIMACTIC.
I THOUGHT HE'D BE TOUGHER THAN--

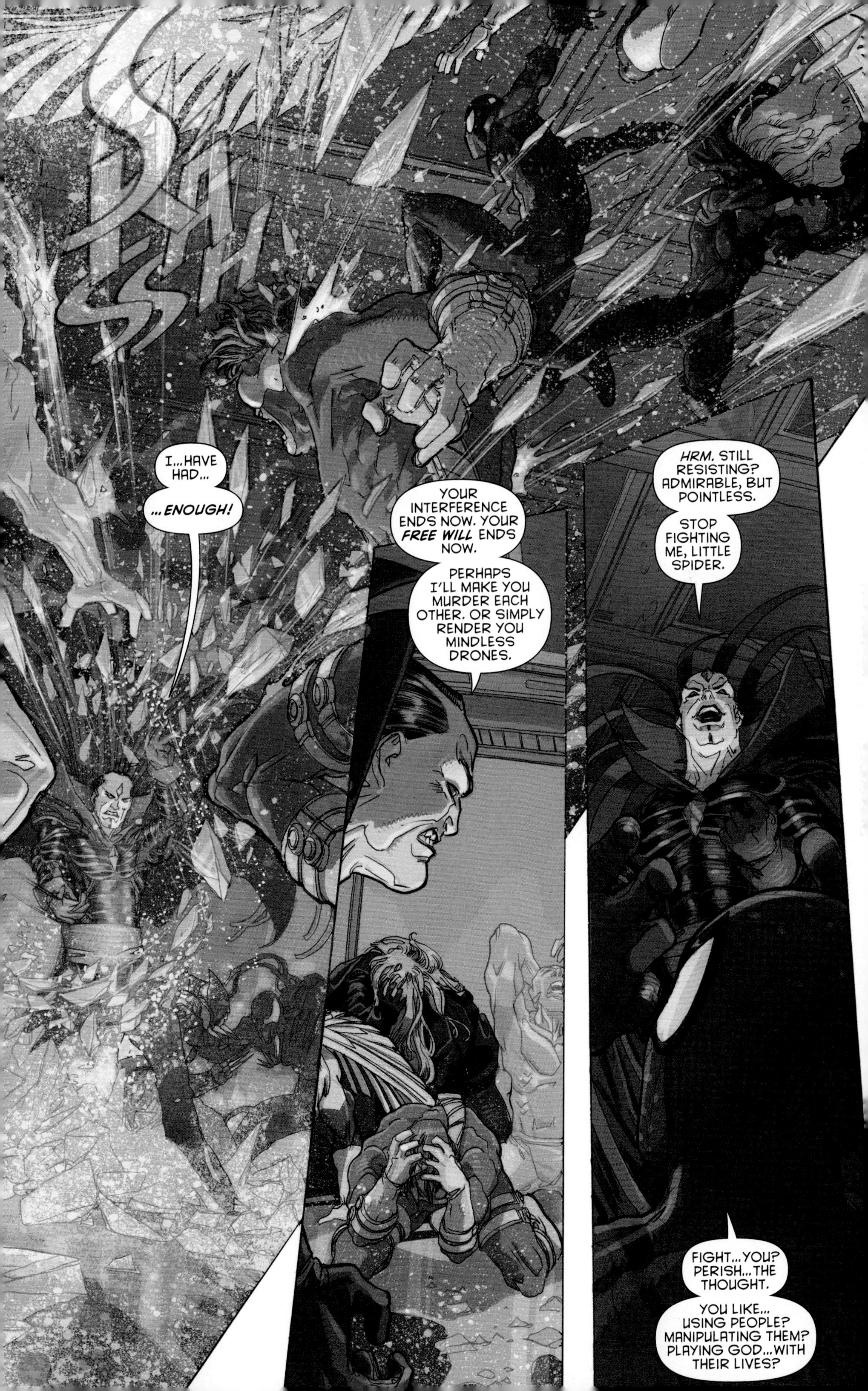
SSSHHH
I...HAVE HAD...
...ENOUGH!
YOUR INTERFERENCE ENDS NOW. YOUR FREE WILL ENDS NOW.
PERHAPS I'LL MAKE YOU MURDER EACH OTHER. OR SIMPLY RENDER YOU MINDLESS DRONES.
HRM. STILL RESISTING? ADMIRABLE, BUT POINTLESS.
STOP FIGHTING ME, LITTLE SPIDER.
FIGHT...YOU? PERISH...THE THOUGHT.
YOU LIKE... USING PEOPLE? MANIPULATING THEM? PLAYING GOD...WITH THEIR LIVES?

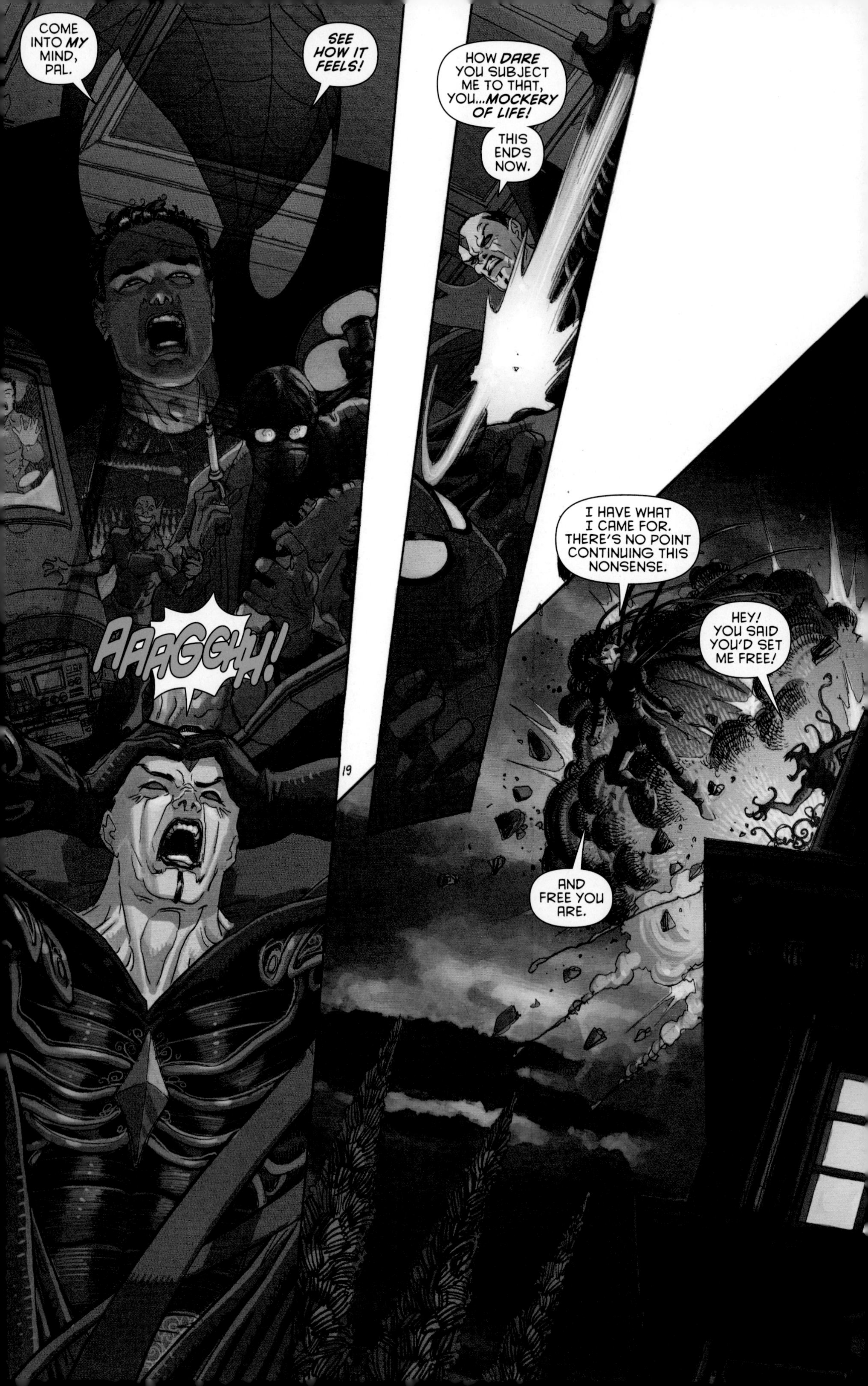
COME INTO *MY* MIND, PAL.
SEE HOW IT FEELS!
AAAGGHH!
HOW *DARE* YOU SUBJECT ME TO THAT, YOU...*MOCKERY OF LIFE!*
THIS ENDS NOW.
I HAVE WHAT I CAME FOR. THERE'S NO POINT CONTINUING THIS NONSENSE.
HEY! YOU SAID YOU'D SET ME FREE!
AND FREE YOU ARE.
19

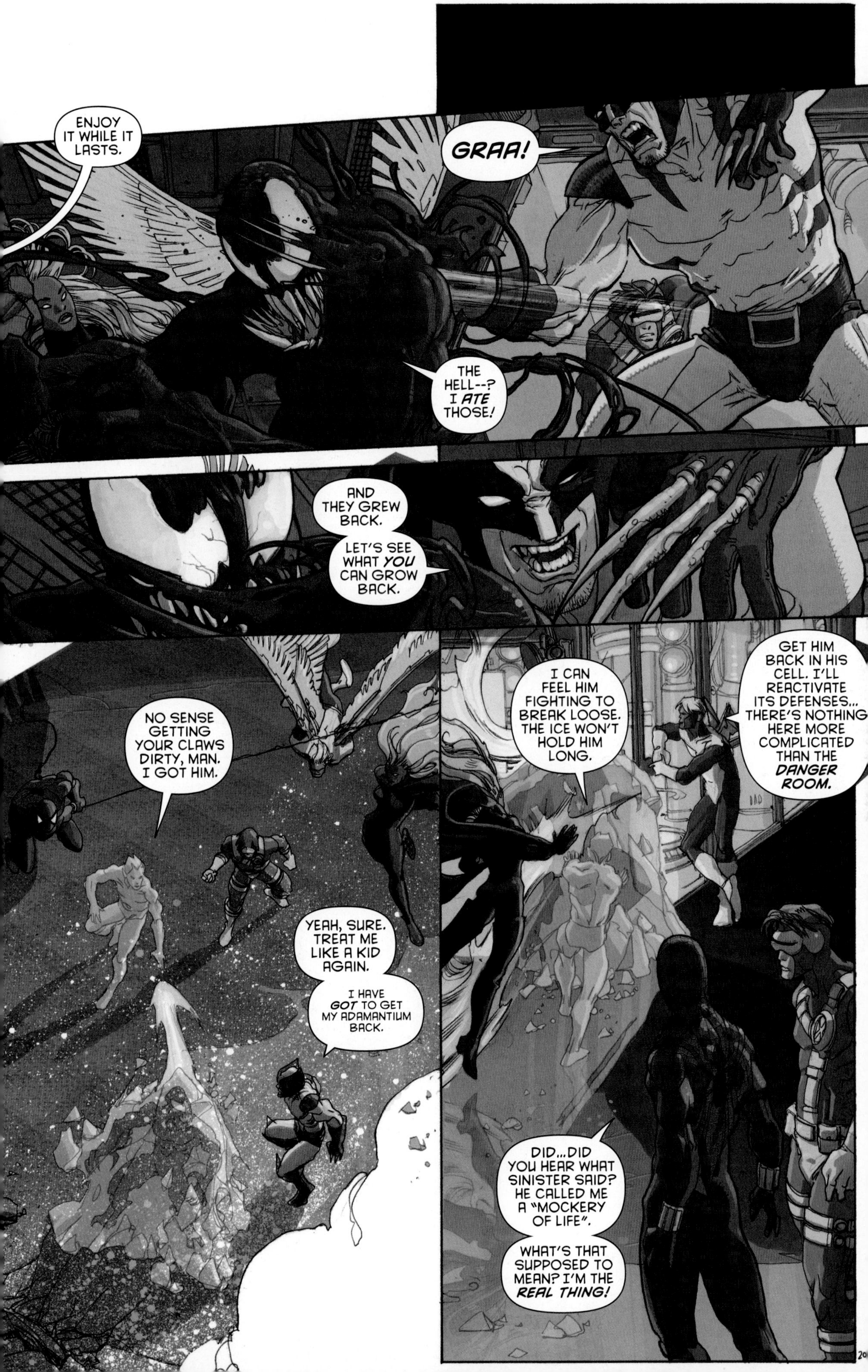
ENJOY IT WHILE IT LASTS.
GRAA!
THE HELL--? I ATE THOSE!
AND THEY GREW BACK.
LET'S SEE WHAT YOU CAN GROW BACK.
NO SENSE GETTING YOUR CLAWS DIRTY, MAN. I GOT HIM.
YEAH, SURE. TREAT ME LIKE A KID AGAIN.
I HAVE GOT TO GET MY ADAMANTIUM BACK.
I CAN FEEL HIM FIGHTING TO BREAK LOOSE. THE ICE WON'T HOLD HIM LONG.
GET HIM BACK IN HIS CELL. I'LL REACTIVATE ITS DEFENSES... THERE'S NOTHING HERE MORE COMPLICATED THAN THE DANGER ROOM.
DID...DID YOU HEAR WHAT SINISTER SAID? HE CALLED ME A "MOCKERY OF LIFE".
WHAT'S THAT SUPPOSED TO MEAN? I'M THE REAL THING!

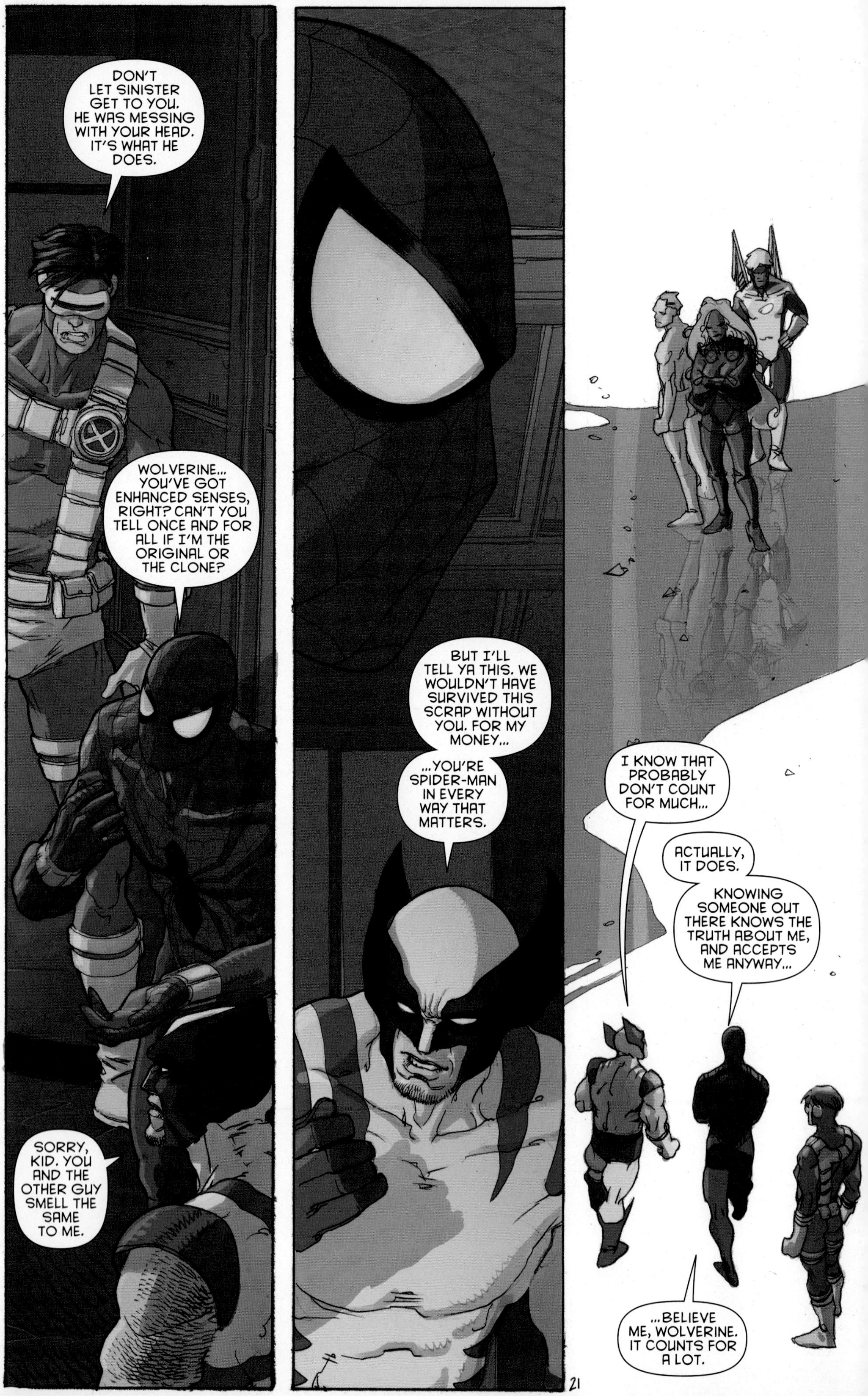
DON'T LET SINISTER GET TO YOU. HE WAS MESSING WITH YOUR HEAD. IT'S WHAT HE DOES.
WOLVERINE... YOU'VE GOT ENHANCED SENSES, RIGHT? CAN'T YOU TELL ONCE AND FOR ALL IF I'M THE ORIGINAL OR THE CLONE?
SORRY, KID. YOU AND THE OTHER GUY SMELL THE SAME TO ME.
BUT I'LL TELL YA THIS. WE WOULDN'T HAVE SURVIVED THIS SCRAP WITHOUT YOU. FOR MY MONEY...
...YOU'RE SPIDER-MAN IN EVERY WAY THAT MATTERS.
I KNOW THAT PROBABLY DON'T COUNT FOR MUCH...
ACTUALLY, IT DOES.
KNOWING SOMEONE OUT THERE KNOWS THE TRUTH ABOUT ME, AND ACCEPTS ME ANYWAY...
...BELIEVE ME, WOLVERINE. IT COUNTS FOR A LOT.

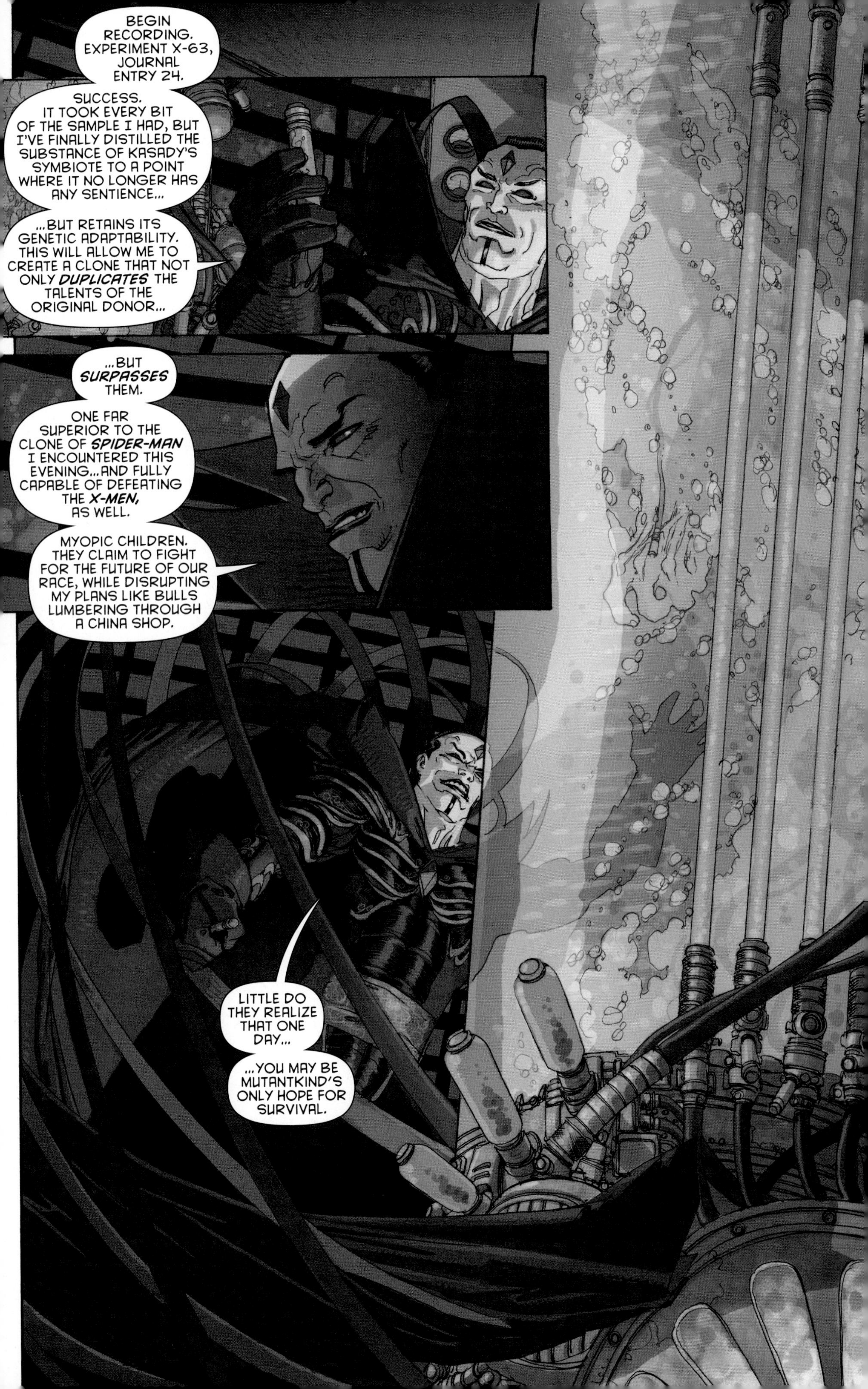
BEGIN RECORDING. EXPERIMENT X-63, JOURNAL ENTRY 24.
SUCCESS. IT TOOK EVERY BIT OF THE SAMPLE I HAD, BUT I'VE FINALLY DISTILLED THE SUBSTANCE OF KASADY'S SYMBIOTE TO A POINT WHERE IT NO LONGER HAS ANY SENTIENCE...
...BUT RETAINS ITS GENETIC ADAPTABILITY. THIS WILL ALLOW ME TO CREATE A CLONE THAT NOT ONLY DUPLICATES THE TALENTS OF THE ORIGINAL DONOR...
...BUT SURPASSES THEM.
ONE FAR SUPERIOR TO THE CLONE OF SPIDER-MAN I ENCOUNTERED THIS EVENING...AND FULLY CAPABLE OF DEFEATING THE X-MEN, AS WELL.
MYOPIC CHILDREN. THEY CLAIM TO FIGHT FOR THE FUTURE OF OUR RACE, WHILE DISRUPTING MY PLANS LIKE BULLS LUMBERING THROUGH A CHINA SHOP.
LITTLE DO THEY REALIZE THAT ONE DAY...
...YOU MAY BE MUTANTKIND'S ONLY HOPE FOR SURVIVAL.

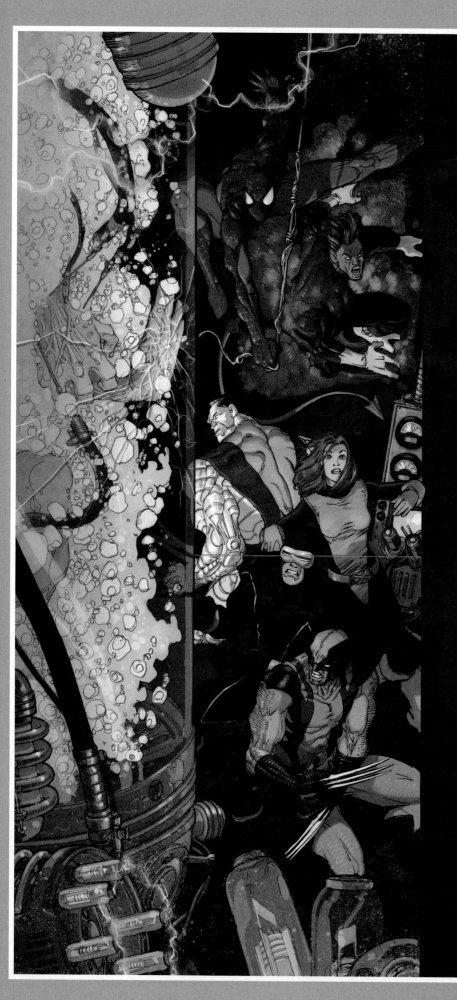

FOUR

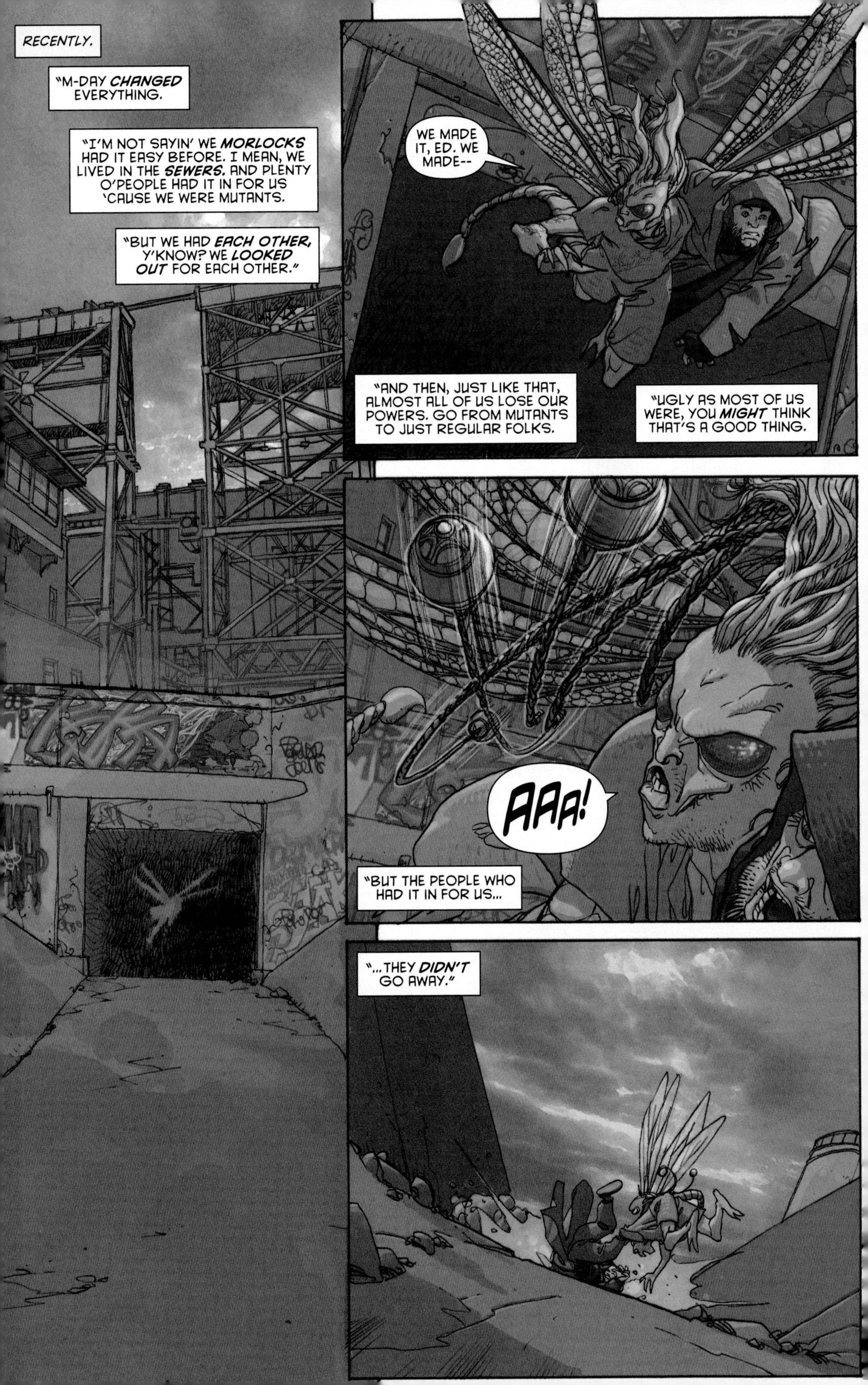
RECENTLY.
"M-DAY CHANGED EVERYTHING.
"I'M NOT SAYIN' WE MORLOCKS HAD IT EASY BEFORE. I MEAN, WE LIVED IN THE SEWERS. AND PLENTY O'PEOPLE HAD IT IN FOR US 'CAUSE WE WERE MUTANTS.
"BUT WE HAD EACH OTHER, Y'KNOW? WE LOOKED OUT FOR EACH OTHER."
WE MADE IT, ED. WE MADE--
"AND THEN, JUST LIKE THAT, ALMOST ALL OF US LOSE OUR POWERS. GO FROM MUTANTS TO JUST REGULAR FOLKS.
"UGLY AS MOST OF US WERE, YOU MIGHT THINK THAT'S A GOOD THING.
AAA!
"BUT THE PEOPLE WHO HAD IT IN FOR US...
"...THEY DIDN'T GO AWAY."

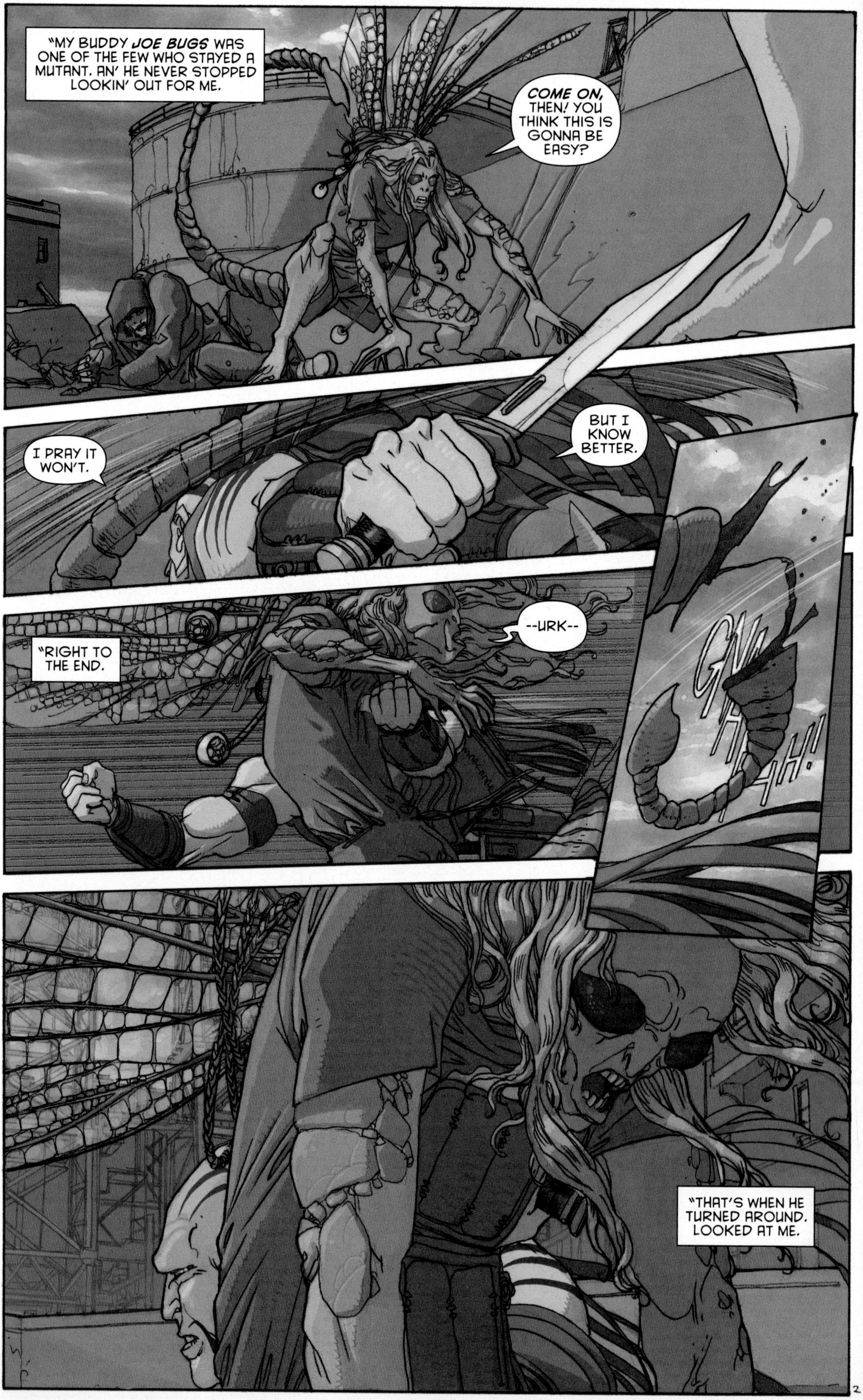
"MY BUDDY JOE BUGS WAS ONE OF THE FEW WHO STAYED A MUTANT. AN' HE NEVER STOPPED LOOKIN' OUT FOR ME.
COME ON, THEN! YOU THINK THIS IS GONNA BE EASY?
I PRAY IT WON'T.
BUT I KNOW BETTER.
"RIGHT TO THE END.
--URK--
"THAT'S WHEN HE TURNED AROUND. LOOKED AT ME.

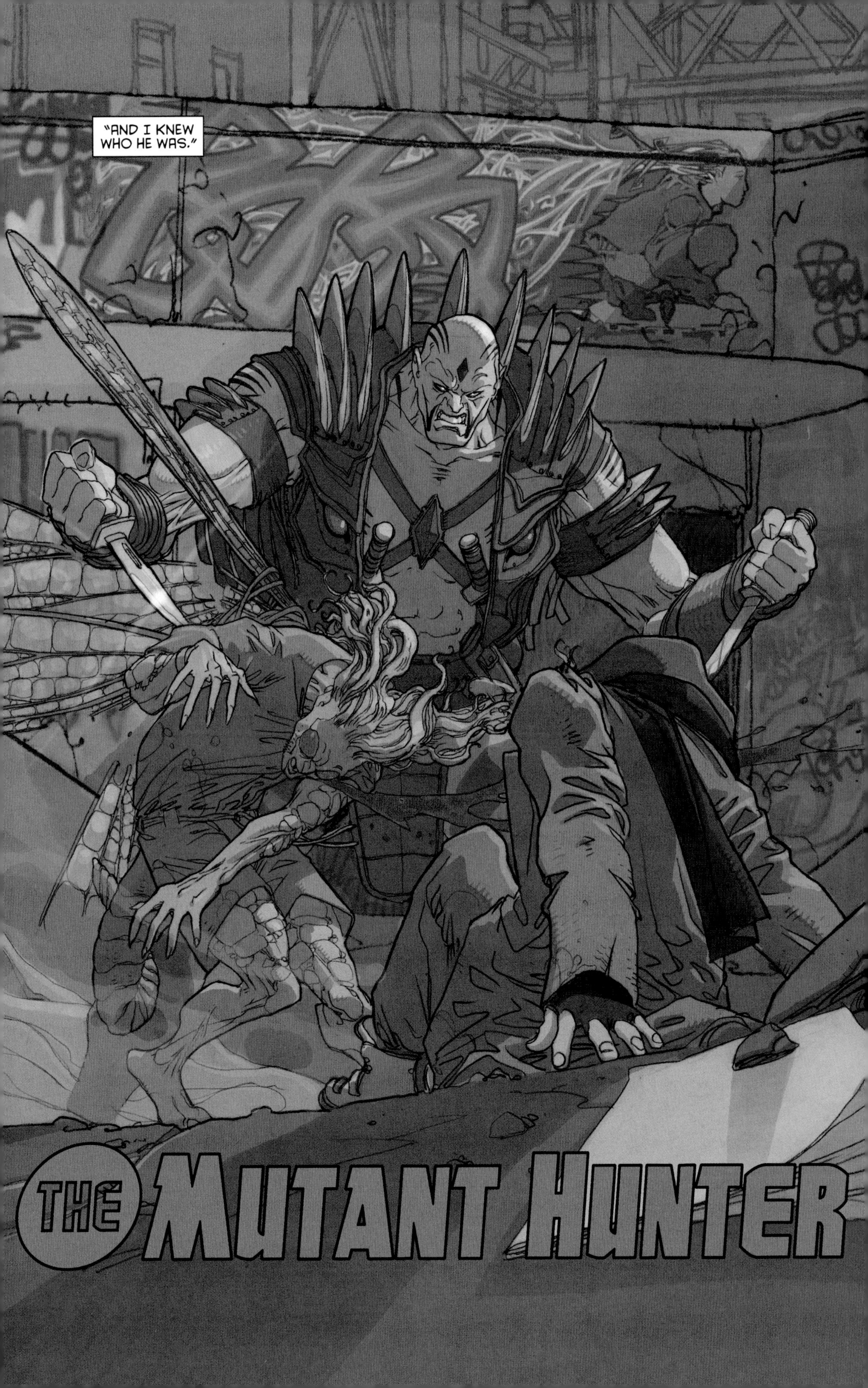
"AND I KNEW WHO HE WAS."
THE MUTANT HUNTER

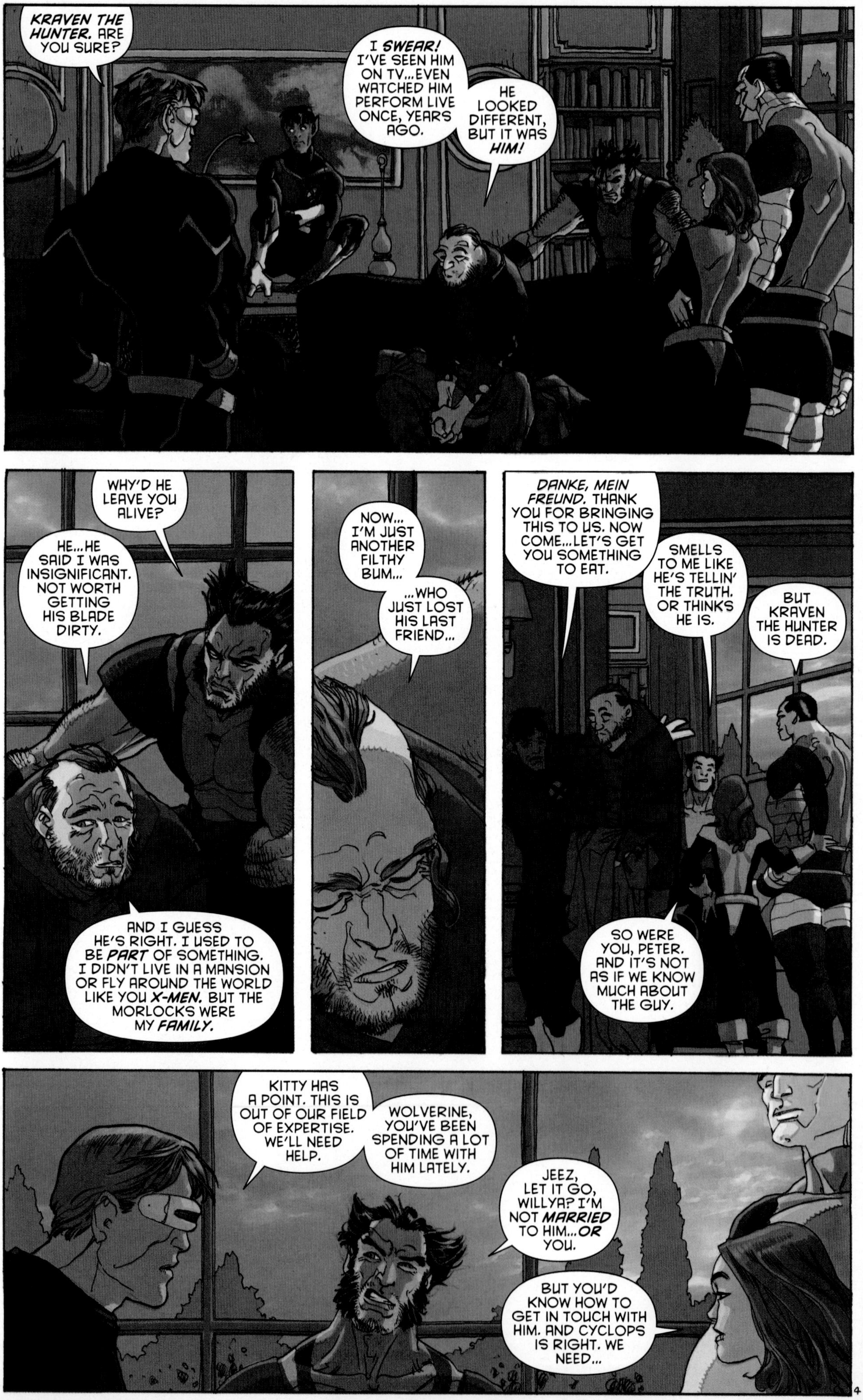
KRAVEN THE HUNTER. ARE YOU SURE?
I SWEAR! I'VE SEEN HIM ON TV...EVEN WATCHED HIM PERFORM LIVE ONCE, YEARS AGO.
HE LOOKED DIFFERENT, BUT IT WAS HIM!
WHY'D HE LEAVE YOU ALIVE?
HE...HE SAID I WAS INSIGNIFICANT. NOT WORTH GETTING HIS BLADE DIRTY.
AND I GUESS HE'S RIGHT. I USED TO BE PART OF SOMETHING. I DIDN'T LIVE IN A MANSION OR FLY AROUND THE WORLD LIKE YOU X-MEN. BUT THE MORLOCKS WERE MY FAMILY.
NOW... I'M JUST ANOTHER FILTHY BUM...
...WHO JUST LOST HIS LAST FRIEND...
DANKE, MEIN FREUND. THANK YOU FOR BRINGING THIS TO US. NOW COME...LET'S GET YOU SOMETHING TO EAT.
SMELLS TO ME LIKE HE'S TELLIN' THE TRUTH. OR THINKS HE IS.
BUT KRAVEN THE HUNTER IS DEAD.
SO WERE YOU, PETER. AND IT'S NOT AS IF WE KNOW MUCH ABOUT THE GUY.
KITTY HAS A POINT. THIS IS OUT OF OUR FIELD OF EXPERTISE. WE'LL NEED HELP.
WOLVERINE, YOU'VE BEEN SPENDING A LOT OF TIME WITH HIM LATELY.
JEEZ, LET IT GO, WILLYA? I'M NOT MARRIED TO HIM...OR YOU.
BUT YOU'D KNOW HOW TO GET IN TOUCH WITH HIM. AND CYCLOPS IS RIGHT. WE NEED...

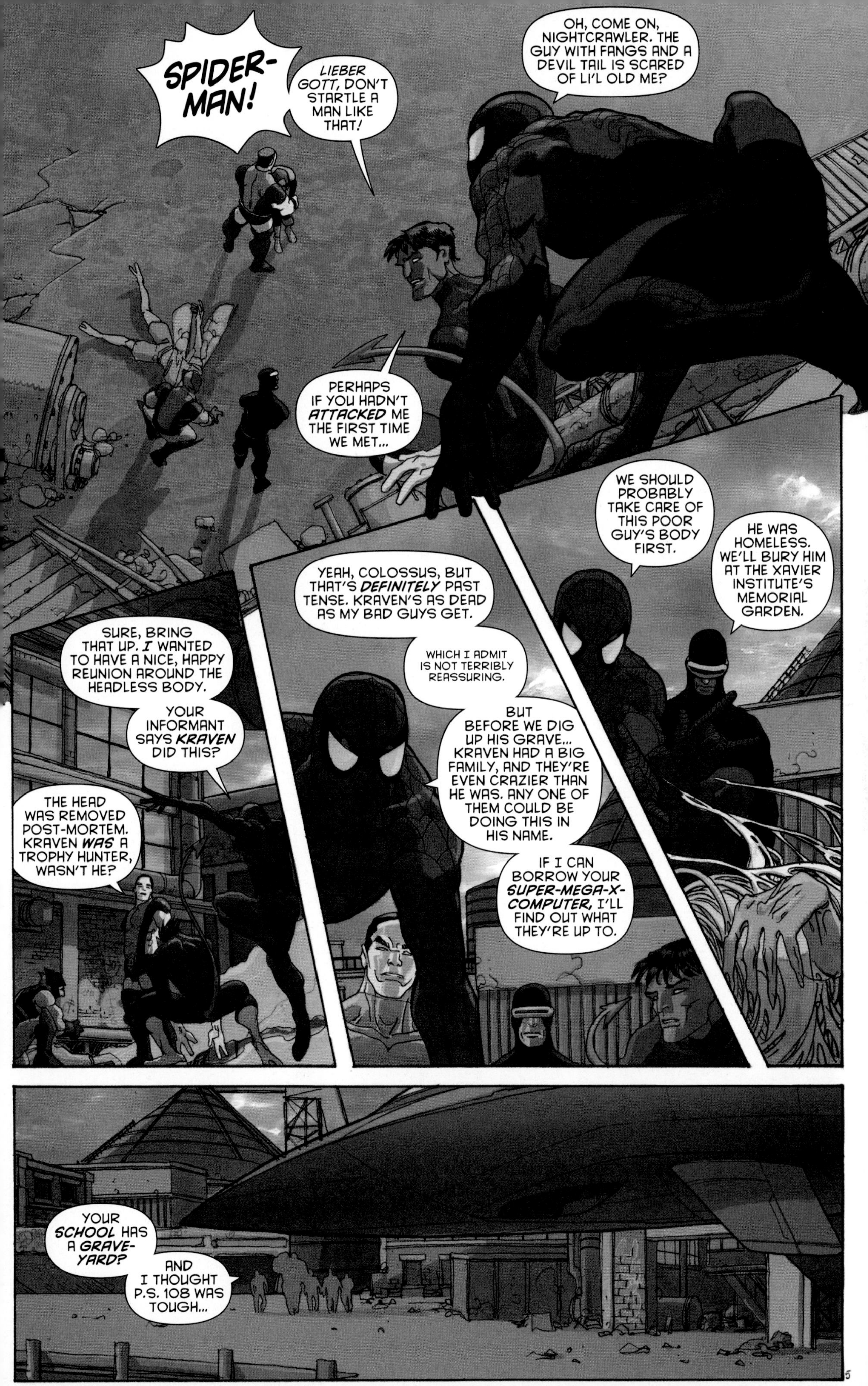
SPIDER-MAN!
LIEBER GOTT, DON'T STARTLE A MAN LIKE THAT!
OH, COME ON, NIGHTCRAWLER. THE GUY WITH FANGS AND A DEVIL TAIL IS SCARED OF LI'L OLD ME?
PERHAPS IF YOU HADN'T ATTACKED ME THE FIRST TIME WE MET...
SURE, BRING THAT UP. I WANTED TO HAVE A NICE, HAPPY REUNION AROUND THE HEADLESS BODY.
YOUR INFORMANT SAYS KRAVEN DID THIS?
THE HEAD WAS REMOVED POST-MORTEM. KRAVEN WAS A TROPHY HUNTER, WASN'T HE?
YEAH, COLOSSUS, BUT THAT'S DEFINITELY PAST TENSE. KRAVEN'S AS DEAD AS MY BAD GUYS GET.
WHICH I ADMIT IS NOT TERRIBLY REASSURING.
BUT BEFORE WE DIG UP HIS GRAVE... KRAVEN HAD A BIG FAMILY, AND THEY'RE EVEN CRAZIER THAN HE WAS. ANY ONE OF THEM COULD BE DOING THIS IN HIS NAME.
IF I CAN BORROW YOUR SUPER-MEGA-X-COMPUTER, I'LL FIND OUT WHAT THEY'RE UP TO.
WE SHOULD PROBABLY TAKE CARE OF THIS POOR GUY'S BODY FIRST.
HE WAS HOMELESS. WE'LL BURY HIM AT THE XAVIER INSTITUTE'S MEMORIAL GARDEN.
YOUR SCHOOL HAS A GRAVEYARD?
AND I THOUGHT P.S. 108 WAS TOUGH...

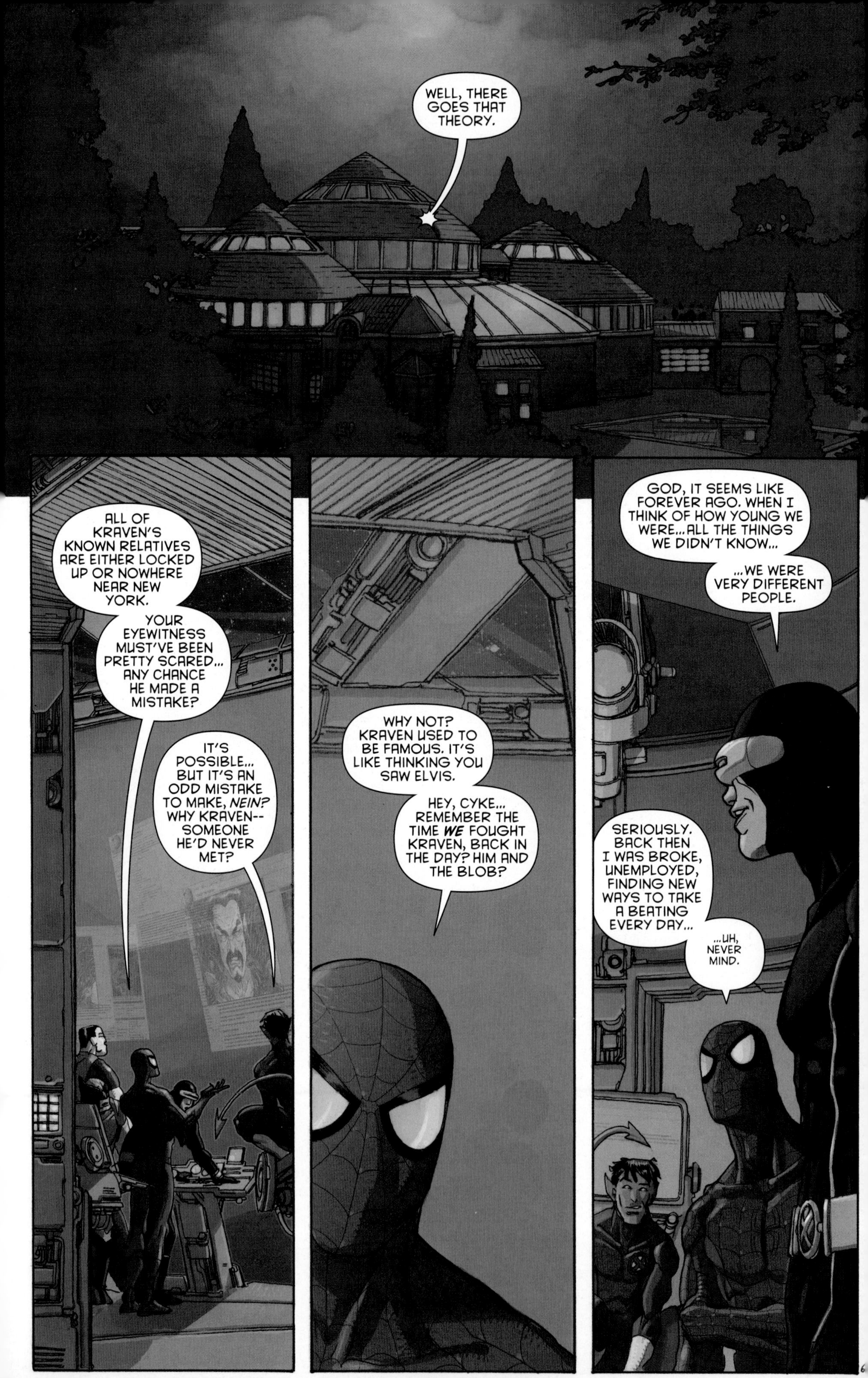

WELL, THERE GOES THAT THEORY.
ALL OF KRAVEN'S KNOWN RELATIVES ARE EITHER LOCKED UP OR NOWHERE NEAR NEW YORK.
YOUR EYEWITNESS MUST'VE BEEN PRETTY SCARED... ANY CHANCE HE MADE A MISTAKE?
IT'S POSSIBLE... BUT IT'S AN ODD MISTAKE TO MAKE, *NEIN?* WHY KRAVEN-- SOMEONE HE'D NEVER MET?
WHY NOT? KRAVEN USED TO BE FAMOUS. IT'S LIKE THINKING YOU SAW ELVIS.
HEY, CYKE... REMEMBER THE TIME ***WE*** FOUGHT KRAVEN, BACK IN THE DAY? HIM AND THE BLOB?
GOD, IT SEEMS LIKE FOREVER AGO. WHEN I THINK OF HOW YOUNG WE WERE... ALL THE THINGS WE DIDN'T KNOW...
...WE WERE VERY DIFFERENT PEOPLE.
SERIOUSLY. BACK THEN I WAS BROKE, UNEMPLOYED, FINDING NEW WAYS TO TAKE A BEATING EVERY DAY...
...UH, NEVER MIND.

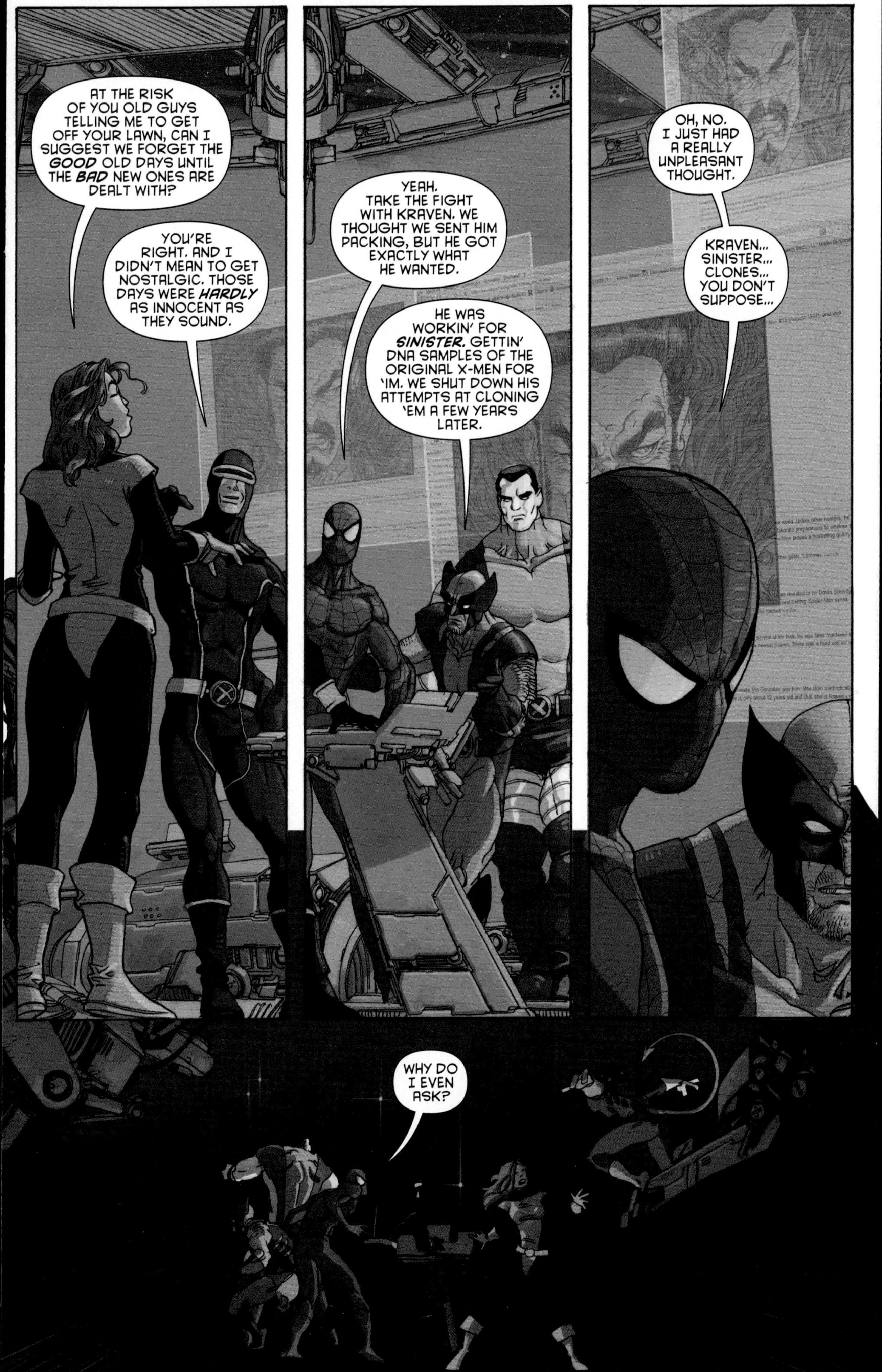

AT THE RISK OF YOU OLD GUYS TELLING ME TO GET OFF YOUR LAWN, CAN I SUGGEST WE FORGET THE GOOD OLD DAYS UNTIL THE BAD NEW ONES ARE DEALT WITH?
YOU'RE RIGHT. AND I DIDN'T MEAN TO GET NOSTALGIC. THOSE DAYS WERE HARDLY AS INNOCENT AS THEY SOUND.
YEAH. TAKE THE FIGHT WITH KRAVEN. WE THOUGHT WE SENT HIM PACKING, BUT HE GOT EXACTLY WHAT HE WANTED.
HE WAS WORKIN' FOR SINISTER. GETTIN' DNA SAMPLES OF THE ORIGINAL X-MEN FOR 'IM. WE SHUT DOWN HIS ATTEMPTS AT CLONING 'EM A FEW YEARS LATER.
OH, NO. I JUST HAD A REALLY UNPLEASANT THOUGHT.
KRAVEN... SINISTER... CLONES... YOU DON'T SUPPOSE...
WHY DO I EVEN ASK?

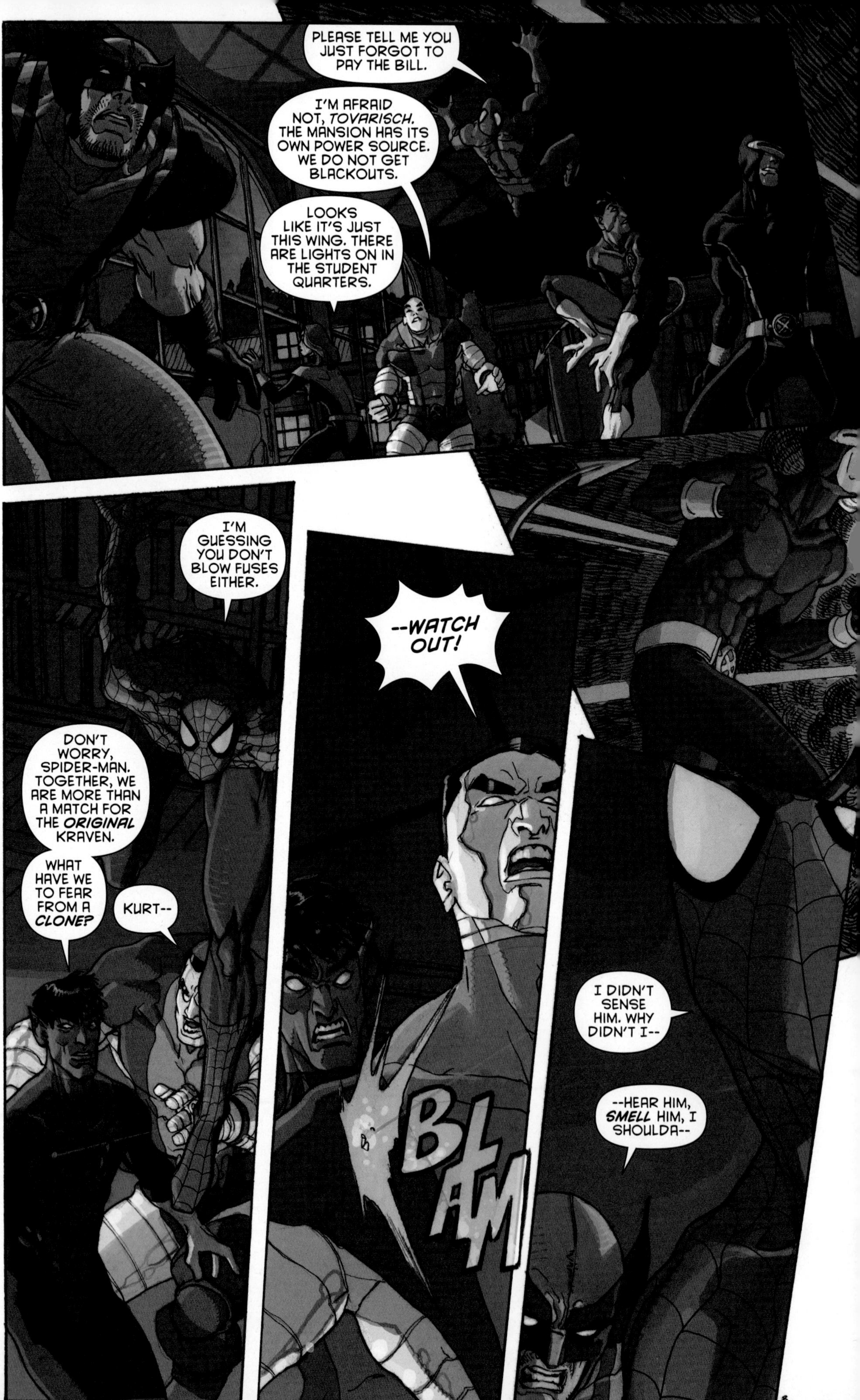
PLEASE TELL ME YOU JUST FORGOT TO PAY THE BILL.
I'M AFRAID NOT, *TOVARISCH*. THE MANSION HAS ITS OWN POWER SOURCE. WE DO NOT GET BLACKOUTS.
LOOKS LIKE IT'S JUST THIS WING. THERE ARE LIGHTS ON IN THE STUDENT QUARTERS.
I'M GUESSING YOU DON'T BLOW FUSES EITHER.
DON'T WORRY, SPIDER-MAN. TOGETHER, WE ARE MORE THAN A MATCH FOR THE *ORIGINAL* KRAVEN.
WHAT HAVE WE TO FEAR FROM A *CLONE?*
KURT--
--*WATCH OUT!*
BLAM
I DIDN'T SENSE HIM. WHY DIDN'T I--
--HEAR HIM, *SMELL* HIM, I SHOULDA--

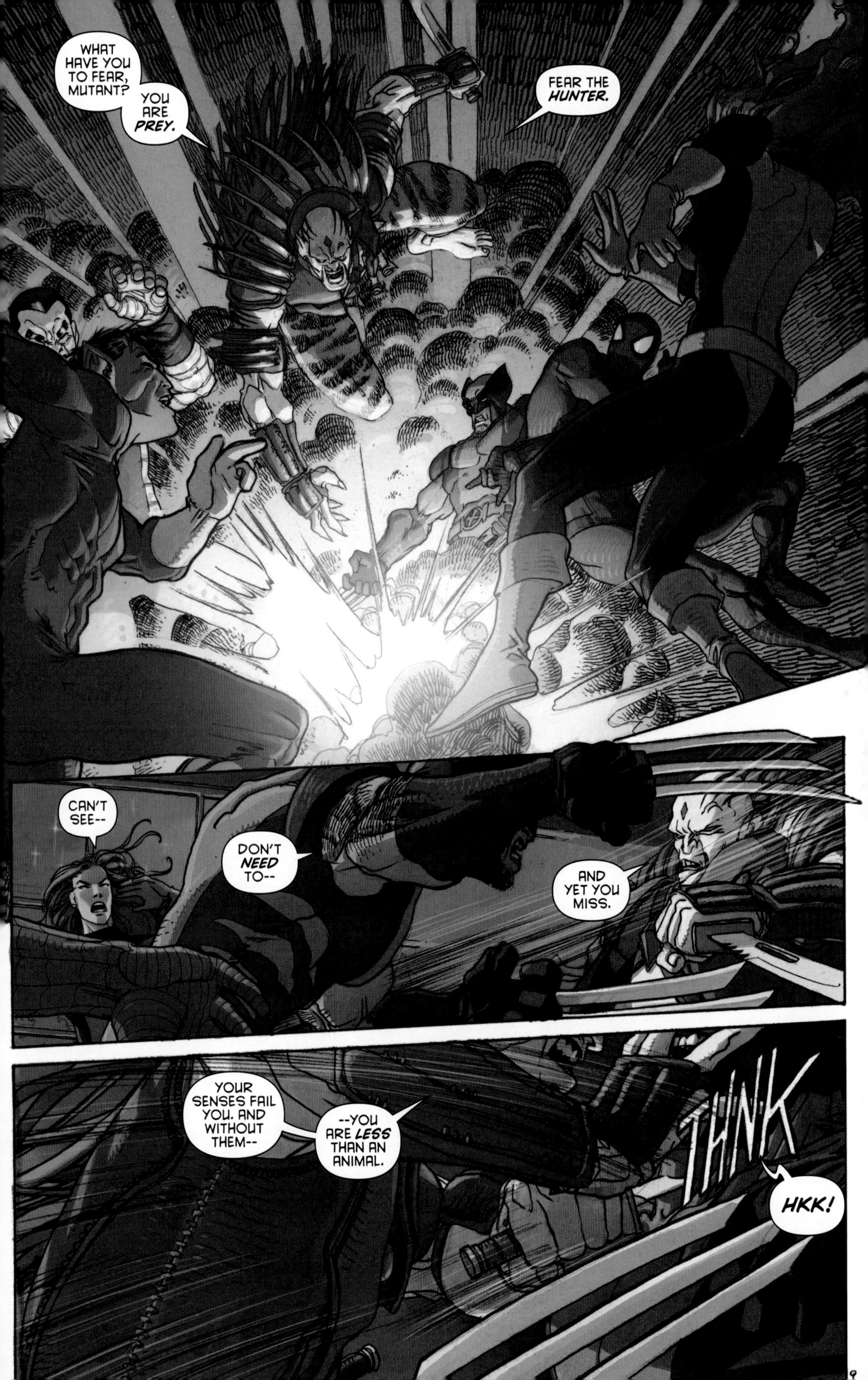
WHAT HAVE YOU TO FEAR, MUTANT?
YOU ARE PREY.
FEAR THE HUNTER.
CAN'T SEE--
DON'T NEED TO--
AND YET YOU MISS.
YOUR SENSES FAIL YOU. AND WITHOUT THEM--
--YOU ARE LESS THAN AN ANIMAL.
THNK
HKK!

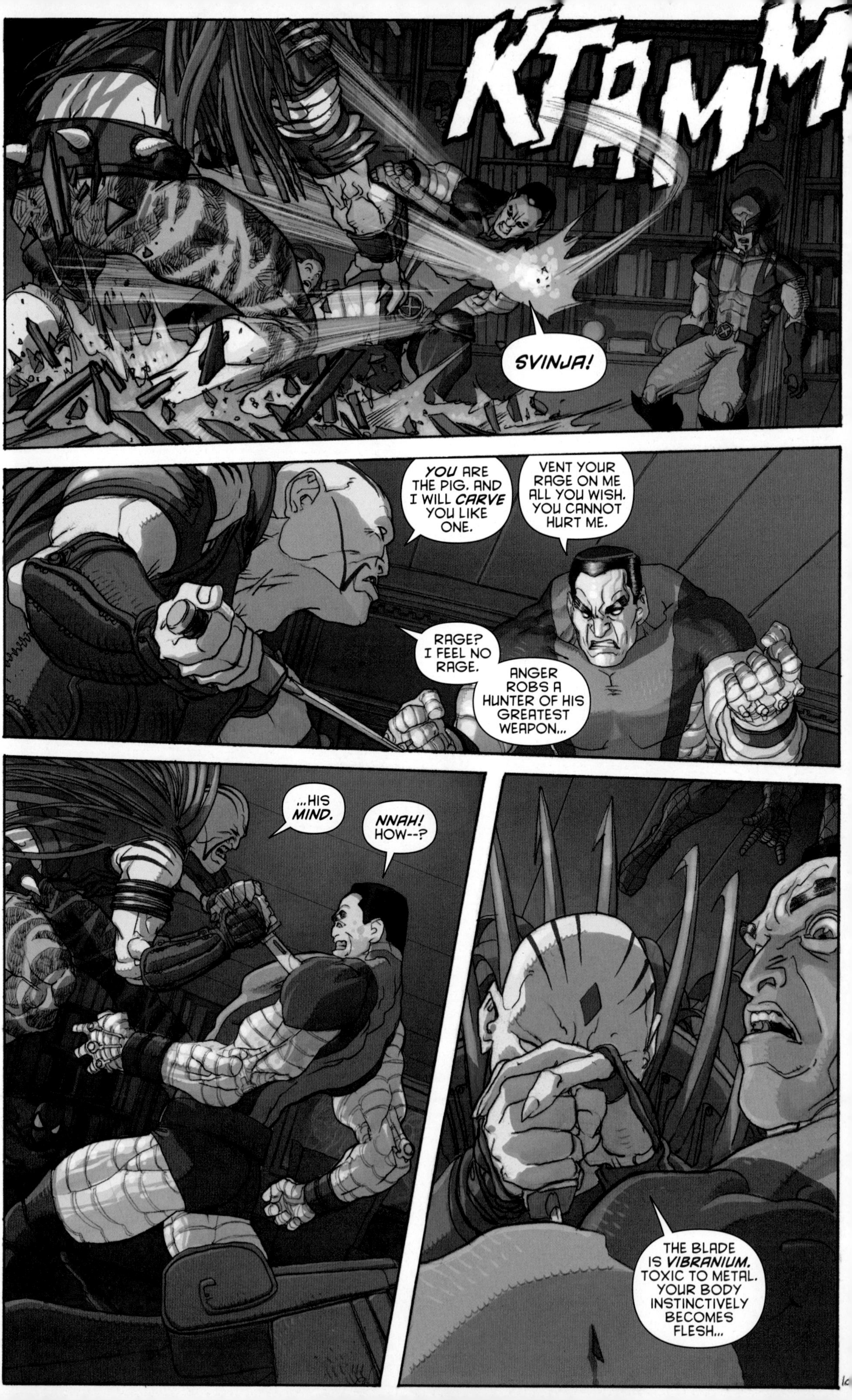
KTAMM
SVINJA!
YOU ARE THE PIG. AND I WILL CARVE YOU LIKE ONE.
VENT YOUR RAGE ON ME ALL YOU WISH. YOU CANNOT HURT ME.
RAGE? I FEEL NO RAGE.
ANGER ROBS A HUNTER OF HIS GREATEST WEAPON...
...HIS MIND.
NNAH! HOW--?
THE BLADE IS VIBRANIUM. TOXIC TO METAL. YOUR BODY INSTINCTIVELY BECOMES FLESH...

...AND BLOOD!
AHH!
OKAY, I CAN SEE AGAIN. AND THAT'S ENOUGH OUT OF YOU.
PETER, ARE YOU--?
I WILL BE FINE, KATYA. HELP ME WITH WOLVERINE... PHASE HIM THROUGH THE KNIFE SO HE CAN HEAL.
LOOK. HIS SKIN... THE SAME SHADE AS SINISTER'S.
AND HAIRLESS... BUT OTHERWISE, HE'S THE MIRROR IMAGE OF KRAVEN. YOU WERE RIGHT, SPIDER-MAN.
I WERE? THAT YOUR STORY, PAL? YOU ONE OF SINISTER'S CLONES?
I...

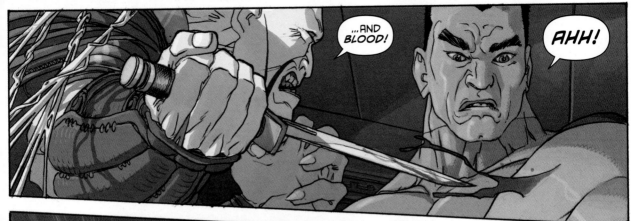

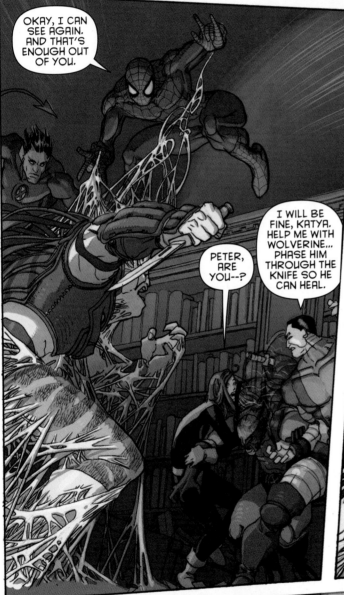

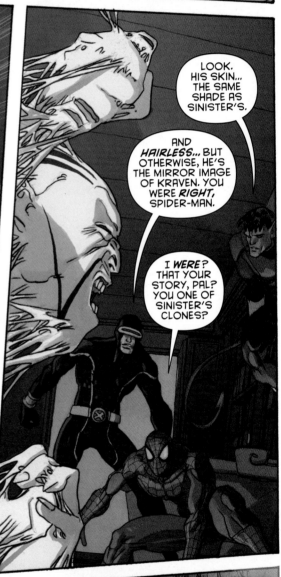

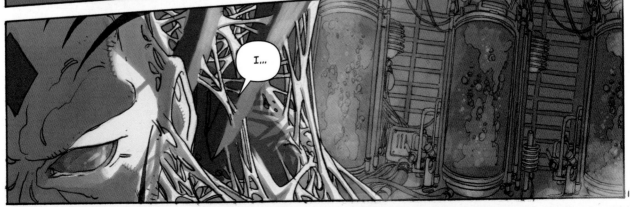

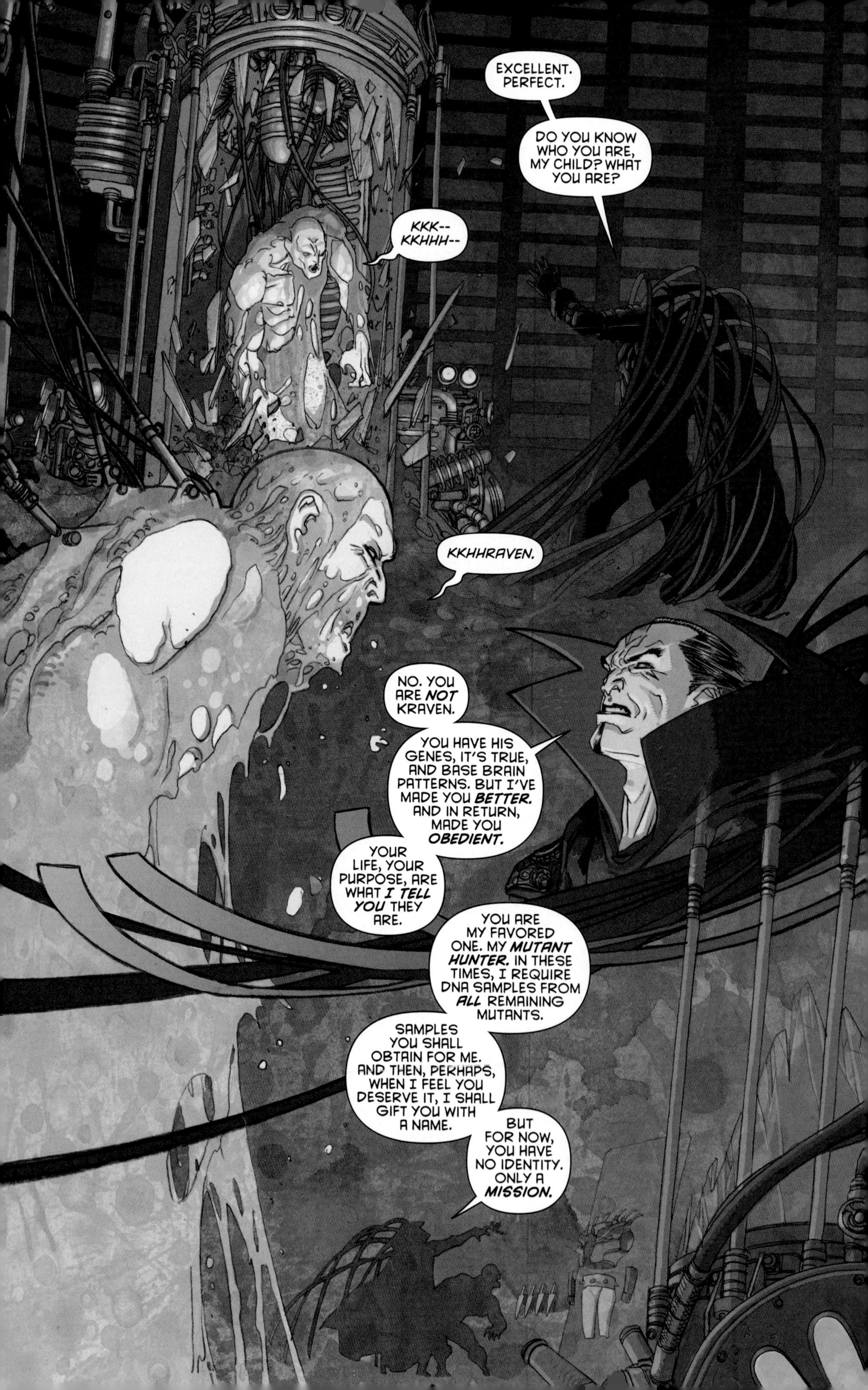
EXCELLENT. PERFECT.
DO YOU KNOW WHO YOU ARE, MY CHILD? WHAT YOU ARE?
KKK-- KKHHH--
KKHHRAVEN.
NO. YOU ARE *NOT* KRAVEN.
YOU HAVE HIS GENES, IT'S TRUE, AND BASE BRAIN PATTERNS. BUT I'VE MADE YOU *BETTER.* AND IN RETURN, MADE YOU *OBEDIENT.*
YOUR LIFE, YOUR PURPOSE, ARE WHAT *I TELL YOU* THEY ARE.
YOU ARE MY FAVORED ONE. MY *MUTANT HUNTER.* IN THESE TIMES, I REQUIRE DNA SAMPLES FROM *ALL* REMAINING MUTANTS.
SAMPLES YOU SHALL OBTAIN FOR ME. AND THEN, PERHAPS, WHEN I FEEL YOU DESERVE IT, I SHALL GIFT YOU WITH A NAME.
BUT FOR NOW, YOU HAVE NO IDENTITY. ONLY A *MISSION.*

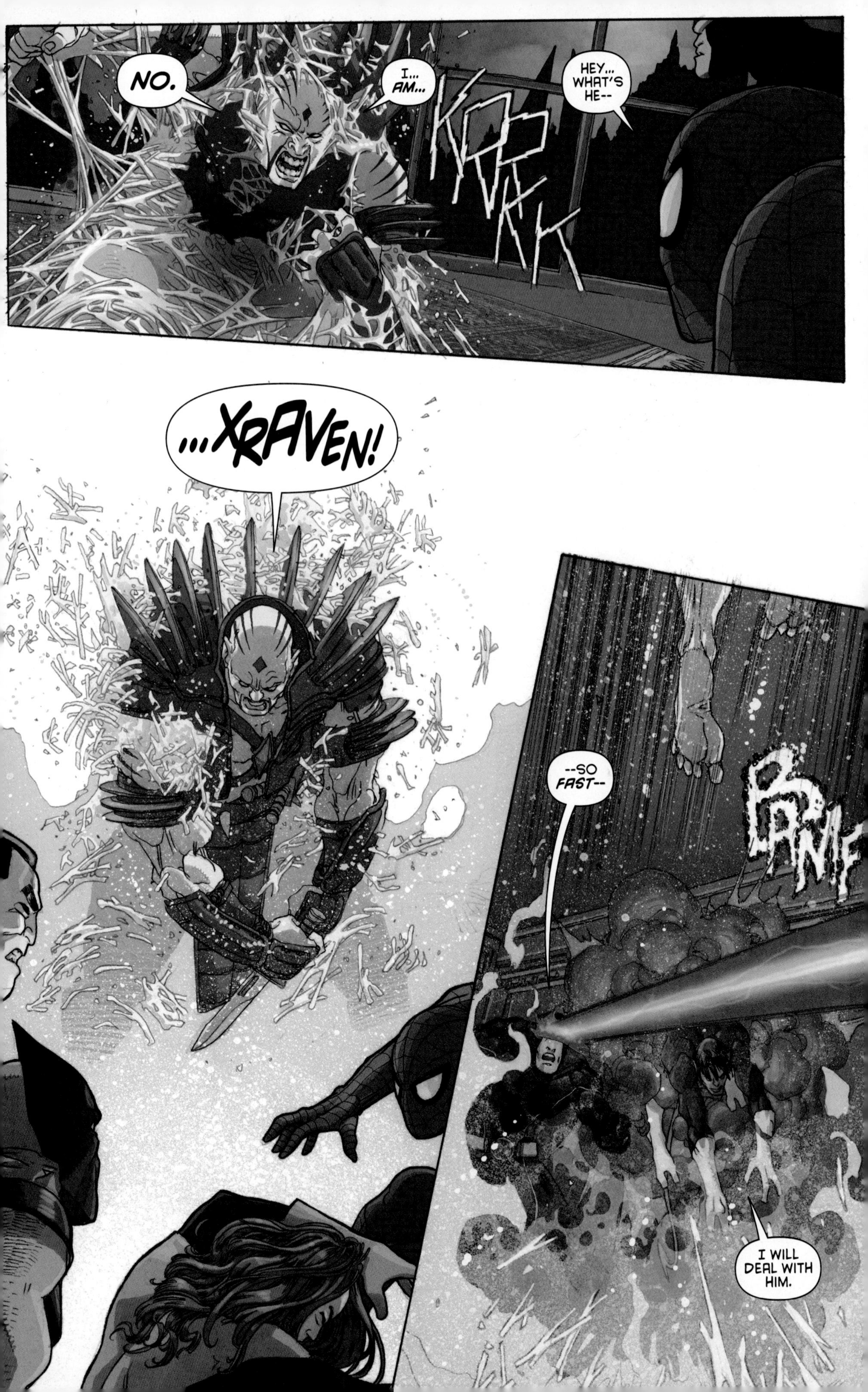

NO.
I... AM...
KRRAKK
HEY... WHAT'S HE--
...XRAVEN!
--SO FAST--
BAMF
I WILL DEAL WITH HIM.

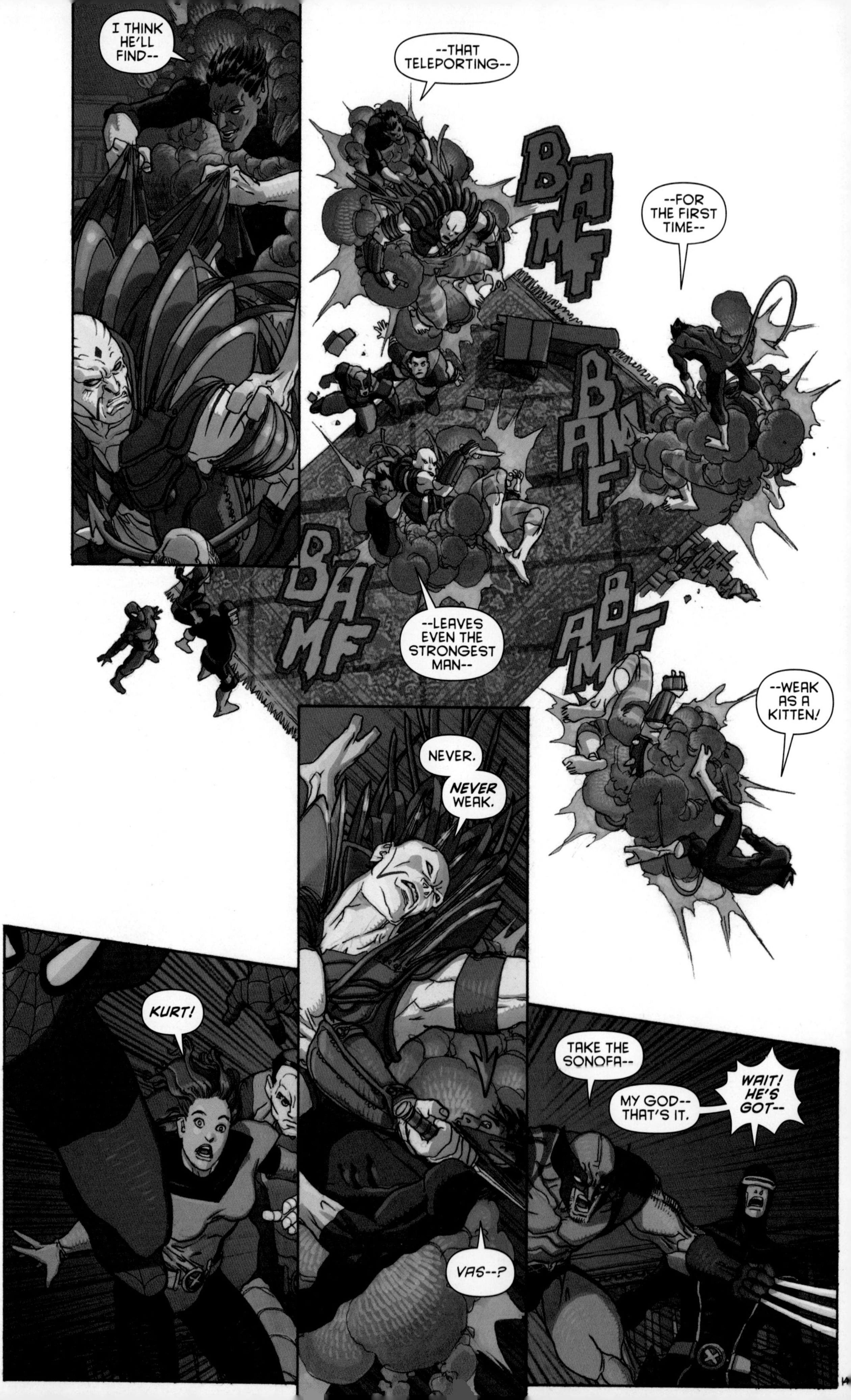
I THINK HE'LL FIND--
--THAT TELEPORTING--
BAMF
--FOR THE FIRST TIME--
BAMF
BAMF
--LEAVES EVEN THE STRONGEST MAN--
BAMF
--WEAK AS A KITTEN!
NEVER.
NEVER WEAK.
KURT!
VAS--?
TAKE THE SONOFA--
MY GOD-- THAT'S IT.
WAIT! HE'S GOT--

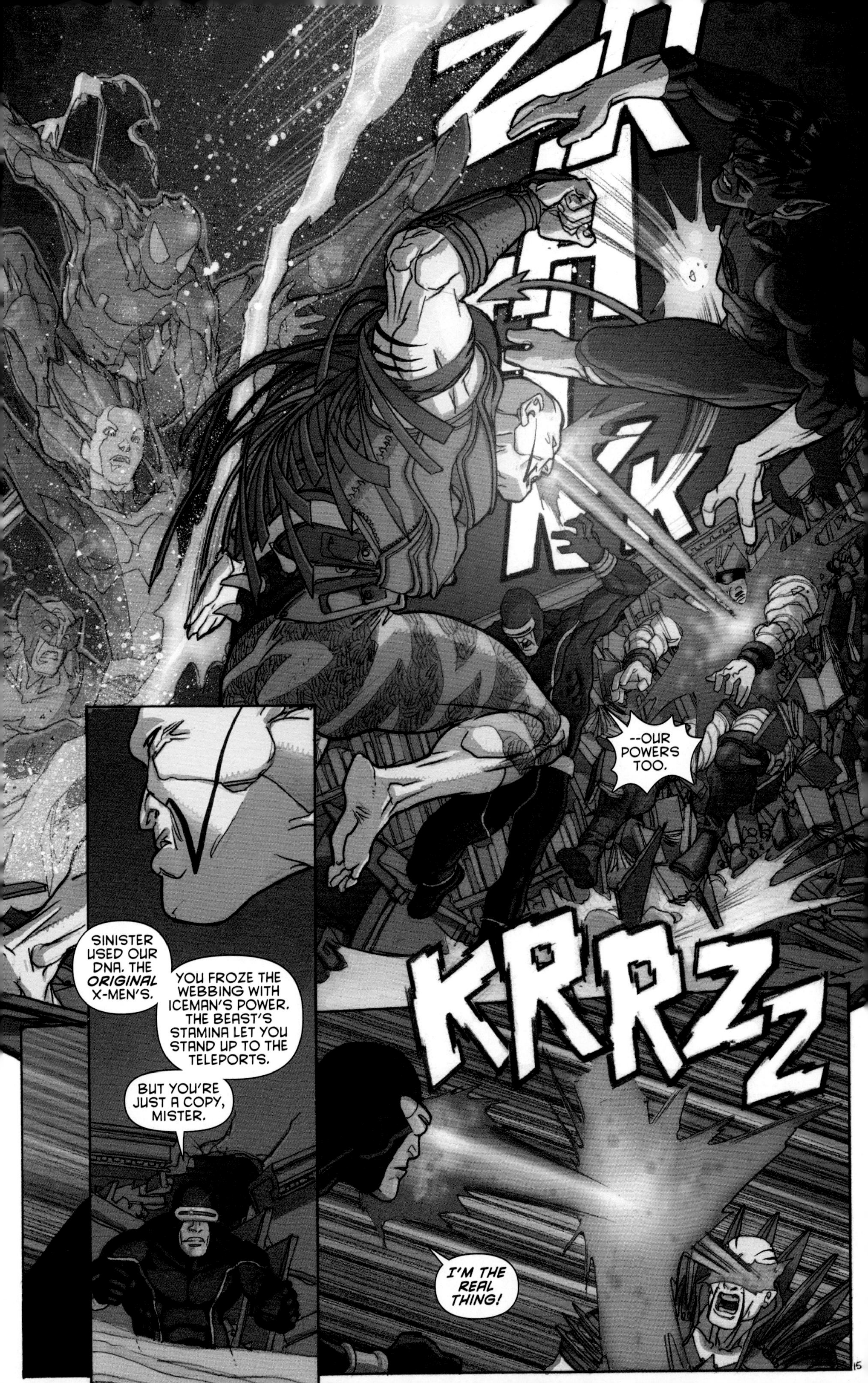
ZZAK
--OUR POWERS TOO.
KRRZZ
SINISTER USED OUR DNA. THE ORIGINAL X-MEN'S.
YOU FROZE THE WEBBING WITH ICEMAN'S POWER. THE BEAST'S STAMINA LET YOU STAND UP TO THE TELEPORTS.
BUT YOU'RE JUST A COPY, MISTER.
I'M THE REAL THING!

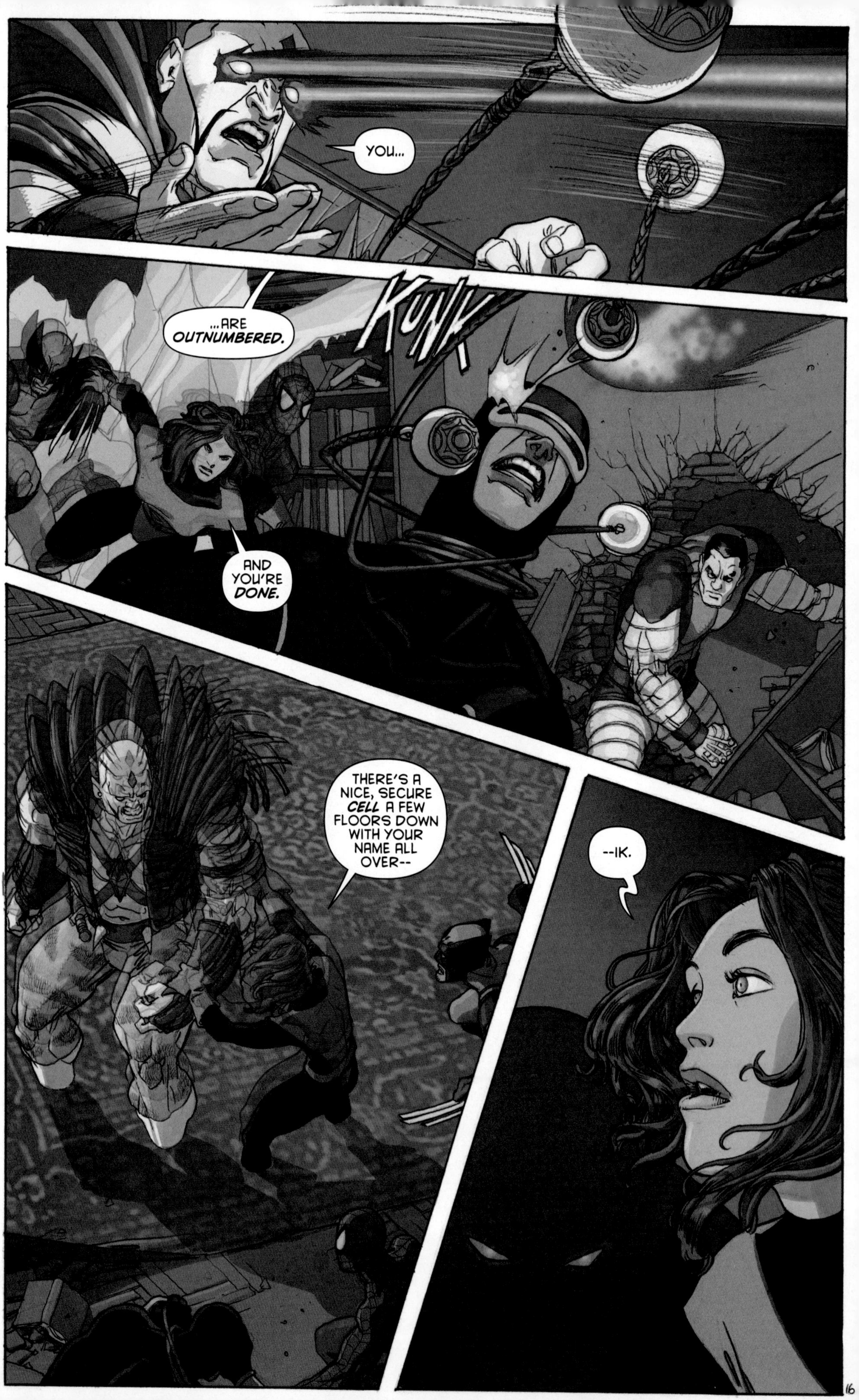
YOU...
...ARE OUTNUMBERED.
KONK
AND YOU'RE DONE.
THERE'S A NICE, SECURE CELL A FEW FLOORS DOWN WITH YOUR NAME ALL OVER--
--IK.

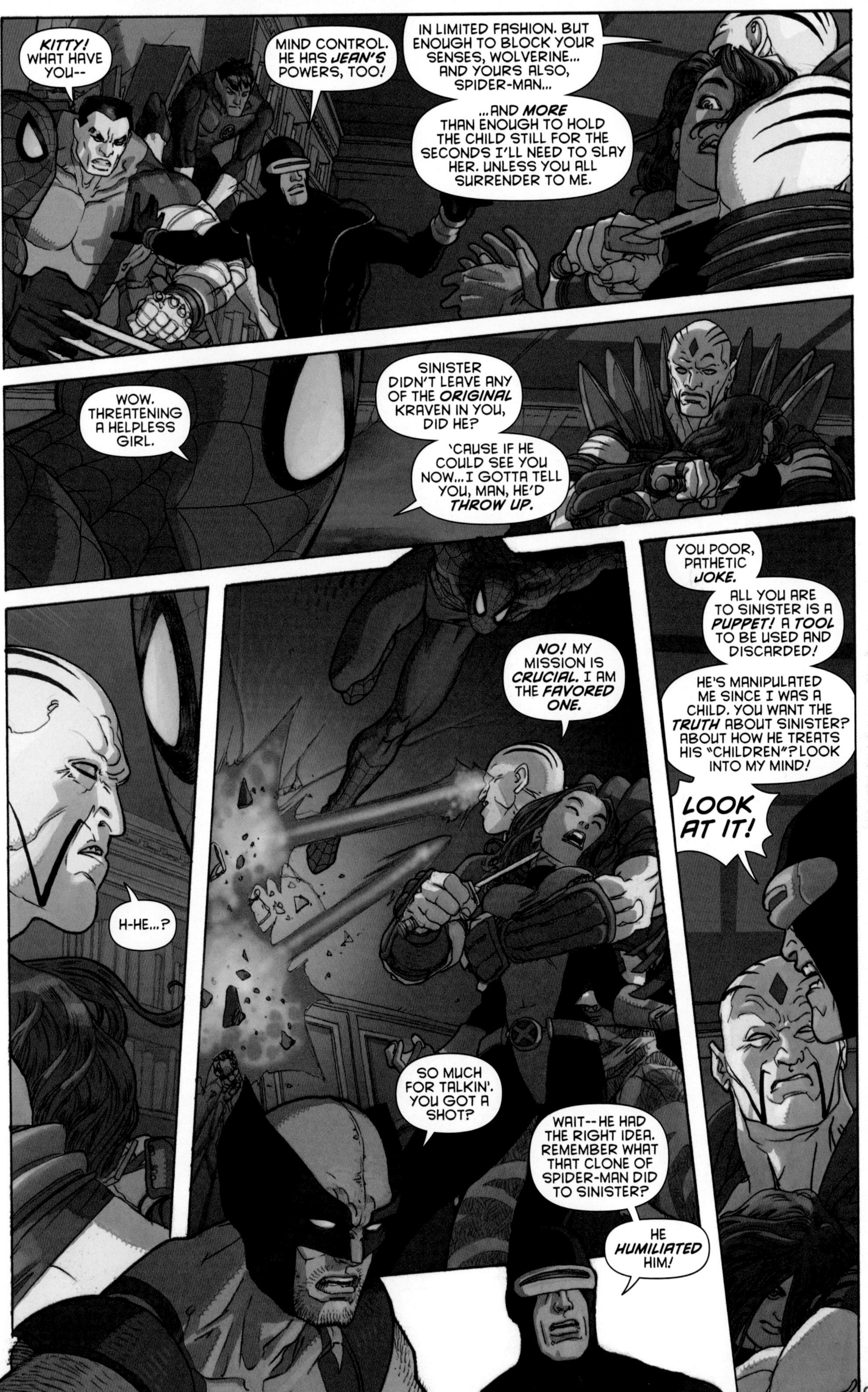
KITTY! WHAT HAVE YOU--
MIND CONTROL. HE HAS JEAN'S POWERS, TOO!
IN LIMITED FASHION. BUT ENOUGH TO BLOCK YOUR SENSES, WOLVERINE... AND YOURS ALSO, SPIDER-MAN...
...AND MORE THAN ENOUGH TO HOLD THE CHILD STILL FOR THE SECONDS I'LL NEED TO SLAY HER. UNLESS YOU ALL SURRENDER TO ME.
WOW. THREATENING A HELPLESS GIRL.
SINISTER DIDN'T LEAVE ANY OF THE ORIGINAL KRAVEN IN YOU, DID HE?
'CAUSE IF HE COULD SEE YOU NOW...I GOTTA TELL YOU, MAN, HE'D THROW UP.
H-HE...?
NO! MY MISSION IS CRUCIAL. I AM THE FAVORED ONE.
SO MUCH FOR TALKIN'. YOU GOT A SHOT?
WAIT--HE HAD THE RIGHT IDEA. REMEMBER WHAT THAT CLONE OF SPIDER-MAN DID TO SINISTER?
HE HUMILIATED HIM!
YOU POOR, PATHETIC JOKE.
ALL YOU ARE TO SINISTER IS A PUPPET! A TOOL TO BE USED AND DISCARDED!
HE'S MANIPULATED ME SINCE I WAS A CHILD. YOU WANT THE TRUTH ABOUT SINISTER? ABOUT HOW HE TREATS HIS "CHILDREN"? LOOK INTO MY MIND!
LOOK AT IT!

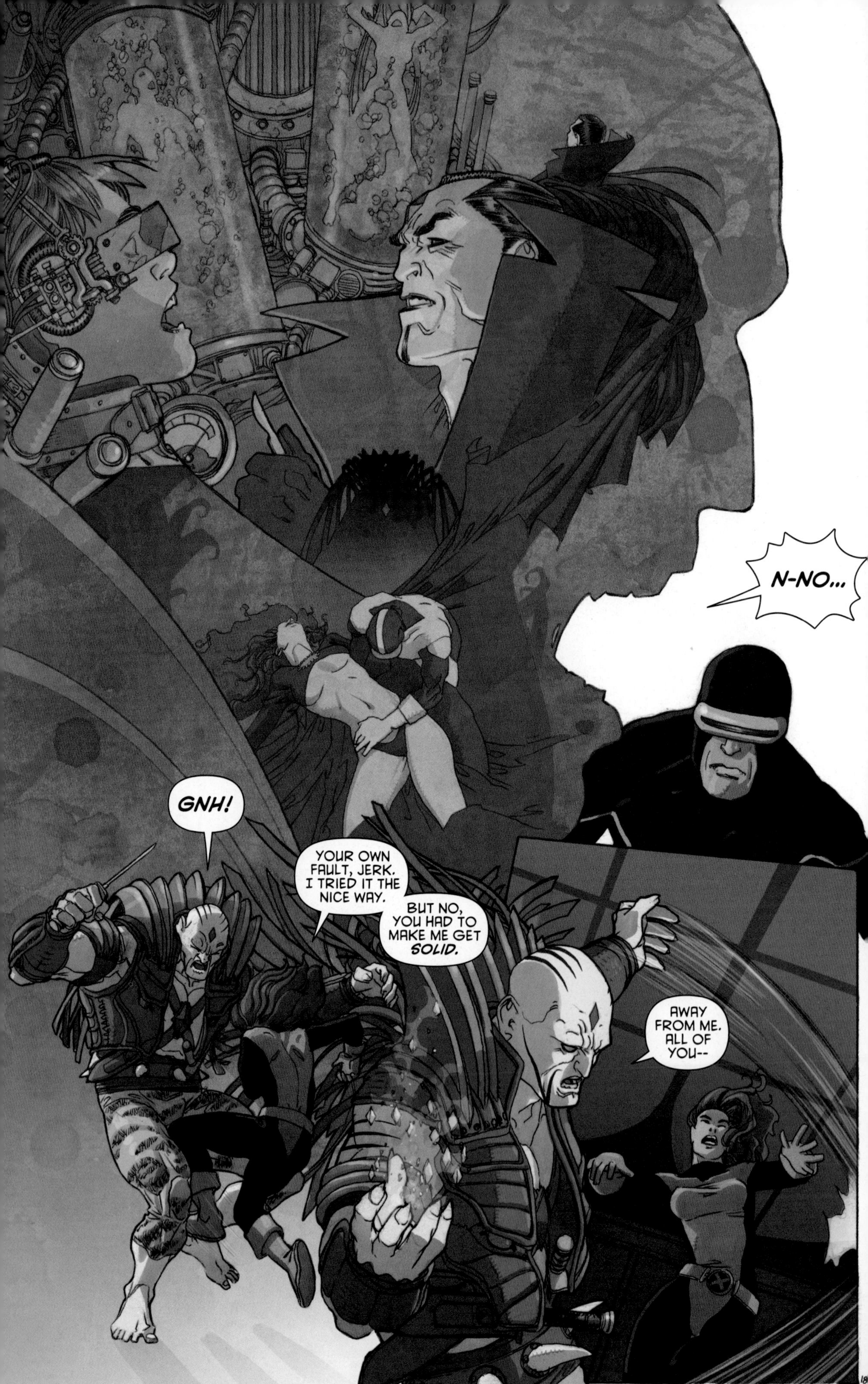
N-NO...
GNH!
YOUR OWN FAULT, JERK. I TRIED IT THE NICE WAY.
BUT NO, YOU HAD TO MAKE ME GET SOLID.
AWAY FROM ME. ALL OF YOU--

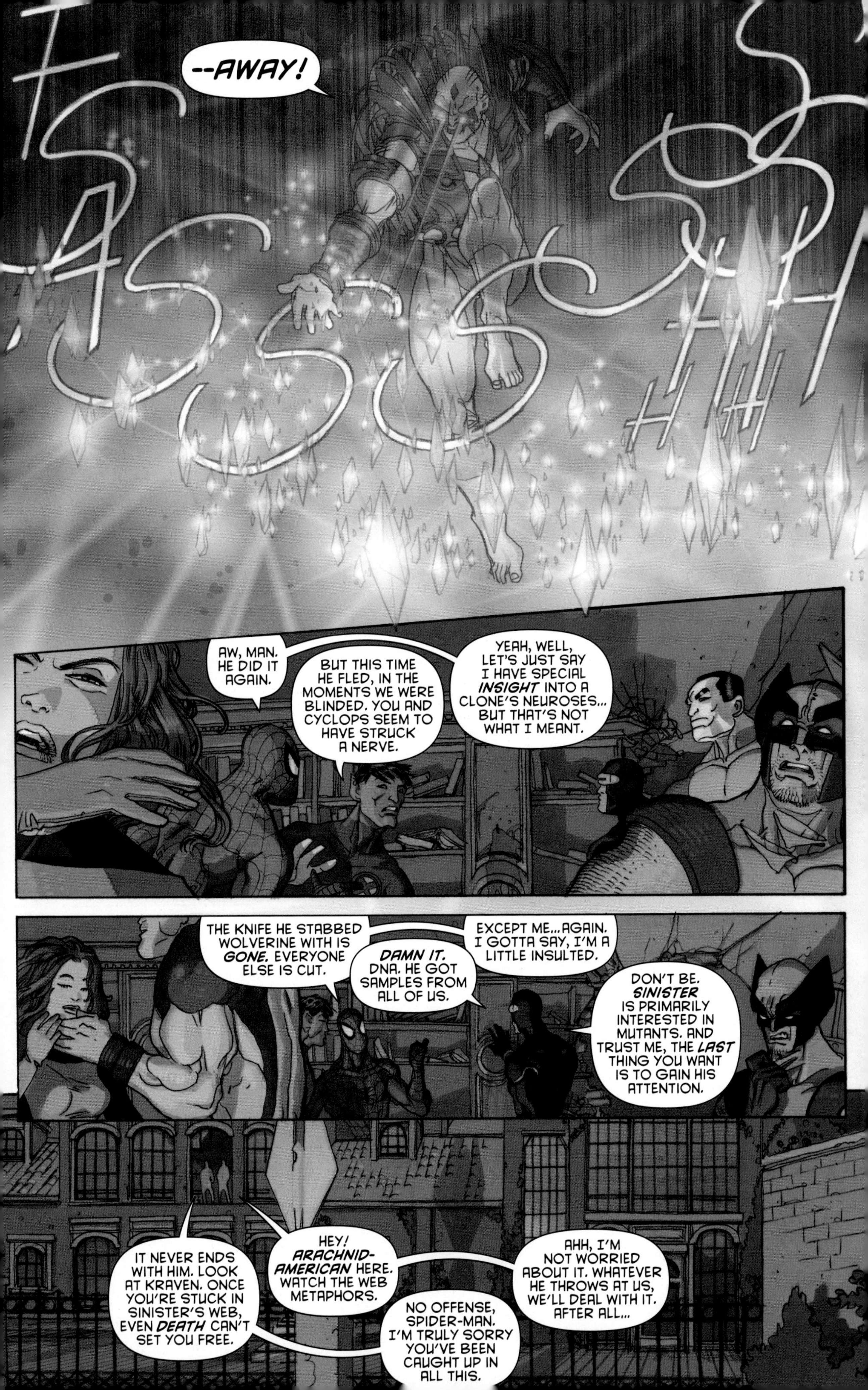
--AWAY!
FASSSSHHH
AW, MAN. HE DID IT AGAIN.
BUT THIS TIME HE FLED, IN THE MOMENTS WE WERE BLINDED. YOU AND CYCLOPS SEEM TO HAVE STRUCK A NERVE.
YEAH, WELL, LET'S JUST SAY I HAVE SPECIAL INSIGHT INTO A CLONE'S NEUROSES... BUT THAT'S NOT WHAT I MEANT.
THE KNIFE HE STABBED WOLVERINE WITH IS GONE. EVERYONE ELSE IS CUT.
EXCEPT ME...AGAIN. I GOTTA SAY, I'M A LITTLE INSULTED.
DAMN IT. DNA. HE GOT SAMPLES FROM ALL OF US.
DON'T BE. SINISTER IS PRIMARILY INTERESTED IN MUTANTS. AND TRUST ME, THE LAST THING YOU WANT IS TO GAIN HIS ATTENTION.
IT NEVER ENDS WITH HIM. LOOK AT KRAVEN. ONCE YOU'RE STUCK IN SINISTER'S WEB, EVEN DEATH CAN'T SET YOU FREE.
HEY! ARACHNID-AMERICAN HERE. WATCH THE WEB METAPHORS.
NO OFFENSE, SPIDER-MAN. I'M TRULY SORRY YOU'VE BEEN CAUGHT UP IN ALL THIS.
AHH, I'M NOT WORRIED ABOUT IT. WHATEVER HE THROWS AT US, WE'LL DEAL WITH IT. AFTER ALL...

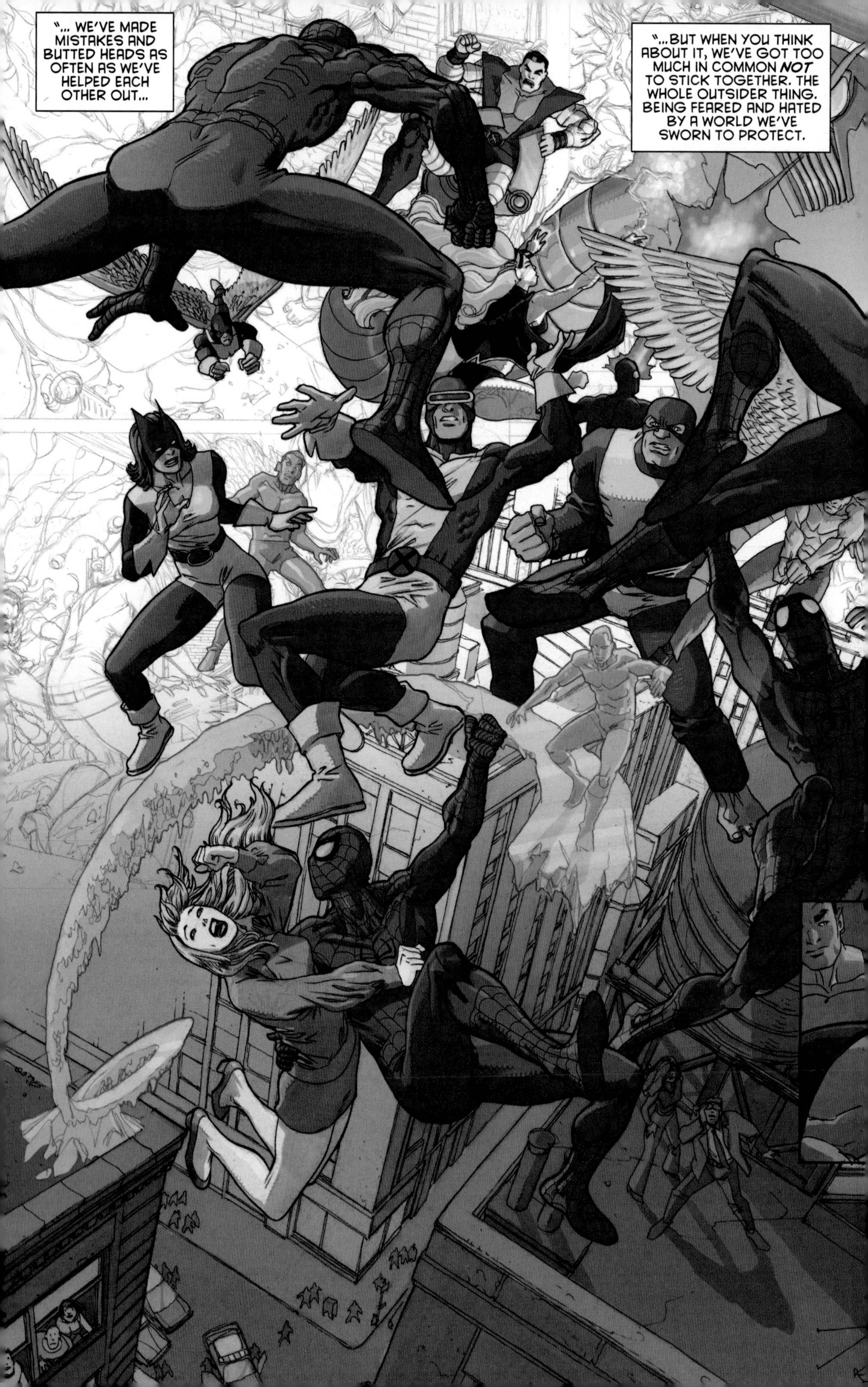
"... WE'VE MADE MISTAKES AND BUTTED HEADS AS OFTEN AS WE'VE HELPED EACH OTHER OUT...
"...BUT WHEN YOU THINK ABOUT IT, WE'VE GOT TOO MUCH IN COMMON NOT TO STICK TOGETHER. THE WHOLE OUTSIDER THING. BEING FEARED AND HATED BY A WORLD WE'VE SWORN TO PROTECT.

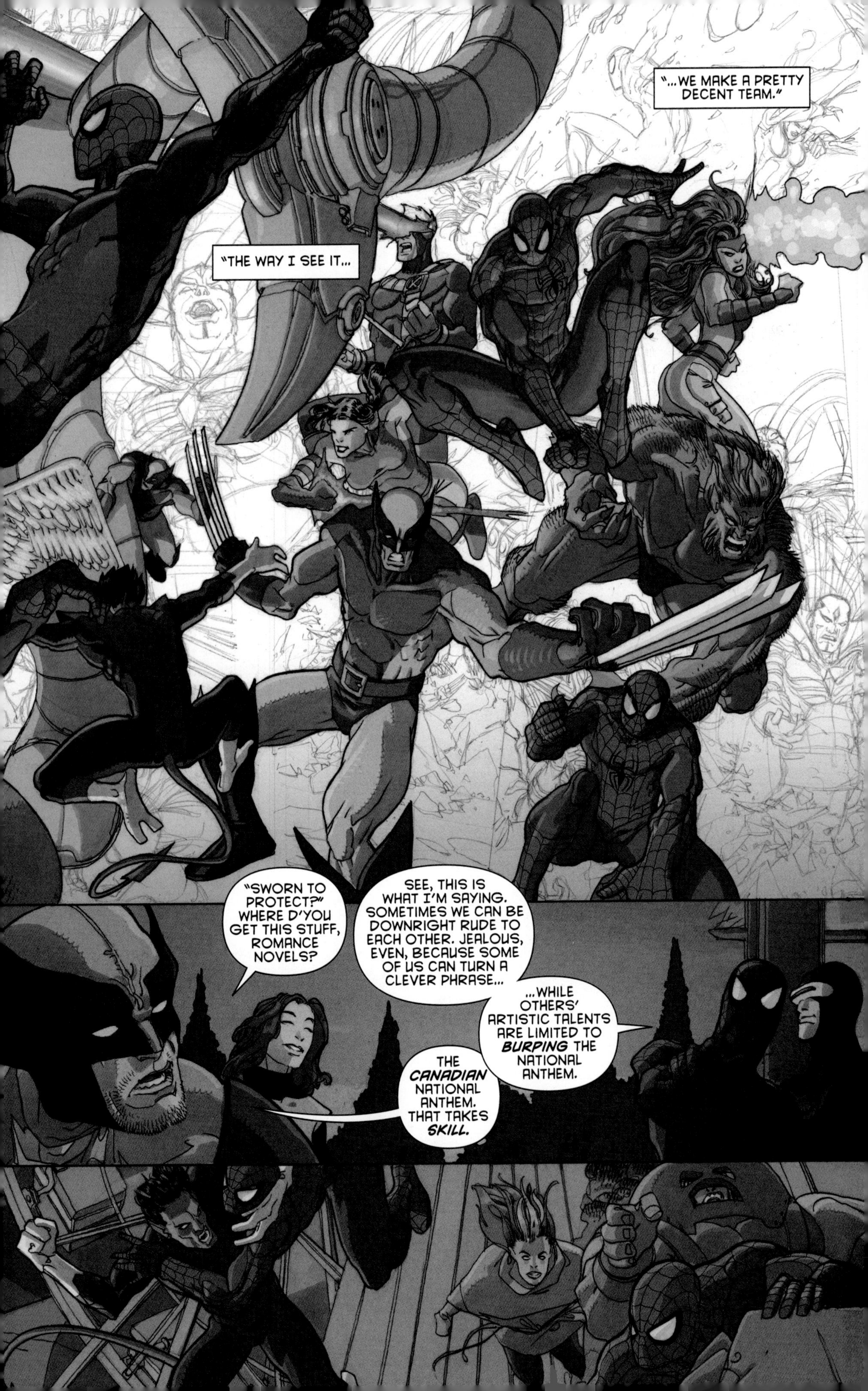
"THE WAY I SEE IT...
"...WE MAKE A PRETTY DECENT TEAM."
"SWORN TO PROTECT?" WHERE D'YOU GET THIS STUFF, ROMANCE NOVELS?
SEE, THIS IS WHAT I'M SAYING. SOMETIMES WE CAN BE DOWNRIGHT RUDE TO EACH OTHER. JEALOUS, EVEN, BECAUSE SOME OF US CAN TURN A CLEVER PHRASE...
...WHILE OTHERS' ARTISTIC TALENTS ARE LIMITED TO ***BURPING*** THE NATIONAL ANTHEM.
THE ***CANADIAN*** NATIONAL ANTHEM. THAT TAKES ***SKILL.***

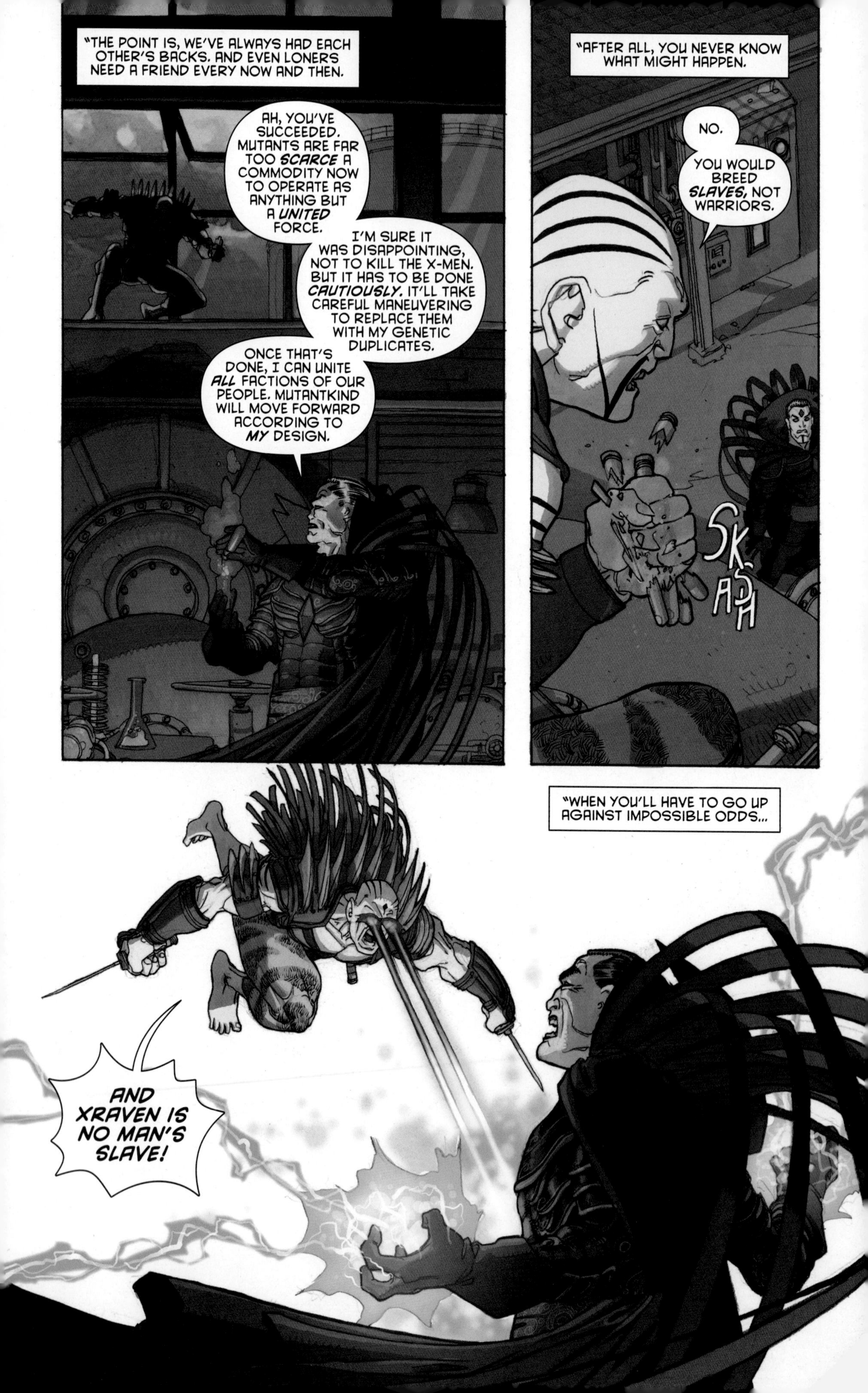
"THE POINT IS, WE'VE ALWAYS HAD EACH OTHER'S BACKS. AND EVEN LONERS NEED A FRIEND EVERY NOW AND THEN.
AH, YOU'VE SUCCEEDED. MUTANTS ARE FAR TOO SCARCE A COMMODITY NOW TO OPERATE AS ANYTHING BUT A UNITED FORCE.
I'M SURE IT WAS DISAPPOINTING, NOT TO KILL THE X-MEN. BUT IT HAS TO BE DONE CAUTIOUSLY. IT'LL TAKE CAREFUL MANEUVERING TO REPLACE THEM WITH MY GENETIC DUPLICATES.
ONCE THAT'S DONE, I CAN UNITE ALL FACTIONS OF OUR PEOPLE. MUTANTKIND WILL MOVE FORWARD ACCORDING TO MY DESIGN.
"AFTER ALL, YOU NEVER KNOW WHAT MIGHT HAPPEN.
NO.
YOU WOULD BREED SLAVES, NOT WARRIORS.
SKSASH
"WHEN YOU'LL HAVE TO GO UP AGAINST IMPOSSIBLE ODDS...
AND XRAVEN IS NO MAN'S SLAVE!

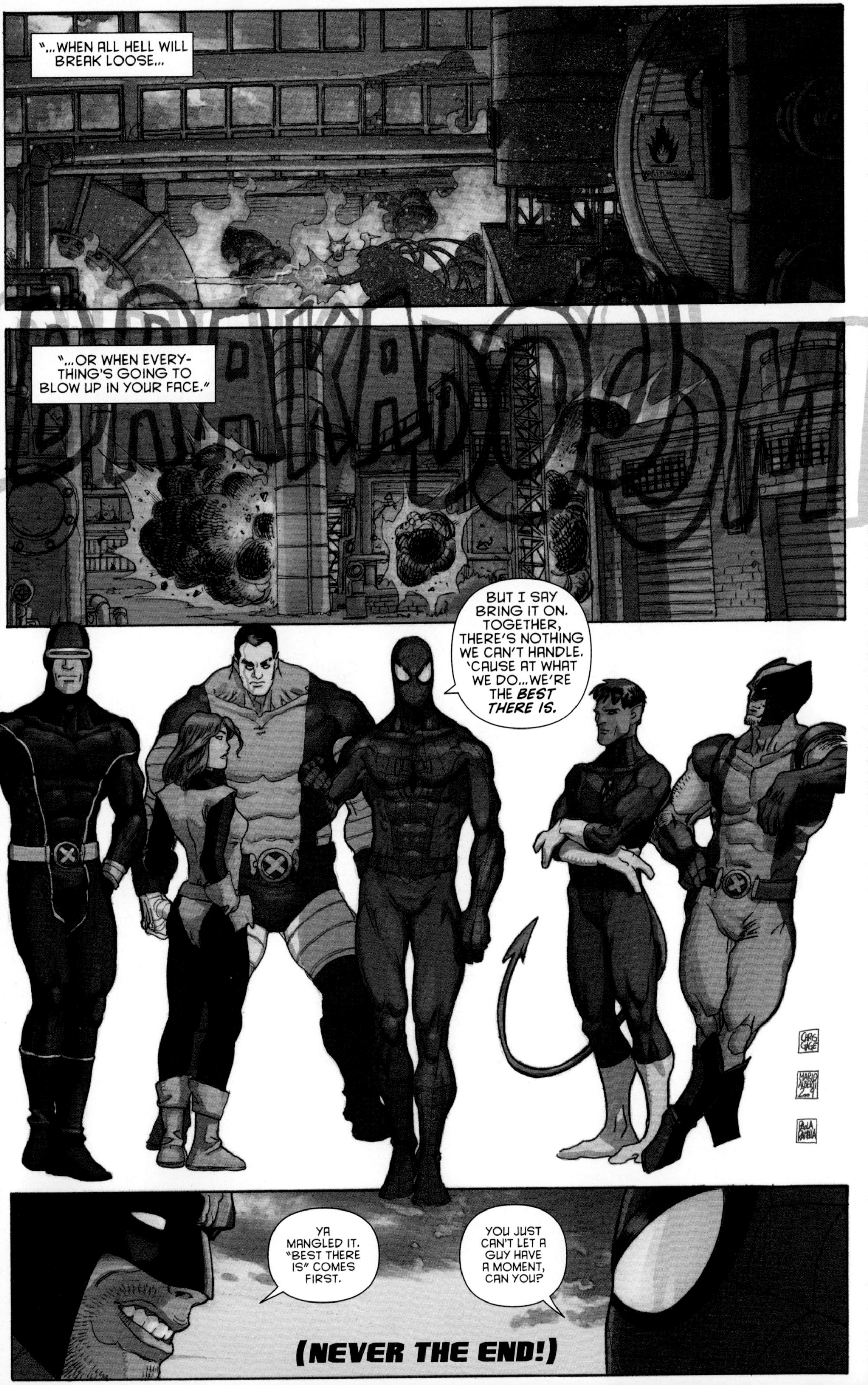
"...WHEN ALL HELL WILL BREAK LOOSE...
"...OR WHEN EVERY-THING'S GOING TO BLOW UP IN YOUR FACE."
BUT I SAY BRING IT ON. TOGETHER, THERE'S NOTHING WE CAN'T HANDLE. 'CAUSE AT WHAT WE DO...WE'RE THE *BEST THERE IS.*
YA MANGLED IT. "BEST THERE IS" COMES FIRST.
YOU JUST CAN'T LET A GUY HAVE A MOMENT, CAN YOU?
(NEVER THE END!)

The X-Men's first meeting with Spider-Man, from *X-Men* #27...

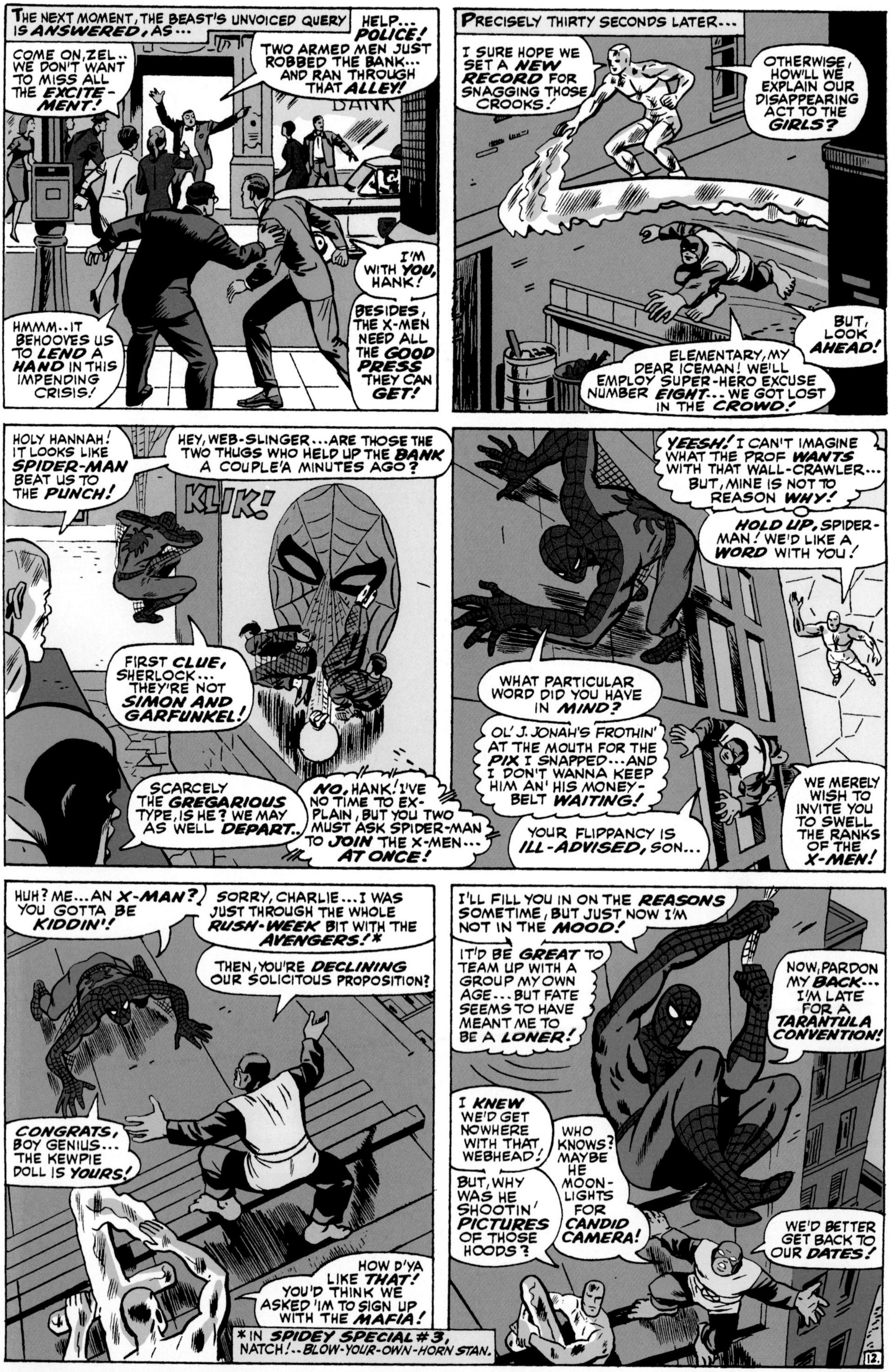
THE NEXT MOMENT, THE BEAST'S UNVOICED QUERY IS ANSWERED, AS...
HELP... POLICE! TWO ARMED MEN JUST ROBBED THE BANK... AND RAN THROUGH THAT ALLEY!
COME ON, ZEL.. WE DON'T WANT TO MISS ALL THE EXCITEMENT!
I'M WITH YOU, HANK!
BESIDES, THE X-MEN NEED ALL THE GOOD PRESS THEY CAN GET!
HMMM.. IT BEHOOVES US TO LEND A HAND IN THIS IMPENDING CRISIS!
PRECISELY THIRTY SECONDS LATER...
I SURE HOPE WE SET A NEW RECORD FOR SNAGGING THOSE CROOKS!
OTHERWISE, HOW'LL WE EXPLAIN OUR DISAPPEARING ACT TO THE GIRLS?
ELEMENTARY, MY DEAR ICEMAN! WE'LL EMPLOY SUPER-HERO EXCUSE NUMBER EIGHT... WE GOT LOST IN THE CROWD!
BUT, LOOK AHEAD!
HOLY HANNAH! IT LOOKS LIKE SPIDER-MAN BEAT US TO THE PUNCH!
HEY, WEB-SLINGER... ARE THOSE THE TWO THUGS WHO HELD UP THE BANK A COUPLE'A MINUTES AGO?
KLIK!
FIRST CLUE, SHERLOCK... THEY'RE NOT SIMON AND GARFUNKEL!
SCARCELY THE GREGARIOUS TYPE, IS HE? WE MAY AS WELL DEPART..
NO, HANK! I'VE NO TIME TO EXPLAIN, BUT YOU TWO MUST ASK SPIDER-MAN TO JOIN THE X-MEN... AT ONCE!
YEESH! I CAN'T IMAGINE WHAT THE PROF WANTS WITH THAT WALL-CRAWLER... BUT, MINE IS NOT TO REASON WHY!
HOLD UP, SPIDER-MAN! WE'D LIKE A WORD WITH YOU!
WHAT PARTICULAR WORD DID YOU HAVE IN MIND?
OL' J. JONAH'S FROTHIN' AT THE MOUTH FOR THE PIX I SNAPPED... AND I DON'T WANNA KEEP HIM AN' HIS MONEY-BELT WAITING!
YOUR FLIPPANCY IS ILL-ADVISED, SON...
WE MERELY WISH TO INVITE YOU TO SWELL THE RANKS OF THE X-MEN!
HUH? ME... AN X-MAN? YOU GOTTA BE KIDDIN'!
SORRY, CHARLIE... I WAS JUST THROUGH THE WHOLE RUSH-WEEK BIT WITH THE AVENGERS!*
THEN, YOU'RE DECLINING OUR SOLICITOUS PROPOSITION?
CONGRATS, BOY GENIUS... THE KEWPIE DOLL IS YOURS!
HOW D'YA LIKE THAT! YOU'D THINK WE ASKED 'IM TO SIGN UP WITH THE MAFIA!
*IN SPIDEY SPECIAL #3, NATCH!.. BLOW-YOUR-OWN-HORN STAN.
I'LL FILL YOU IN ON THE REASONS SOMETIME, BUT JUST NOW I'M NOT IN THE MOOD!
IT'D BE GREAT TO TEAM UP WITH A GROUP MY OWN AGE... BUT FATE SEEMS TO HAVE MEANT ME TO BE A LONER!
NOW, PARDON MY BACK... I'M LATE FOR A TARANTULA CONVENTION!
I KNEW WE'D GET NOWHERE WITH THAT WEBHEAD!
BUT, WHY WAS HE SHOOTIN' PICTURES OF THOSE HOODS?
WHO KNOWS? MAYBE HE MOONLIGHTS FOR CANDID CAMERA!
WE'D BETTER GET BACK TO OUR DATES!
12.

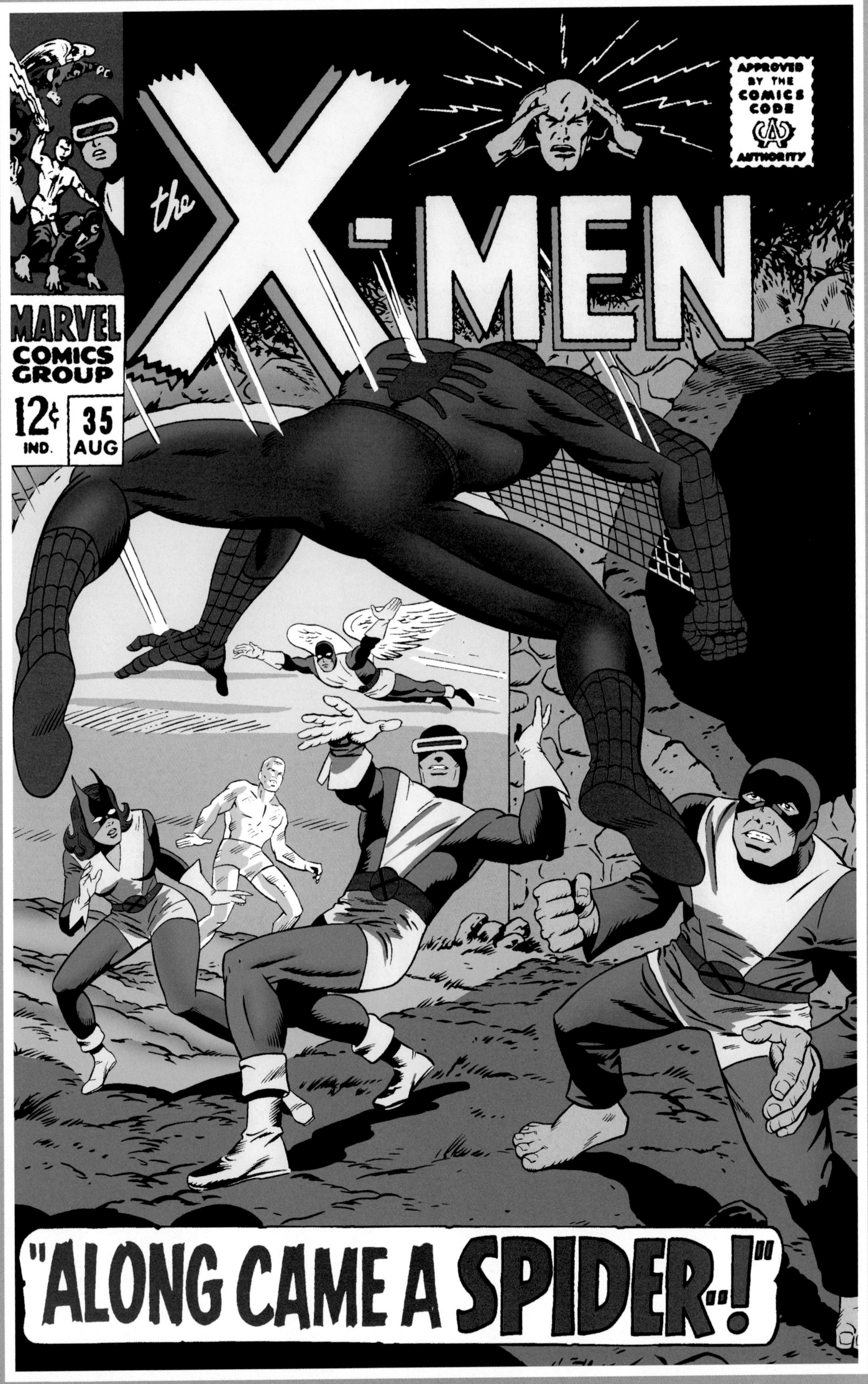
APPROVED BY THE COMICS CODE AUTHORITY
the X-MEN
MARVEL COMICS GROUP
12¢ IND.
35 AUG
"ALONG CAME A SPIDER..!"

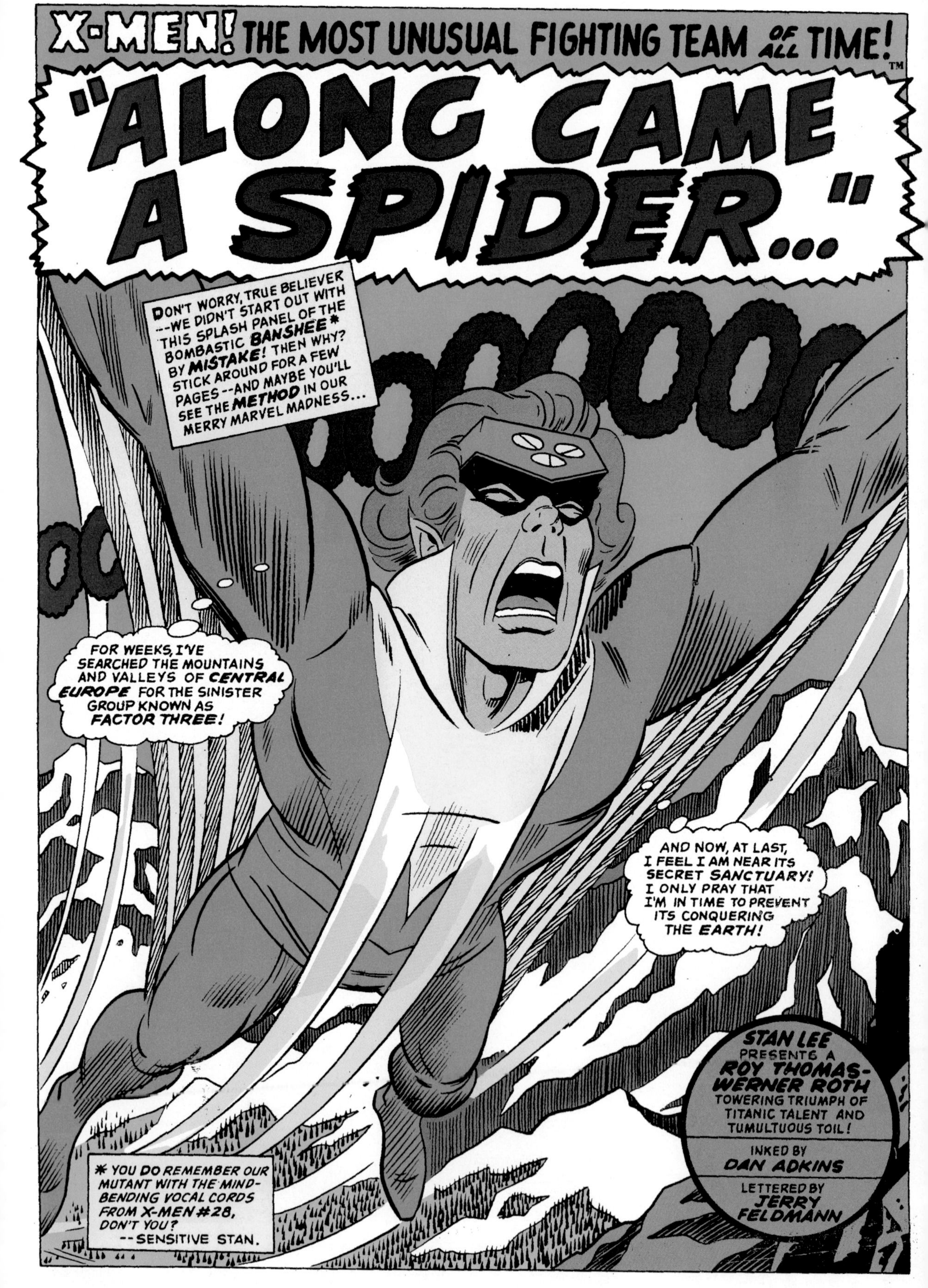
X-MEN! THE MOST UNUSUAL FIGHTING TEAM OF ALL TIME!
"ALONG CAME A SPIDER..."
DON'T WORRY, TRUE BELIEVER --WE DIDN'T START OUT WITH THIS SPLASH PANEL OF THE BOMBASTIC BANSHEE* BY MISTAKE! THEN WHY? STICK AROUND FOR A FEW PAGES --AND MAYBE YOU'LL SEE THE METHOD IN OUR MERRY MARVEL MADNESS...
FOR WEEKS, I'VE SEARCHED THE MOUNTAINS AND VALLEYS OF CENTRAL EUROPE FOR THE SINISTER GROUP KNOWN AS FACTOR THREE!
AND NOW, AT LAST, I FEEL I AM NEAR ITS SECRET SANCTUARY! I ONLY PRAY THAT I'M IN TIME TO PREVENT ITS CONQUERING THE EARTH!
STAN LEE PRESENTS A ROY THOMAS-WERNER ROTH TOWERING TRIUMPH OF TITANIC TALENT AND TUMULTUOUS TOIL!
INKED BY DAN ADKINS
LETTERED BY JERRY FELDMANN
* YOU DO REMEMBER OUR MUTANT WITH THE MIND-BENDING VOCAL CORDS FROM X-MEN #28, DON'T YOU? --SENSITIVE STAN.

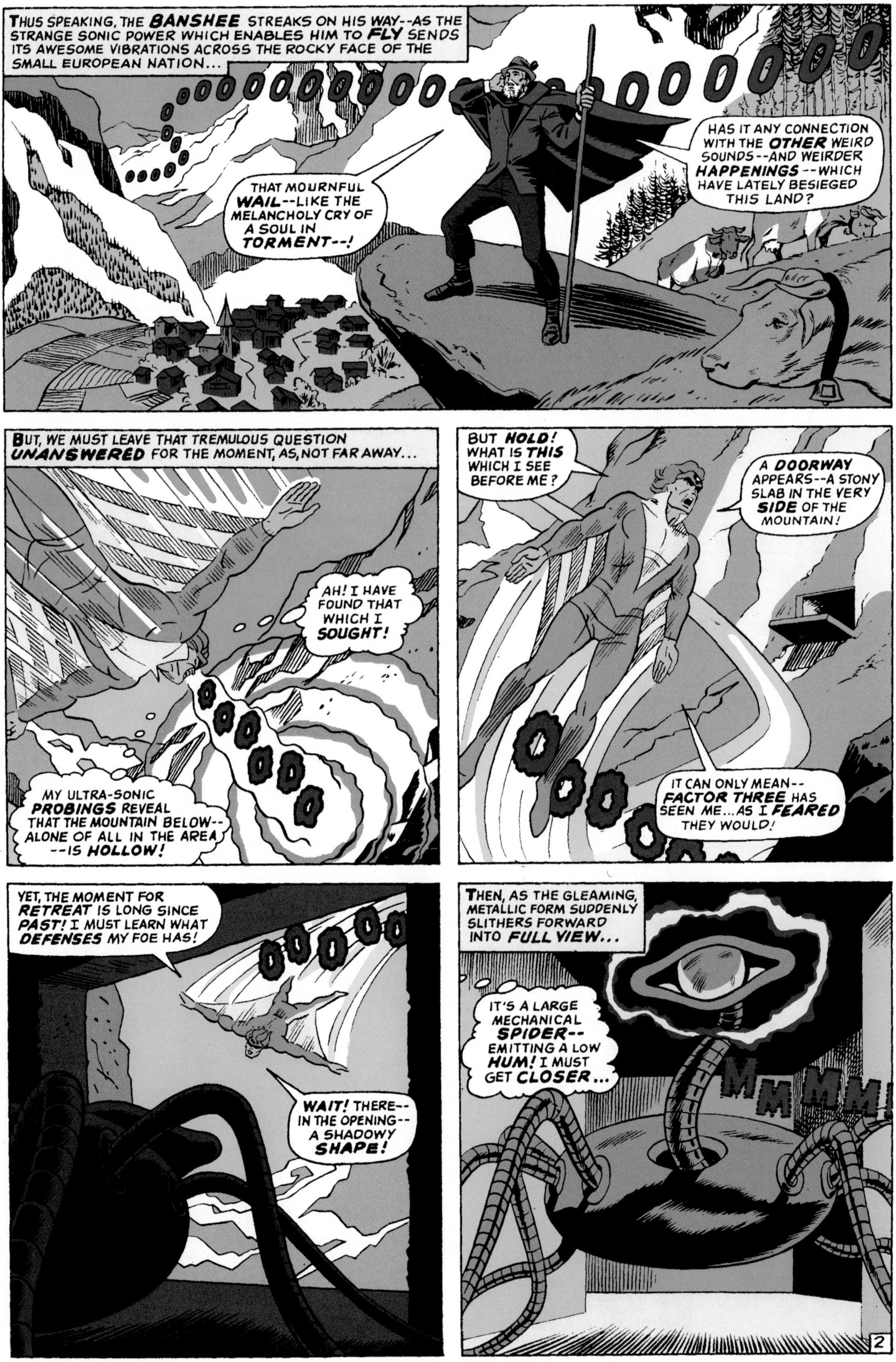
THUS SPEAKING, THE BANSHEE STREAKS ON HIS WAY--AS THE STRANGE SONIC POWER WHICH ENABLES HIM TO FLY SENDS ITS AWESOME VIBRATIONS ACROSS THE ROCKY FACE OF THE SMALL EUROPEAN NATION...
THAT MOURNFUL WAIL--LIKE THE MELANCHOLY CRY OF A SOUL IN TORMENT--!
HAS IT ANY CONNECTION WITH THE OTHER WEIRD SOUNDS--AND WEIRDER HAPPENINGS--WHICH HAVE LATELY BESIEGED THIS LAND?
BUT, WE MUST LEAVE THAT TREMULOUS QUESTION UNANSWERED FOR THE MOMENT, AS, NOT FAR AWAY...
AH! I HAVE FOUND THAT WHICH I SOUGHT!
MY ULTRA-SONIC PROBINGS REVEAL THAT THE MOUNTAIN BELOW--ALONE OF ALL IN THE AREA--IS HOLLOW!
BUT HOLD! WHAT IS THIS WHICH I SEE BEFORE ME?
A DOORWAY APPEARS--A STONY SLAB IN THE VERY SIDE OF THE MOUNTAIN!
IT CAN ONLY MEAN--FACTOR THREE HAS SEEN ME...AS I FEARED THEY WOULD!
YET, THE MOMENT FOR RETREAT IS LONG SINCE PAST! I MUST LEARN WHAT DEFENSES MY FOE HAS!
WAIT! THERE--IN THE OPENING--A SHADOWY SHAPE!
THEN, AS THE GLEAMING, METALLIC FORM SUDDENLY SLITHERS FORWARD INTO FULL VIEW...
IT'S A LARGE MECHANICAL SPIDER--EMITTING A LOW HUM! I MUST GET CLOSER...
MMMMM
2

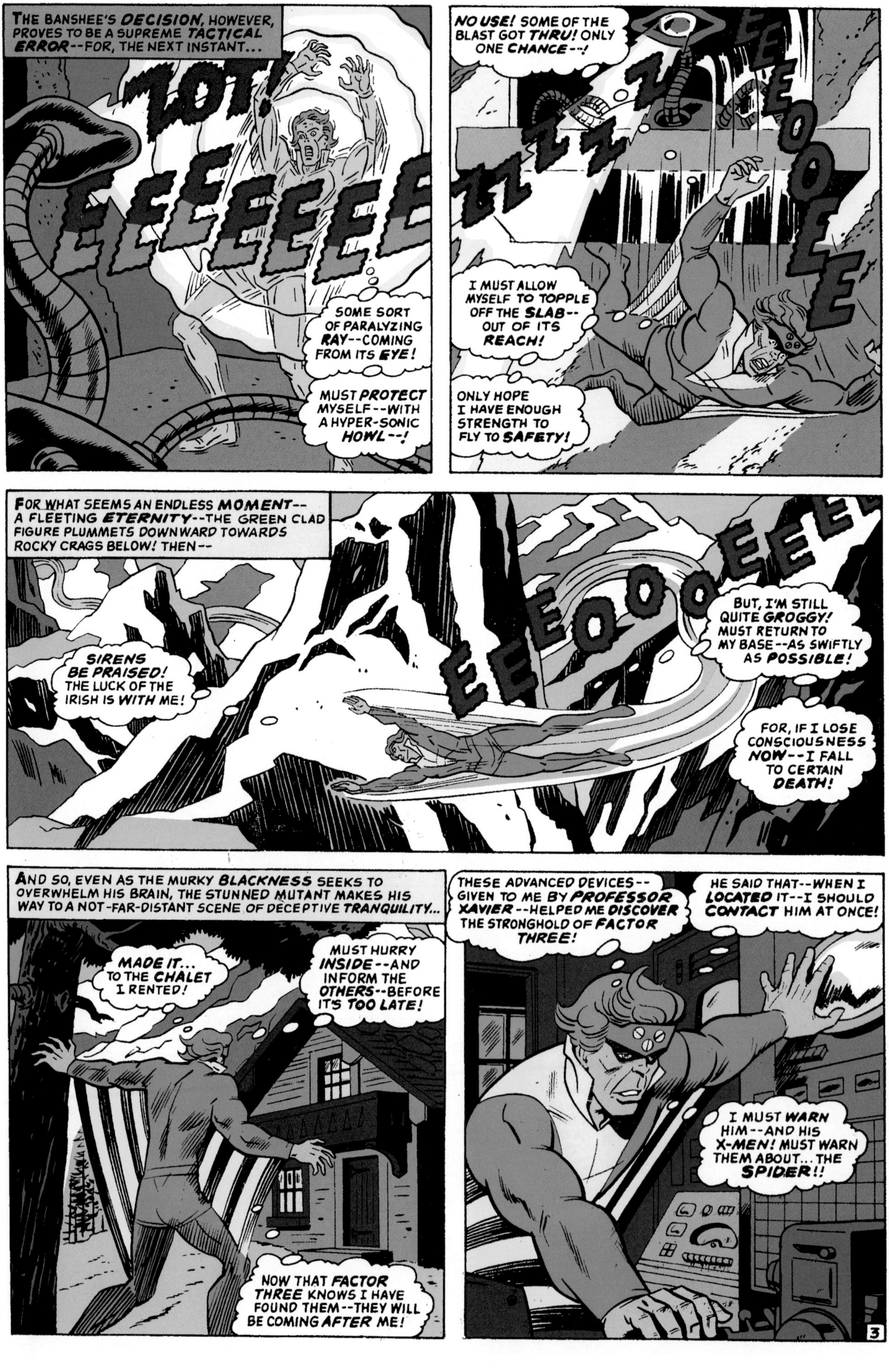
THE BANSHEE'S DECISION, HOWEVER, PROVES TO BE A SUPREME TACTICAL ERROR--FOR, THE NEXT INSTANT...
ZOT!
EEEEEEEE
SOME SORT OF PARALYZING RAY--COMING FROM ITS EYE!
MUST PROTECT MYSELF--WITH A HYPER-SONIC HOWL--!
NO USE! SOME OF THE BLAST GOT THRU! ONLY ONE CHANCE--!
ZZZZZZ
EEEOOOEEE
I MUST ALLOW MYSELF TO TOPPLE OFF THE SLAB--OUT OF ITS REACH!
ONLY HOPE I HAVE ENOUGH STRENGTH TO FLY TO SAFETY!
FOR WHAT SEEMS AN ENDLESS MOMENT--A FLEETING ETERNITY--THE GREEN CLAD FIGURE PLUMMETS DOWNWARD TOWARDS ROCKY CRAGS BELOW! THEN--
EEEOOOEEEE
SIRENS BE PRAISED! THE LUCK OF THE IRISH IS WITH ME!
BUT, I'M STILL QUITE GROGGY! MUST RETURN TO MY BASE--AS SWIFTLY AS POSSIBLE!
FOR, IF I LOSE CONSCIOUSNESS NOW--I FALL TO CERTAIN DEATH!
AND SO, EVEN AS THE MURKY BLACKNESS SEEKS TO OVERWHELM HIS BRAIN, THE STUNNED MUTANT MAKES HIS WAY TO A NOT-FAR-DISTANT SCENE OF DECEPTIVE TRANQUILITY...
MADE IT... TO THE CHALET I RENTED!
MUST HURRY INSIDE--AND INFORM THE OTHERS--BEFORE IT'S TOO LATE!
NOW THAT FACTOR THREE KNOWS I HAVE FOUND THEM--THEY WILL BE COMING AFTER ME!
THESE ADVANCED DEVICES--GIVEN TO ME BY PROFESSOR XAVIER--HELPED ME DISCOVER THE STRONGHOLD OF FACTOR THREE!
HE SAID THAT--WHEN I LOCATED IT--I SHOULD CONTACT HIM AT ONCE!
I MUST WARN HIM--AND HIS X-MEN! MUST WARN THEM ABOUT... THE SPIDER!!

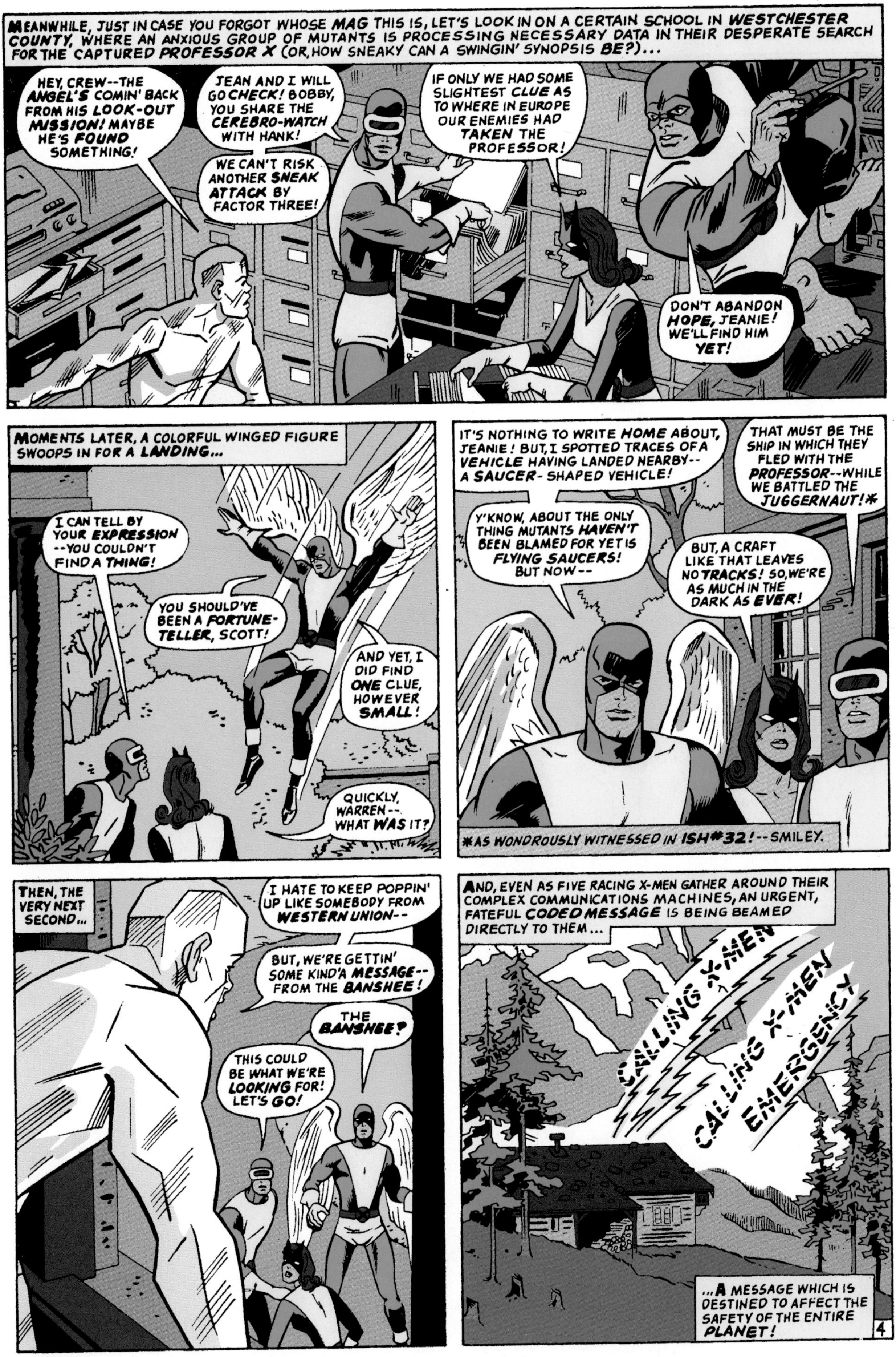
MEANWHILE, JUST IN CASE YOU FORGOT WHOSE MAG THIS IS, LET'S LOOK IN ON A CERTAIN SCHOOL IN WESTCHESTER COUNTY, WHERE AN ANXIOUS GROUP OF MUTANTS IS PROCESSING NECESSARY DATA IN THEIR DESPERATE SEARCH FOR THE CAPTURED PROFESSOR X (OR, HOW SNEAKY CAN A SWINGIN' SYNOPSIS BE?)...
HEY, CREW--THE ANGEL'S COMIN' BACK FROM HIS LOOK-OUT MISSION! MAYBE HE'S FOUND SOMETHING!
JEAN AND I WILL GO CHECK! BOBBY, YOU SHARE THE CEREBRO-WATCH WITH HANK!
WE CAN'T RISK ANOTHER SNEAK ATTACK BY FACTOR THREE!
IF ONLY WE HAD SOME SLIGHTEST CLUE AS TO WHERE IN EUROPE OUR ENEMIES HAD TAKEN THE PROFESSOR!
DON'T ABANDON HOPE, JEANIE! WE'LL FIND HIM YET!
MOMENTS LATER, A COLORFUL WINGED FIGURE SWOOPS IN FOR A LANDING...
I CAN TELL BY YOUR EXPRESSION --YOU COULDN'T FIND A THING!
YOU SHOULD'VE BEEN A FORTUNE-TELLER, SCOTT!
AND YET, I DID FIND ONE CLUE, HOWEVER SMALL!
QUICKLY, WARREN-- WHAT WAS IT?
IT'S NOTHING TO WRITE HOME ABOUT, JEANIE! BUT, I SPOTTED TRACES OF A VEHICLE HAVING LANDED NEARBY-- A SAUCER-SHAPED VEHICLE!
THAT MUST BE THE SHIP IN WHICH THEY FLED WITH THE PROFESSOR--WHILE WE BATTLED THE JUGGERNAUT!*
Y'KNOW, ABOUT THE ONLY THING MUTANTS HAVEN'T BEEN BLAMED FOR YET IS FLYING SAUCERS! BUT NOW--
BUT, A CRAFT LIKE THAT LEAVES NO TRACKS! SO, WE'RE AS MUCH IN THE DARK AS EVER!
*AS WONDROUSLY WITNESSED IN ISH #32! --SMILEY.
THEN, THE VERY NEXT SECOND...
I HATE TO KEEP POPPIN' UP LIKE SOMEBODY FROM WESTERN UNION--
BUT, WE'RE GETTIN' SOME KIND'A MESSAGE-- FROM THE BANSHEE!
THE BANSHEE?
THIS COULD BE WHAT WE'RE LOOKING FOR! LET'S GO!
AND, EVEN AS FIVE RACING X-MEN GATHER AROUND THEIR COMPLEX COMMUNICATIONS MACHINES, AN URGENT, FATEFUL CODED MESSAGE IS BEING BEAMED DIRECTLY TO THEM...
CALLING X-MEN
CALLING X-MEN
EMERGENCY
...A MESSAGE WHICH IS DESTINED TO AFFECT THE SAFETY OF THE ENTIRE PLANET!
4

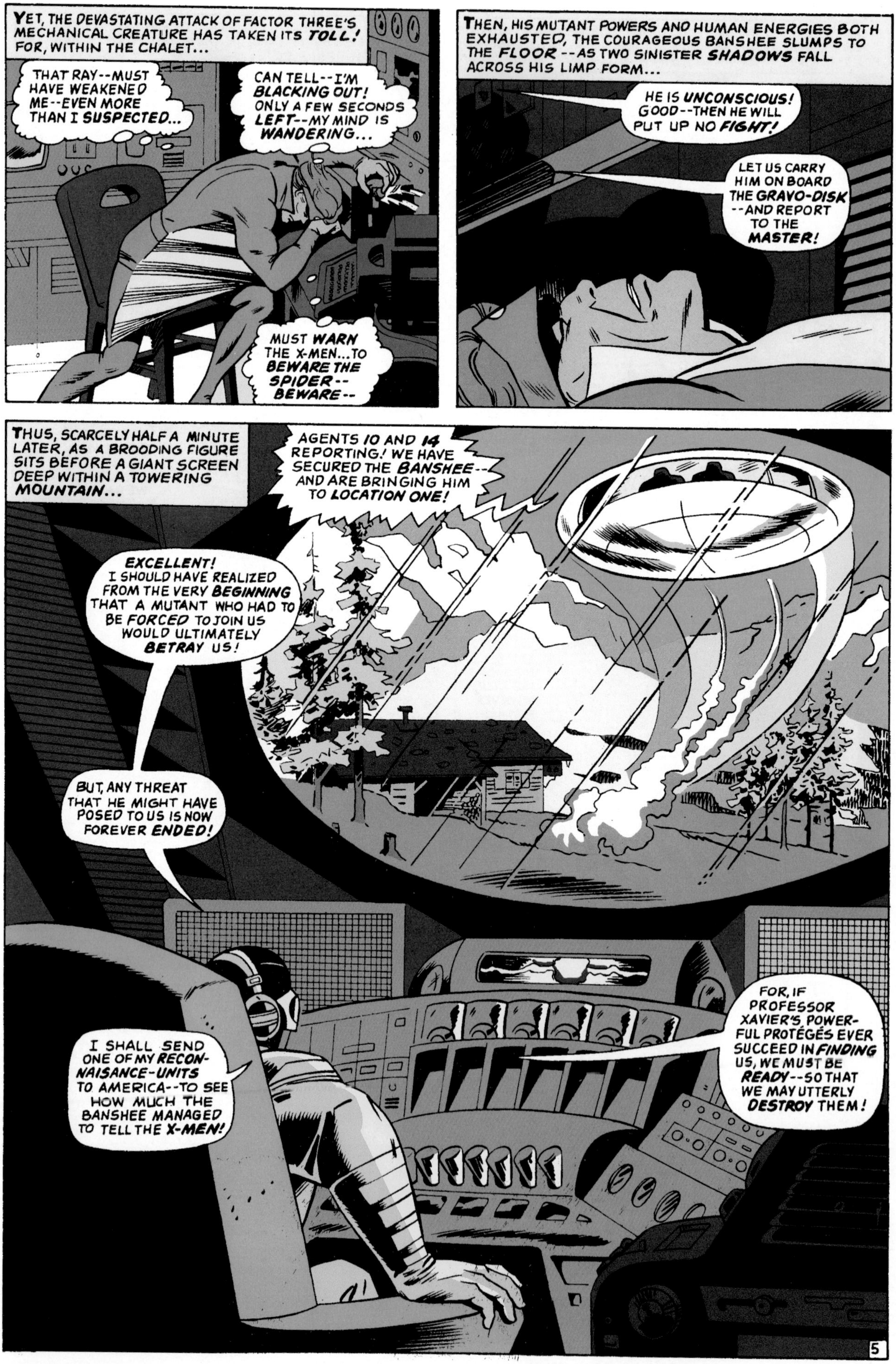

YET, THE DEVASTATING ATTACK OF FACTOR THREE'S MECHANICAL CREATURE HAS TAKEN ITS TOLL! FOR, WITHIN THE CHALET...
THAT RAY--MUST HAVE WEAKENED ME--EVEN MORE THAN I SUSPECTED...
CAN TELL--I'M BLACKING OUT! ONLY A FEW SECONDS LEFT--MY MIND IS WANDERING...
MUST WARN THE X-MEN...TO BEWARE THE SPIDER-- BEWARE--
THEN, HIS MUTANT POWERS AND HUMAN ENERGIES BOTH EXHAUSTED, THE COURAGEOUS BANSHEE SLUMPS TO THE FLOOR --AS TWO SINISTER SHADOWS FALL ACROSS HIS LIMP FORM...
HE IS UNCONSCIOUS! GOOD--THEN HE WILL PUT UP NO FIGHT!
LET US CARRY HIM ON BOARD THE GRAVO-DISK --AND REPORT TO THE MASTER!
THUS, SCARCELY HALF A MINUTE LATER, AS A BROODING FIGURE SITS BEFORE A GIANT SCREEN DEEP WITHIN A TOWERING MOUNTAIN...
AGENTS 10 AND 14 REPORTING! WE HAVE SECURED THE BANSHEE-- AND ARE BRINGING HIM TO LOCATION ONE!
EXCELLENT! I SHOULD HAVE REALIZED FROM THE VERY BEGINNING THAT A MUTANT WHO HAD TO BE FORCED TO JOIN US WOULD ULTIMATELY BETRAY US!
BUT, ANY THREAT THAT HE MIGHT HAVE POSED TO US IS NOW FOREVER ENDED!
I SHALL SEND ONE OF MY RECON-NAISANCE-UNITS TO AMERICA--TO SEE HOW MUCH THE BANSHEE MANAGED TO TELL THE X-MEN!
FOR, IF PROFESSOR XAVIER'S POWER-FUL PROTÉGÉS EVER SUCCEED IN FINDING US, WE MUST BE READY--SO THAT WE MAY UTTERLY DESTROY THEM!

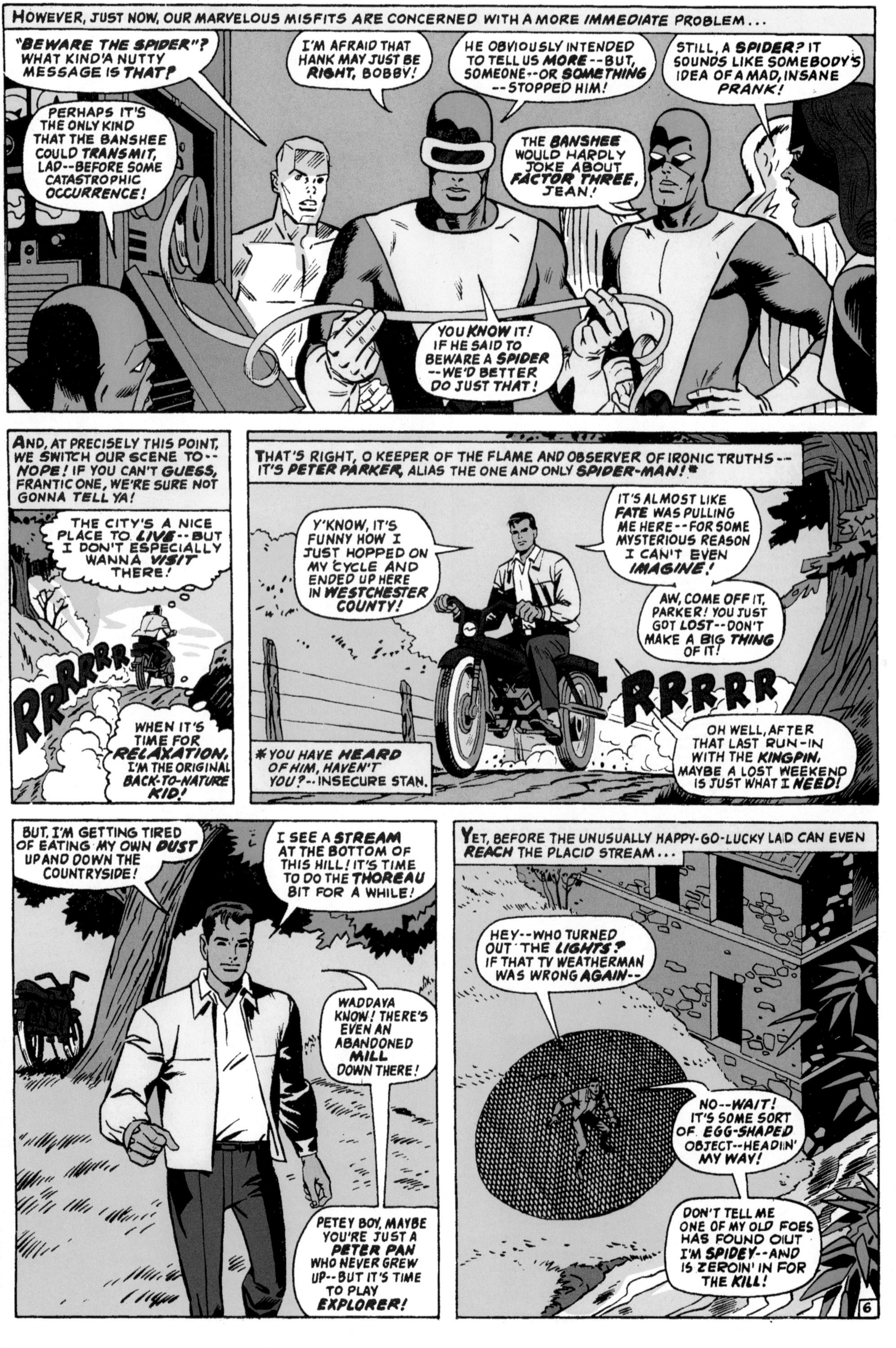
HOWEVER, JUST NOW, OUR MARVELOUS MISFITS ARE CONCERNED WITH A MORE IMMEDIATE PROBLEM...
"BEWARE THE SPIDER"? WHAT KIND'A NUTTY MESSAGE IS THAT?
PERHAPS IT'S THE ONLY KIND THAT THE BANSHEE COULD TRANSMIT, LAD--BEFORE SOME CATASTROPHIC OCCURRENCE!
I'M AFRAID THAT HANK MAY JUST BE RIGHT, BOBBY!
HE OBVIOUSLY INTENDED TO TELL US MORE--BUT, SOMEONE--OR SOMETHING--STOPPED HIM!
STILL, A SPIDER? IT SOUNDS LIKE SOMEBODY'S IDEA OF A MAD, INSANE PRANK!
THE BANSHEE WOULD HARDLY JOKE ABOUT FACTOR THREE, JEAN!
YOU KNOW IT! IF HE SAID TO BEWARE A SPIDER--WE'D BETTER DO JUST THAT!
AND, AT PRECISELY THIS POINT, WE SWITCH OUR SCENE TO--NOPE! IF YOU CAN'T GUESS, FRANTIC ONE, WE'RE SURE NOT GONNA TELL YA!
THE CITY'S A NICE PLACE TO LIVE--BUT I DON'T ESPECIALLY WANNA VISIT THERE!
RRRRRR
WHEN IT'S TIME FOR RELAXATION, I'M THE ORIGINAL BACK-TO-NATURE KID!
THAT'S RIGHT, O KEEPER OF THE FLAME AND OBSERVER OF IRONIC TRUTHS--IT'S PETER PARKER, ALIAS THE ONE AND ONLY SPIDER-MAN!*
Y'KNOW, IT'S FUNNY HOW I JUST HOPPED ON MY CYCLE AND ENDED UP HERE IN WESTCHESTER COUNTY!
IT'S ALMOST LIKE FATE WAS PULLING ME HERE--FOR SOME MYSTERIOUS REASON I CAN'T EVEN IMAGINE!
AW, COME OFF IT, PARKER! YOU JUST GOT LOST--DON'T MAKE A BIG THING OF IT!
RRRRR
OH WELL, AFTER THAT LAST RUN-IN WITH THE KINGPIN, MAYBE A LOST WEEKEND IS JUST WHAT I NEED!
*YOU HAVE HEARD OF HIM, HAVEN'T YOU?--INSECURE STAN.
BUT, I'M GETTING TIRED OF EATING MY OWN DUST UP AND DOWN THE COUNTRYSIDE!
I SEE A STREAM AT THE BOTTOM OF THIS HILL! IT'S TIME TO DO THE THOREAU BIT FOR A WHILE!
WADDAYA KNOW! THERE'S EVEN AN ABANDONED MILL DOWN THERE!
PETEY BOY, MAYBE YOU'RE JUST A PETER PAN WHO NEVER GREW UP--BUT IT'S TIME TO PLAY EXPLORER!
YET, BEFORE THE UNUSUALLY HAPPY-GO-LUCKY LAD CAN EVEN REACH THE PLACID STREAM...
HEY--WHO TURNED OUT THE LIGHTS? IF THAT TV WEATHERMAN WAS WRONG AGAIN--
NO--WAIT! IT'S SOME SORT OF EGG-SHAPED OBJECT--HEADIN' MY WAY!
DON'T TELL ME ONE OF MY OLD FOES HAS FOUND OUT I'M SPIDEY--AND IS ZEROIN' IN FOR THE KILL!
6

AND SO...

I'LL DUCK INTO THE *MILL*, OUT OF SIGHT, AND SEE IF--*HEY!* NOW, IT'S JUST *CIRCLING AROUND!*

IT'S PROBABLY NOT AFTER *ME* AT ALL!

PARKER, YOU'RE TURNING INTO A WALKING, TALKING *PERSECUTION COMPLEX!*

THEN, WHAT *IS* IT AFTER?

IN FACT, TO PUT THE QUESTION *ANOTHER* WAY--WHAT *IS* IT, *PERIOD?*

WELL, I JUST MIGHT HAVE A CHANCE TO *FIND OUT!* IT'S *LANDING!*

LUCKY I PUT ON MY *SPIDEY* OUTFIT THIS MORNING!

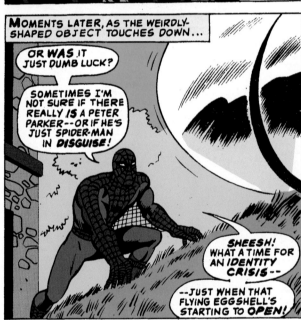

MOMENTS LATER, AS THE WEIRDLY-SHAPED OBJECT TOUCHES DOWN...

OR WAS IT JUST DUMB LUCK?

SOMETIMES I'M NOT SURE IF THERE REALLY *IS* A PETER PARKER--OR IF HE'S JUST SPIDER-MAN IN *DISGUISE!*

SHEESH! WHAT A TIME FOR AN *IDENTITY CRISIS--*

--JUST WHEN THAT FLYING EGGSHELL'S STARTING TO *OPEN!*

THE NEXT MICROSECOND...

I WAS *RIGHT!* BUT, WHAT'S THAT *COMING OUT?*

IT LOOKS LIKE A *SPIDER*--ONE MADE OUT OF *METAL!*

AND, IT'S GOT SOME SORT OF ELECTRONIC *EYE*--STUCK ON A STEEL *TENTACLE!*

BUT, WHY AM I STANDING HERE *ADMIRING* IT--

MMMM MM

--WHEN MY *SPIDER-SENSE* TELLS ME IT'S ABOUT TO *ATTACK--* AND I'M ITS ONLY POSSIBLE *TARGET!*

SORRY, PAL! WE MAY BE *RELATED*, FOR ALL I KNOW--

THWP!

STILL, I DON'T FEEL LIKE STICKING AROUND FOR A *FAMILY FEUD!*

ZAPT!

GOOD THING THAT *MILL* WAS HERE--TO SHOOT MY *WEBBING* ONTO!

THOSE *STUN-RAYS* MY LITTLE PAL IS USING LOOK *POWERFUL!*

FZT!

I DON'T KNOW IF YOU CAN *HEAR* ME OR NOT, CHUM--BUT, I'LL SEE YOU AROUND THE *COBWEBS!*

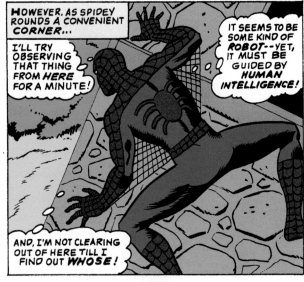

HOWEVER, AS SPIDEY ROUNDS A CONVENIENT *CORNER...*

I'LL TRY *OBSERVING* THAT THING FROM *HERE* FOR A MINUTE!

IT SEEMS TO BE SOME KIND OF *ROBOT*--YET, IT MUST BE GUIDED BY *HUMAN INTELLIGENCE!*

AND, I'M NOT CLEARING OUT OF HERE TILL I FIND OUT *WHOSE!*

BUT THEN, SUDDENLY--

BRAK!

WH--? THE *SONUVAGUN* SNEAKED AROUND *BEHIND* ME--AT FANTASTIC *SPEED!*

IT KNOCKED OFF THE CORNER OF THE *MILL!* MUST GET OUT OF ITS *WAY--!*

MADE IT! GOOD THING THAT *WINDOW* WAS HANDY!

NOW, THAT RAY-BLASTING CREEP'S GONNA BE *SORRY* --'CAUSE IT MADE ME LOSE MY *TEMPER!*

I'M GONNA TAKE IT *APART*--AND SEE WHAT MAKES IT *TICK!*

THERE'S JUST ONE LITTLE THING I WISH--

I WISH I *FELT* AS CONFIDENT AS I *SOUND!*

YET, AT THAT PRECISE WEB-SPINNING INSTANT, A *NEW* ELEMENT IS ABOUT TO ENTER THE SCENE--AND ALTER SPIDEY'S *PLANS...*

REEEEEEEEEEEEEEEE

LISTEN, GROUP! CEREBRO IS INDICATING THE PRESENCE OF... A *MUTANT!*

BUT--IT'S ONLY *MONITORING* THE SURROUNDING *AREA!*

THEN, THAT'S WHERE THE MUTANT *IS!* MAYBE HE'S COME AFTER *US!*

IF SO, HE'S GONNA BE *SORRY*--SINCE WE'RE READY AND *WAITING* FOR HIM!

I'LL TURN OFF THE *SOUND*--WHILE YOU CHECK HIS EXACT *LOCATION!*

8

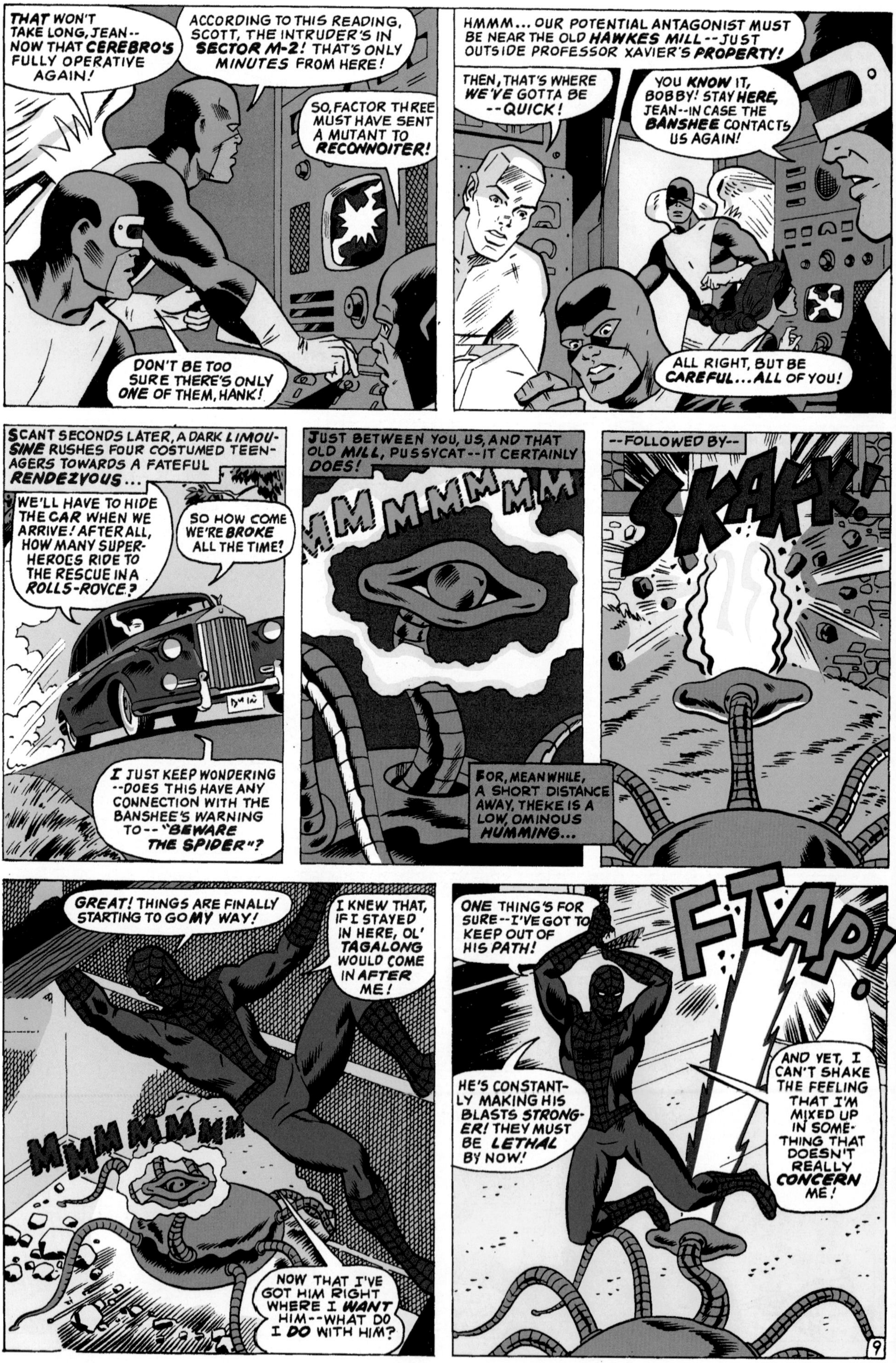
THAT WON'T TAKE LONG, JEAN-- NOW THAT CEREBRO'S FULLY OPERATIVE AGAIN!
ACCORDING TO THIS READING, SCOTT, THE INTRUDER'S IN SECTOR M-2! THAT'S ONLY MINUTES FROM HERE!
SO, FACTOR THREE MUST HAVE SENT A MUTANT TO RECONNOITER!
DON'T BE TOO SURE THERE'S ONLY ONE OF THEM, HANK!
HMMM... OUR POTENTIAL ANTAGONIST MUST BE NEAR THE OLD HAWKES MILL--JUST OUTSIDE PROFESSOR XAVIER'S PROPERTY!
THEN, THAT'S WHERE WE'VE GOTTA BE --QUICK!
YOU KNOW IT, BOBBY! STAY HERE, JEAN--IN CASE THE BANSHEE CONTACTS US AGAIN!
ALL RIGHT, BUT BE CAREFUL...ALL OF YOU!
SCANT SECONDS LATER, A DARK LIMOUSINE RUSHES FOUR COSTUMED TEENAGERS TOWARDS A FATEFUL RENDEZVOUS...
WE'LL HAVE TO HIDE THE CAR WHEN WE ARRIVE! AFTER ALL, HOW MANY SUPER-HEROES RIDE TO THE RESCUE IN A ROLLS-ROYCE?
SO HOW COME WE'RE BROKE ALL THE TIME?
I JUST KEEP WONDERING --DOES THIS HAVE ANY CONNECTION WITH THE BANSHEE'S WARNING TO--"BEWARE THE SPIDER"?
JUST BETWEEN YOU, US, AND THAT OLD MILL, PUSSYCAT--IT CERTAINLY DOES!
MMMMMMMMM
FOR, MEANWHILE, A SHORT DISTANCE AWAY, THERE IS A LOW, OMINOUS HUMMING...
--FOLLOWED BY--
SKAKK!
GREAT! THINGS ARE FINALLY STARTING TO GO MY WAY!
I KNEW THAT, IF I STAYED IN HERE, OL' TAGALONG WOULD COME IN AFTER ME!
MMMMMMM
NOW THAT I'VE GOT HIM RIGHT WHERE I WANT HIM--WHAT DO I DO WITH HIM?
ONE THING'S FOR SURE--I'VE GOT TO KEEP OUT OF HIS PATH!
FTAP!
HE'S CONSTANTLY MAKING HIS BLASTS STRONGER! THEY MUST BE LETHAL BY NOW!
AND YET, I CAN'T SHAKE THE FEELING THAT I'M MIXED UP IN SOMETHING THAT DOESN'T REALLY CONCERN ME!

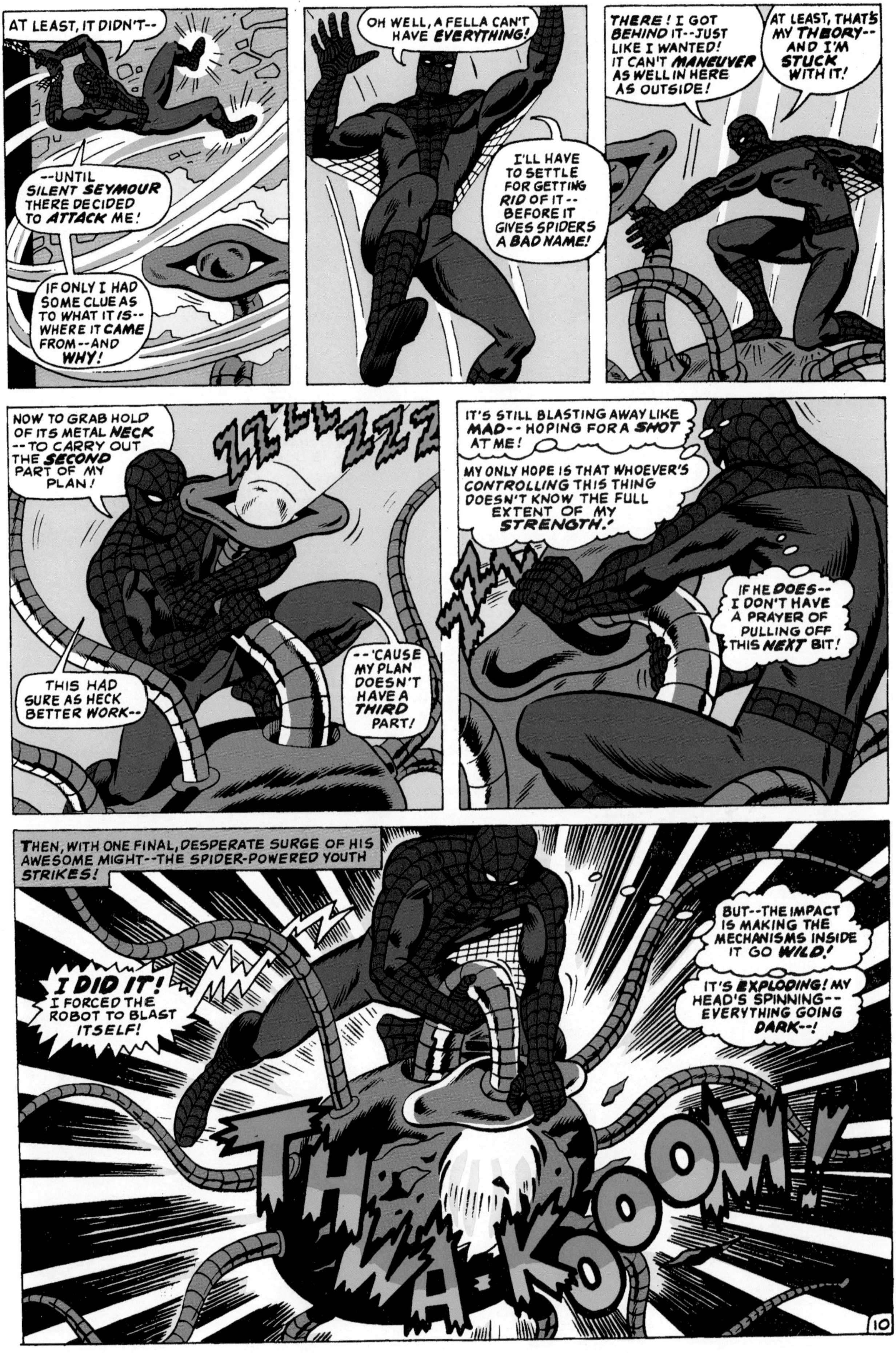
AT LEAST, IT DIDN'T--
--UNTIL SILENT SEYMOUR THERE DECIDED TO ATTACK ME!
IF ONLY I HAD SOME CLUE AS TO WHAT IT IS-- WHERE IT CAME FROM--AND WHY!
OH WELL, A FELLA CAN'T HAVE EVERYTHING!
I'LL HAVE TO SETTLE FOR GETTING RID OF IT-- BEFORE IT GIVES SPIDERS A BAD NAME!
THERE! I GOT BEHIND IT--JUST LIKE I WANTED! IT CAN'T MANEUVER AS WELL IN HERE AS OUTSIDE!
AT LEAST, THAT'S MY THEORY-- AND I'M STUCK WITH IT!
NOW TO GRAB HOLD OF ITS METAL NECK --TO CARRY OUT THE SECOND PART OF MY PLAN!
ZZZZ ZZZ
THIS HAD SURE AS HECK BETTER WORK--
--'CAUSE MY PLAN DOESN'T HAVE A THIRD PART!
IT'S STILL BLASTING AWAY LIKE MAD-- HOPING FOR A SHOT AT ME!
MY ONLY HOPE IS THAT WHOEVER'S CONTROLLING THIS THING DOESN'T KNOW THE FULL EXTENT OF MY STRENGTH!
IF HE DOES-- I DON'T HAVE A PRAYER OF PULLING OFF THIS NEXT BIT!
THEN, WITH ONE FINAL, DESPERATE SURGE OF HIS AWESOME MIGHT--THE SPIDER-POWERED YOUTH STRIKES!
I DID IT! I FORCED THE ROBOT TO BLAST ITSELF!
BUT--THE IMPACT IS MAKING THE MECHANISMS INSIDE IT GO WILD!
IT'S EXPLODING! MY HEAD'S SPINNING-- EVERYTHING GOING DARK--!
THWA-KOOOM!
10

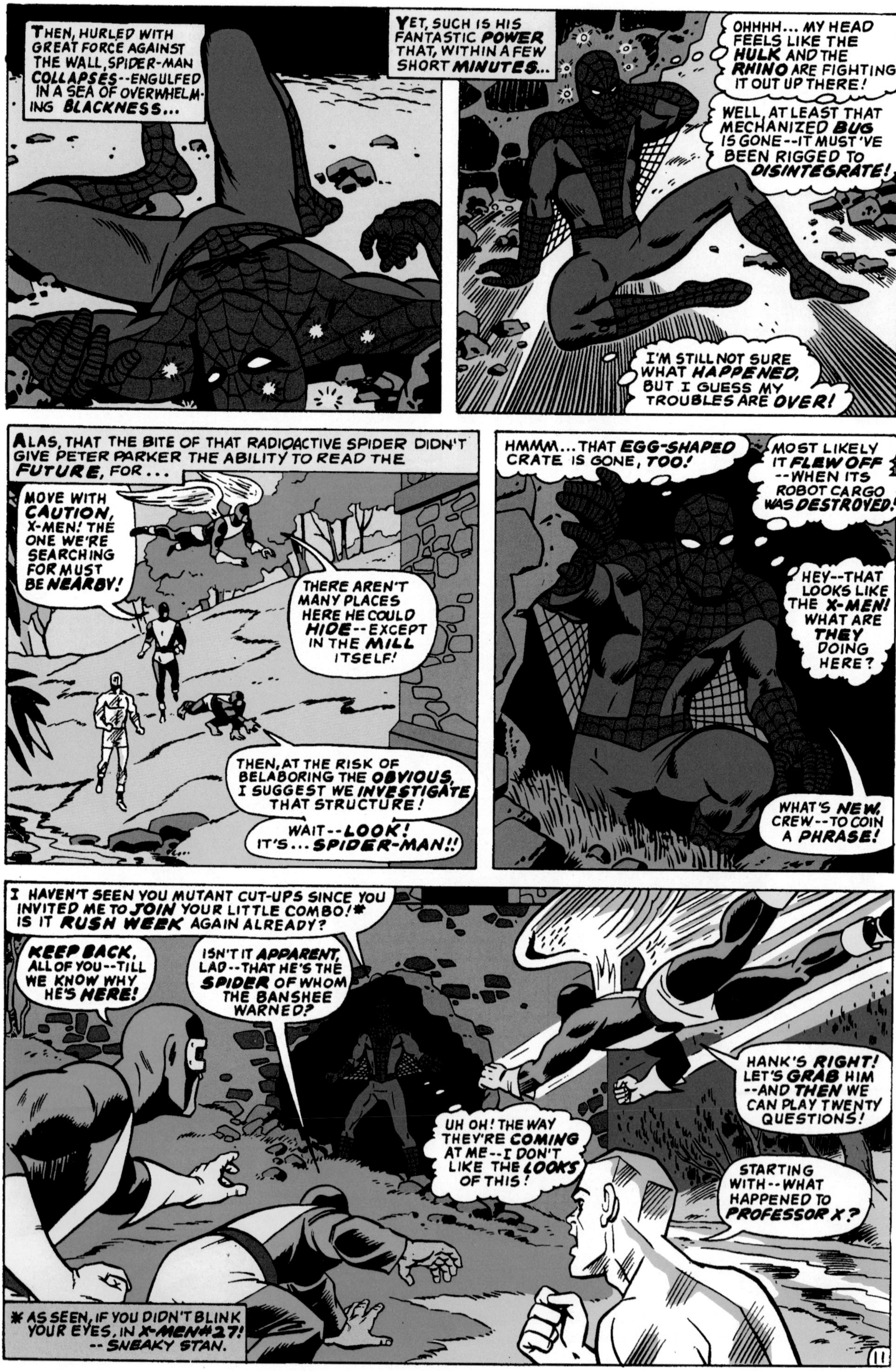
THEN, HURLED WITH GREAT FORCE AGAINST THE WALL, SPIDER-MAN COLLAPSES--ENGULFED IN A SEA OF OVERWHELMING BLACKNESS...
YET, SUCH IS HIS FANTASTIC POWER THAT, WITHIN A FEW SHORT MINUTES...
OHHHH... MY HEAD FEELS LIKE THE HULK AND THE RHINO ARE FIGHTING IT OUT UP THERE!
WELL, AT LEAST THAT MECHANIZED BUG IS GONE--IT MUST'VE BEEN RIGGED TO DISINTEGRATE!
I'M STILL NOT SURE WHAT HAPPENED, BUT I GUESS MY TROUBLES ARE OVER!
ALAS, THAT THE BITE OF THAT RADIOACTIVE SPIDER DIDN'T GIVE PETER PARKER THE ABILITY TO READ THE FUTURE, FOR...
MOVE WITH CAUTION, X-MEN! THE ONE WE'RE SEARCHING FOR MUST BE NEARBY!
THERE AREN'T MANY PLACES HERE HE COULD HIDE--EXCEPT IN THE MILL ITSELF!
THEN, AT THE RISK OF BELABORING THE OBVIOUS, I SUGGEST WE INVESTIGATE THAT STRUCTURE!
WAIT--LOOK! IT'S... SPIDER-MAN!!
HMMM... THAT EGG-SHAPED CRATE IS GONE, TOO!
MOST LIKELY IT FLEW OFF --WHEN ITS ROBOT CARGO WAS DESTROYED!
HEY--THAT LOOKS LIKE THE X-MEN! WHAT ARE THEY DOING HERE?
WHAT'S NEW, CREW--TO COIN A PHRASE!
I HAVEN'T SEEN YOU MUTANT CUT-UPS SINCE YOU INVITED ME TO JOIN YOUR LITTLE COMBO!* IS IT RUSH WEEK AGAIN ALREADY?
KEEP BACK, ALL OF YOU--TILL WE KNOW WHY HE'S HERE!
ISN'T IT APPARENT, LAD--THAT HE'S THE SPIDER OF WHOM THE BANSHEE WARNED?
UH OH! THE WAY THEY'RE COMING AT ME--I DON'T LIKE THE LOOKS OF THIS!
HANK'S RIGHT! LET'S GRAB HIM --AND THEN WE CAN PLAY TWENTY QUESTIONS!
STARTING WITH--WHAT HAPPENED TO PROFESSOR X?
* AS SEEN, IF YOU DIDN'T BLINK YOUR EYES, IN X-MEN #27! --SNEAKY STAN.
11

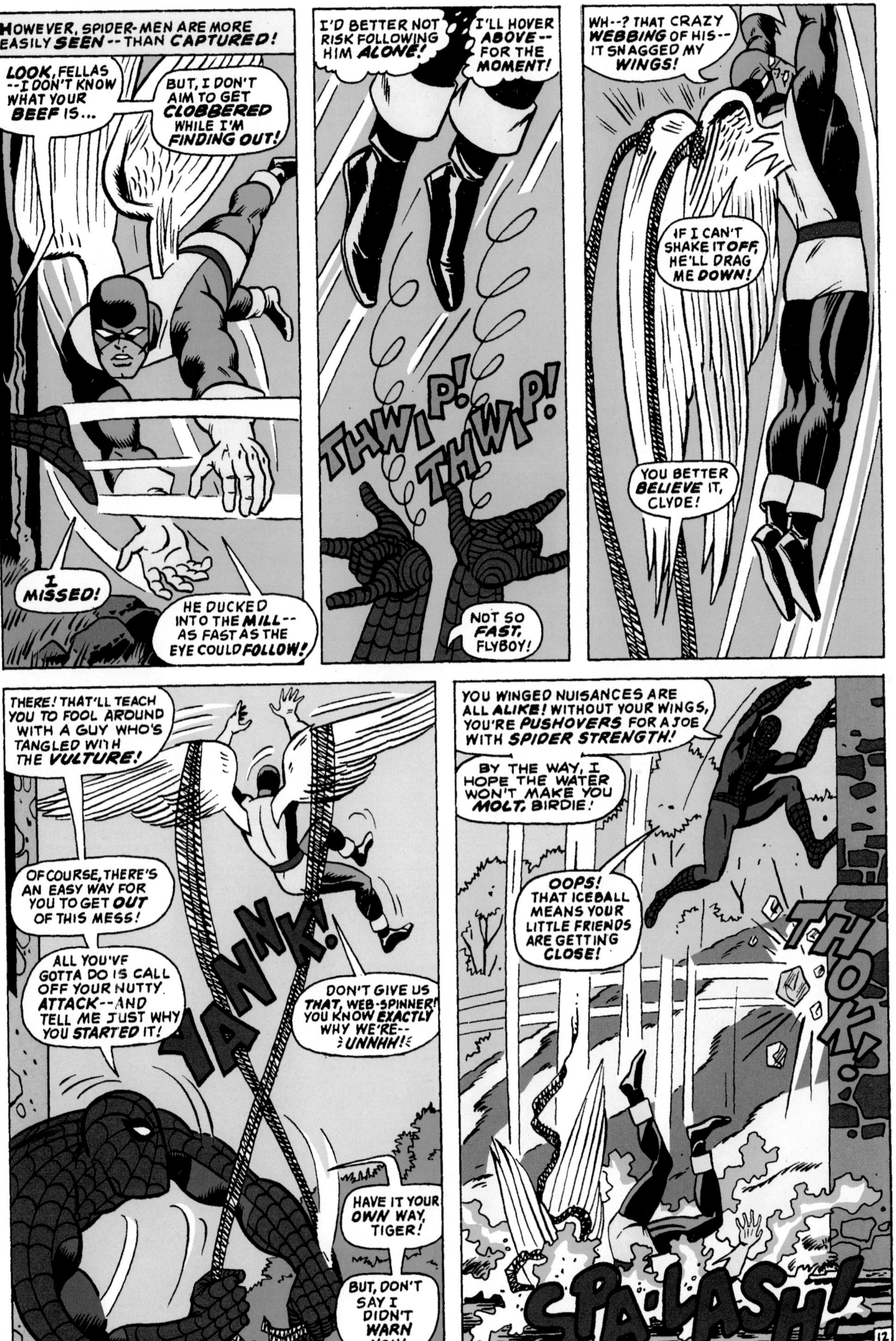
HOWEVER, SPIDER-MEN ARE MORE EASILY SEEN -- THAN CAPTURED!
LOOK, FELLAS --I DON'T KNOW WHAT YOUR BEEF IS...
BUT, I DON'T AIM TO GET CLOBBERED WHILE I'M FINDING OUT!
I MISSED!
HE DUCKED INTO THE MILL-- AS FAST AS THE EYE COULD FOLLOW!
I'D BETTER NOT RISK FOLLOWING HIM ALONE!
I'LL HOVER ABOVE -- FOR THE MOMENT!
THWIP! THWIP!
NOT SO FAST, FLYBOY!
WH--? THAT CRAZY WEBBING OF HIS-- IT SNAGGED MY WINGS!
IF I CAN'T SHAKE IT OFF, HE'LL DRAG ME DOWN!
YOU BETTER BELIEVE IT, CLYDE!
THERE! THAT'LL TEACH YOU TO FOOL AROUND WITH A GUY WHO'S TANGLED WITH THE VULTURE!
OF COURSE, THERE'S AN EASY WAY FOR YOU TO GET OUT OF THIS MESS!
ALL YOU'VE GOTTA DO IS CALL OFF YOUR NUTTY ATTACK--AND TELL ME JUST WHY YOU STARTED IT!
YANNK!
DON'T GIVE US THAT, WEB-SPINNER! YOU KNOW EXACTLY WHY WE'RE-- UNNHH!
HAVE IT YOUR OWN WAY, TIGER!
BUT, DON'T SAY I DIDN'T WARN YOU!
YOU WINGED NUISANCES ARE ALL ALIKE! WITHOUT YOUR WINGS, YOU'RE PUSHOVERS FOR A JOE WITH SPIDER STRENGTH!
BY THE WAY, I HOPE THE WATER WON'T MAKE YOU MOLT, BIRDIE!
OOPS! THAT ICEBALL MEANS YOUR LITTLE FRIENDS ARE GETTING CLOSE!
THOK!
SPA-LASH!
12

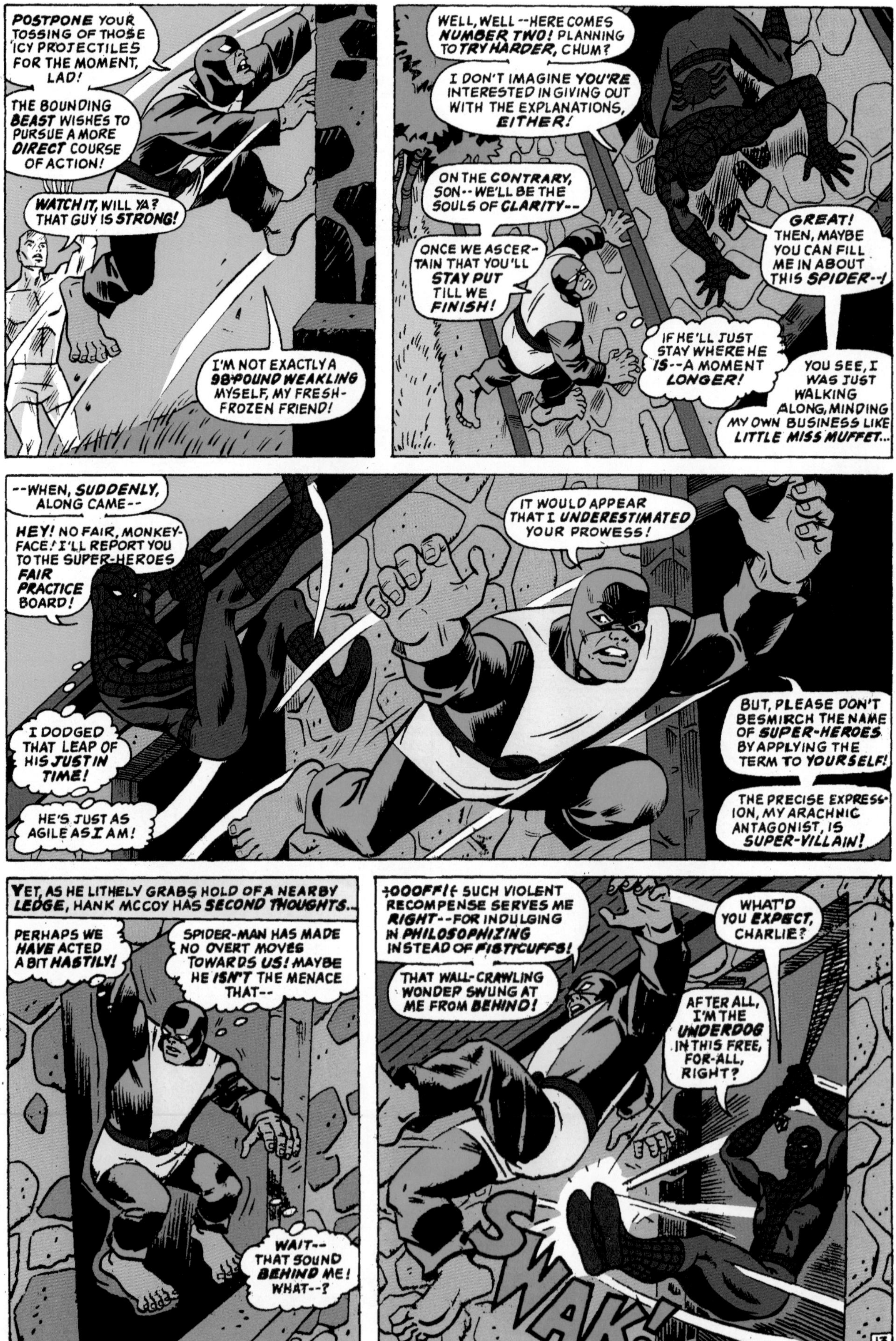
POSTPONE YOUR TOSSING OF THOSE ICY PROJECTILES FOR THE MOMENT, LAD!
THE BOUNDING BEAST WISHES TO PURSUE A MORE DIRECT COURSE OF ACTION!
WATCH IT, WILL YA? THAT GUY IS STRONG!
I'M NOT EXACTLY A 98-POUND WEAKLING MYSELF, MY FRESH-FROZEN FRIEND!
WELL, WELL--HERE COMES NUMBER TWO! PLANNING TO TRY HARDER, CHUM?
I DON'T IMAGINE YOU'RE INTERESTED IN GIVING OUT WITH THE EXPLANATIONS, EITHER!
ON THE CONTRARY, SON--WE'LL BE THE SOULS OF CLARITY--
ONCE WE ASCERTAIN THAT YOU'LL STAY PUT TILL WE FINISH!
GREAT! THEN, MAYBE YOU CAN FILL ME IN ABOUT THIS SPIDER--!
IF HE'LL JUST STAY WHERE HE IS--A MOMENT LONGER!
YOU SEE, I WAS JUST WALKING ALONG, MINDING MY OWN BUSINESS LIKE LITTLE MISS MUFFET...
--WHEN, SUDDENLY, ALONG CAME--
HEY! NO FAIR, MONKEY-FACE! I'LL REPORT YOU TO THE SUPER-HEROES FAIR PRACTICE BOARD!
IT WOULD APPEAR THAT I UNDERESTIMATED YOUR PROWESS!
I DODGED THAT LEAP OF HIS JUST IN TIME!
HE'S JUST AS AGILE AS I AM!
BUT, PLEASE DON'T BESMIRCH THE NAME OF SUPER-HEROES BY APPLYING THE TERM TO YOURSELF!
THE PRECISE EXPRESSION, MY ARACHNIC ANTAGONIST, IS SUPER-VILLAIN!
YET, AS HE LITHELY GRABS HOLD OF A NEARBY LEDGE, HANK MCCOY HAS SECOND THOUGHTS...
PERHAPS WE HAVE ACTED A BIT HASTILY!
SPIDER-MAN HAS MADE NO OVERT MOVES TOWARDS US! MAYBE HE ISN'T THE MENACE THAT--
WAIT--THAT SOUND BEHIND ME! WHAT--?
OOOFF! SUCH VIOLENT RECOMPENSE SERVES ME RIGHT--FOR INDULGING IN PHILOSOPHIZING INSTEAD OF FISTICUFFS!
THAT WALL-CRAWLING WONDER SWUNG AT ME FROM BEHIND!
WHAT'D YOU EXPECT, CHARLIE?
AFTER ALL, I'M THE UNDERDOG IN THIS FREE-FOR-ALL, RIGHT?
SWAK!
13

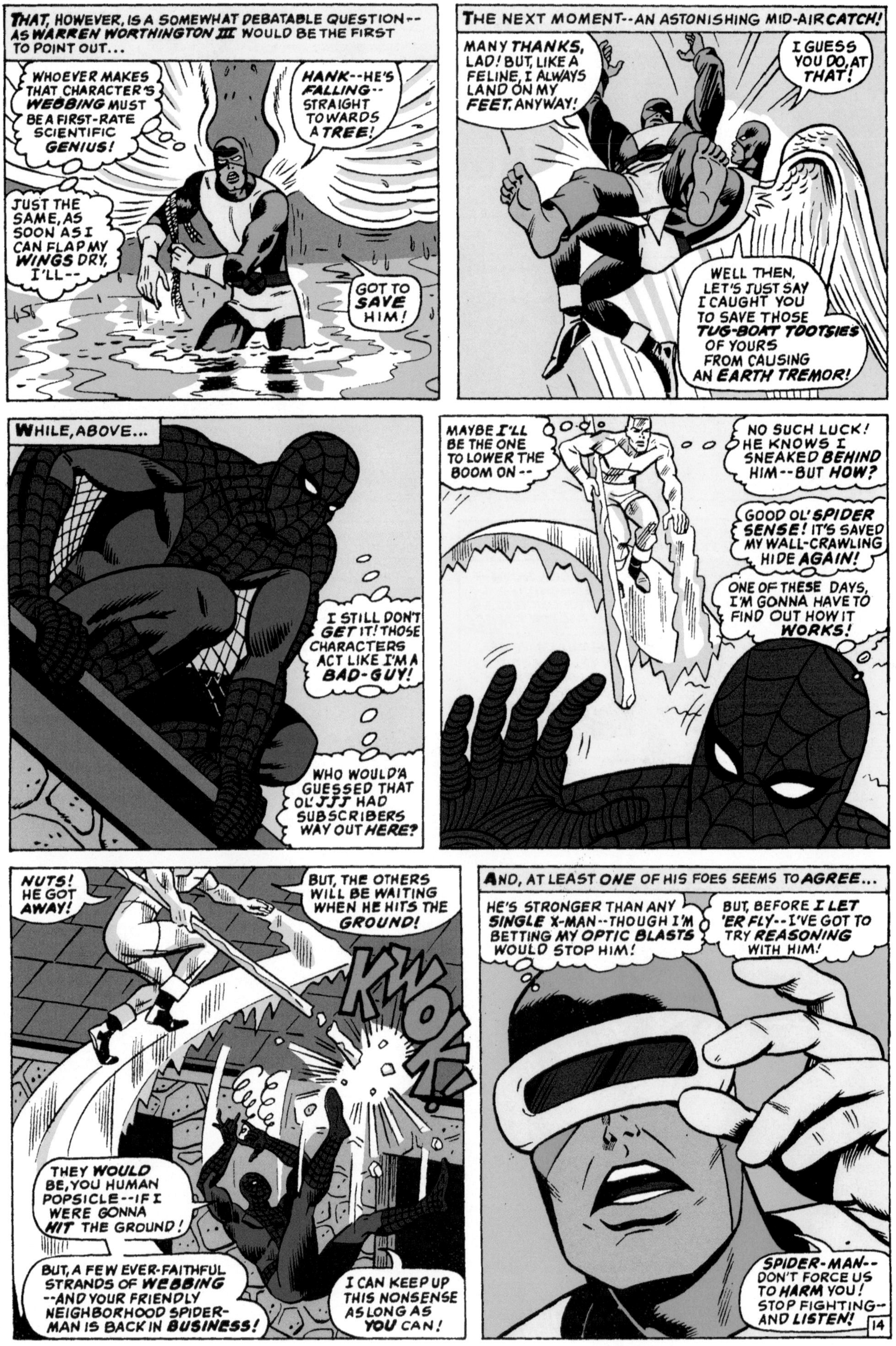
THAT, HOWEVER, IS A SOMEWHAT DEBATABLE QUESTION-- AS WARREN WORTHINGTON III WOULD BE THE FIRST TO POINT OUT...
WHOEVER MAKES THAT CHARACTER'S WEBBING MUST BE A FIRST-RATE SCIENTIFIC GENIUS!
JUST THE SAME, AS SOON AS I CAN FLAP MY WINGS DRY, I'LL--
HANK--HE'S FALLING-- STRAIGHT TOWARDS A TREE!
GOT TO SAVE HIM!
THE NEXT MOMENT--AN ASTONISHING MID-AIR CATCH!
MANY THANKS, LAD! BUT, LIKE A FELINE, I ALWAYS LAND ON MY FEET, ANYWAY!
I GUESS YOU DO, AT THAT!
WELL THEN, LET'S JUST SAY I CAUGHT YOU TO SAVE THOSE TUG-BOAT TOOTSIES OF YOURS FROM CAUSING AN EARTH TREMOR!
WHILE, ABOVE...
I STILL DON'T GET IT! THOSE CHARACTERS ACT LIKE I'M A BAD-GUY!
WHO WOULD'A GUESSED THAT OL' JJJ HAD SUBSCRIBERS WAY OUT HERE?
MAYBE I'LL BE THE ONE TO LOWER THE BOOM ON --
NO SUCH LUCK! HE KNOWS I SNEAKED BEHIND HIM--BUT HOW?
GOOD OL' SPIDER SENSE! IT'S SAVED MY WALL-CRAWLING HIDE AGAIN!
ONE OF THESE DAYS, I'M GONNA HAVE TO FIND OUT HOW IT WORKS!
NUTS! HE GOT AWAY!
BUT, THE OTHERS WILL BE WAITING WHEN HE HITS THE GROUND!
KWOK!
THEY WOULD BE, YOU HUMAN POPSICLE--IF I WERE GONNA HIT THE GROUND!
BUT, A FEW EVER-FAITHFUL STRANDS OF WEBBING --AND YOUR FRIENDLY NEIGHBORHOOD SPIDER-MAN IS BACK IN BUSINESS!
I CAN KEEP UP THIS NONSENSE AS LONG AS YOU CAN!
AND, AT LEAST ONE OF HIS FOES SEEMS TO AGREE...
HE'S STRONGER THAN ANY SINGLE X-MAN--THOUGH I'M BETTING MY OPTIC BLASTS WOULD STOP HIM!
BUT, BEFORE I LET 'ER FLY--I'VE GOT TO TRY REASONING WITH HIM!
SPIDER-MAN-- DON'T FORCE US TO HARM YOU! STOP FIGHTING-- AND LISTEN!

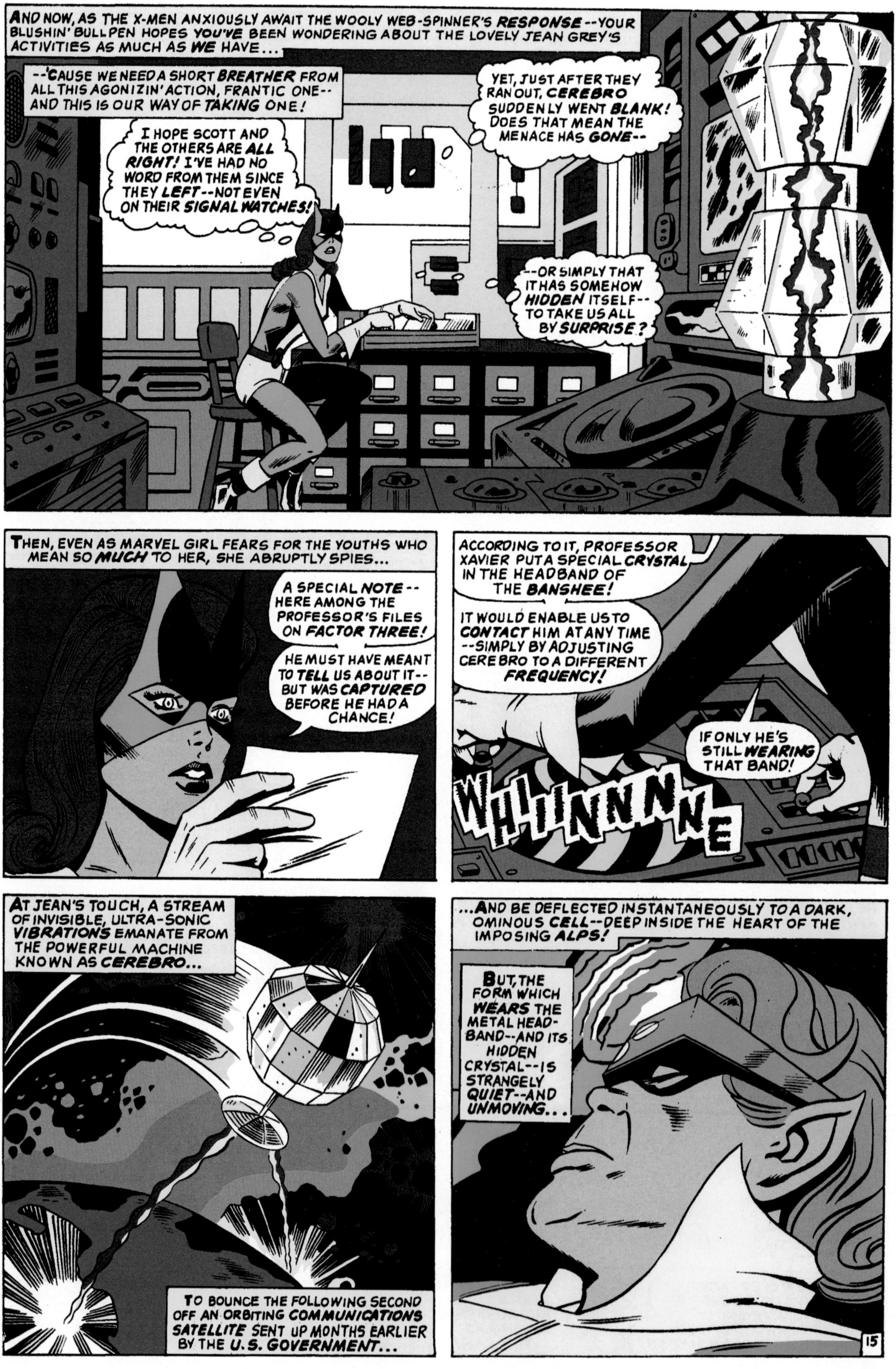
AND NOW, AS THE X-MEN ANXIOUSLY AWAIT THE WOOLY WEB-SPINNER'S RESPONSE--YOUR BLUSHIN' BULLPEN HOPES YOU'VE BEEN WONDERING ABOUT THE LOVELY JEAN GREY'S ACTIVITIES AS MUCH AS WE HAVE...
--'CAUSE WE NEED A SHORT BREATHER FROM ALL THIS AGONIZIN' ACTION, FRANTIC ONE--AND THIS IS OUR WAY OF TAKING ONE!
I HOPE SCOTT AND THE OTHERS ARE ALL RIGHT! I'VE HAD NO WORD FROM THEM SINCE THEY LEFT--NOT EVEN ON THEIR SIGNAL WATCHES!
YET, JUST AFTER THEY RAN OUT, CEREBRO SUDDENLY WENT BLANK! DOES THAT MEAN THE MENACE HAS GONE--
--OR SIMPLY THAT IT HAS SOMEHOW HIDDEN ITSELF--TO TAKE US ALL BY SURPRISE?
THEN, EVEN AS MARVEL GIRL FEARS FOR THE YOUTHS WHO MEAN SO MUCH TO HER, SHE ABRUPTLY SPIES...
A SPECIAL NOTE--HERE AMONG THE PROFESSOR'S FILES ON FACTOR THREE!
HE MUST HAVE MEANT TO TELL US ABOUT IT--BUT WAS CAPTURED BEFORE HE HAD A CHANCE!
ACCORDING TO IT, PROFESSOR XAVIER PUT A SPECIAL CRYSTAL IN THE HEADBAND OF THE BANSHEE!
IT WOULD ENABLE US TO CONTACT HIM AT ANY TIME--SIMPLY BY ADJUSTING CEREBRO TO A DIFFERENT FREQUENCY!
IF ONLY HE'S STILL WEARING THAT BAND!
WHHINNNNNE
AT JEAN'S TOUCH, A STREAM OF INVISIBLE, ULTRA-SONIC VIBRATIONS EMANATE FROM THE POWERFUL MACHINE KNOWN AS CEREBRO...
TO BOUNCE THE FOLLOWING SECOND OFF AN ORBITING COMMUNICATIONS SATELLITE SENT UP MONTHS EARLIER BY THE U.S. GOVERNMENT...
...AND BE DEFLECTED INSTANTANEOUSLY TO A DARK, OMINOUS CELL--DEEP INSIDE THE HEART OF THE IMPOSING ALPS!
BUT, THE FORM WHICH WEARS THE METAL HEAD-BAND--AND ITS HIDDEN CRYSTAL--IS STRANGELY QUIET--AND UNMOVING...
15

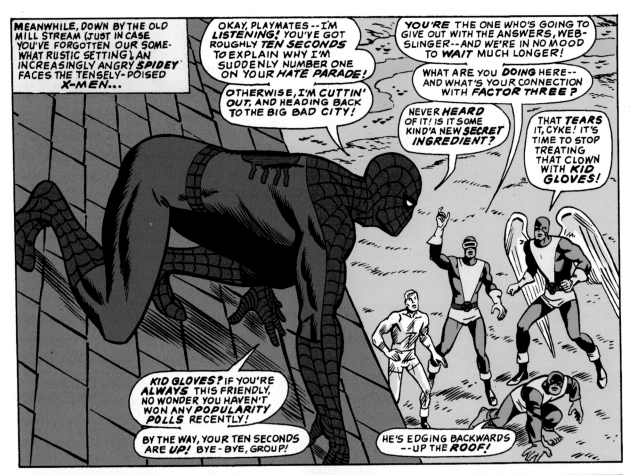

MEANWHILE, DOWN BY THE OLD MILL STREAM (JUST IN CASE YOU'VE FORGOTTEN OUR SOMEWHAT RUSTIC SETTING) AN INCREASINGLY ANGRY *SPIDEY* FACES THE TENSELY-POISED *X-MEN*...

OKAY, PLAYMATES--I'M *LISTENING!* YOU'VE GOT ROUGHLY *TEN SECONDS* TO EXPLAIN WHY I'M SUDDENLY NUMBER ONE ON YOUR *HATE PARADE!*

OTHERWISE, I'M *CUTTIN' OUT,* AND HEADING BACK TO THE BIG BAD CITY!

YOU'RE THE ONE WHO'S GOING TO GIVE OUT WITH THE ANSWERS, WEB-SLINGER--AND WE'RE IN NO MOOD TO *WAIT* MUCH LONGER!

WHAT ARE YOU *DOING* HERE-- AND WHAT'S YOUR CONNECTION WITH *FACTOR THREE?*

NEVER *HEARD* OF IT! IS IT SOME KIND'A NEW *SECRET INGREDIENT?*

THAT *TEARS* IT, CYKE! IT'S TIME TO STOP TREATING THAT CLOWN WITH *KID GLOVES!*

KID GLOVES? IF YOU'RE *ALWAYS* THIS FRIENDLY, NO WONDER YOU HAVEN'T WON ANY *POPULARITY POLLS* RECENTLY!

BY THE WAY, YOUR TEN SECONDS ARE *UP!* BYE-BYE, GROUP!

HE'S EDGING BACKWARDS --UP THE *ROOF!*

HE *MAY* BE TELLING THE TRUTH-- BUT WE CAN'T TAKE THE *CHANCE!*

ALRIGHT, X-MEN! LET'S GO *GET* HIM --AS A *TEAM!*

NOW YOU'RE TALKIN; LEADER-MAN!

BUT *REMEMBER,* BOBBY--WE ONLY WANT TO CAPTURE HIM FOR *INTERROGATION!*

I'LL BOUND INTO THE MILL THRU THIS *HOLE*-- AND TRY TO TAKE HIM BY *SURPRISE!*

FUNNY--SPIDER-MAN DOESN'T *ACT* LIKE AN EVIL MUTANT --OR LIKE ANYBODY'S *MERCENARY!*

STILL, IF HE *ISN'T*--THEN WHY DID *CEREBRO* SEND US TO THIS EXACT SPOT?

OH WELL, FOR THE MOMENT, MINE NOT TO REASON *WHY...*

AND, ABOVE...

ADMIT IT, FRIEND-- WE'VE GOT YOU *SURROUNDED!*

AS A MATTER OF FACT, THEY *DO!*

BUT, WHEN SPIDER-MAN DECIDES TO *SPLIT,* IT'LL TAKE MORE THAN FIVE *MASKED MUTANTS* TO STOP HIM-- I HOPE!

16

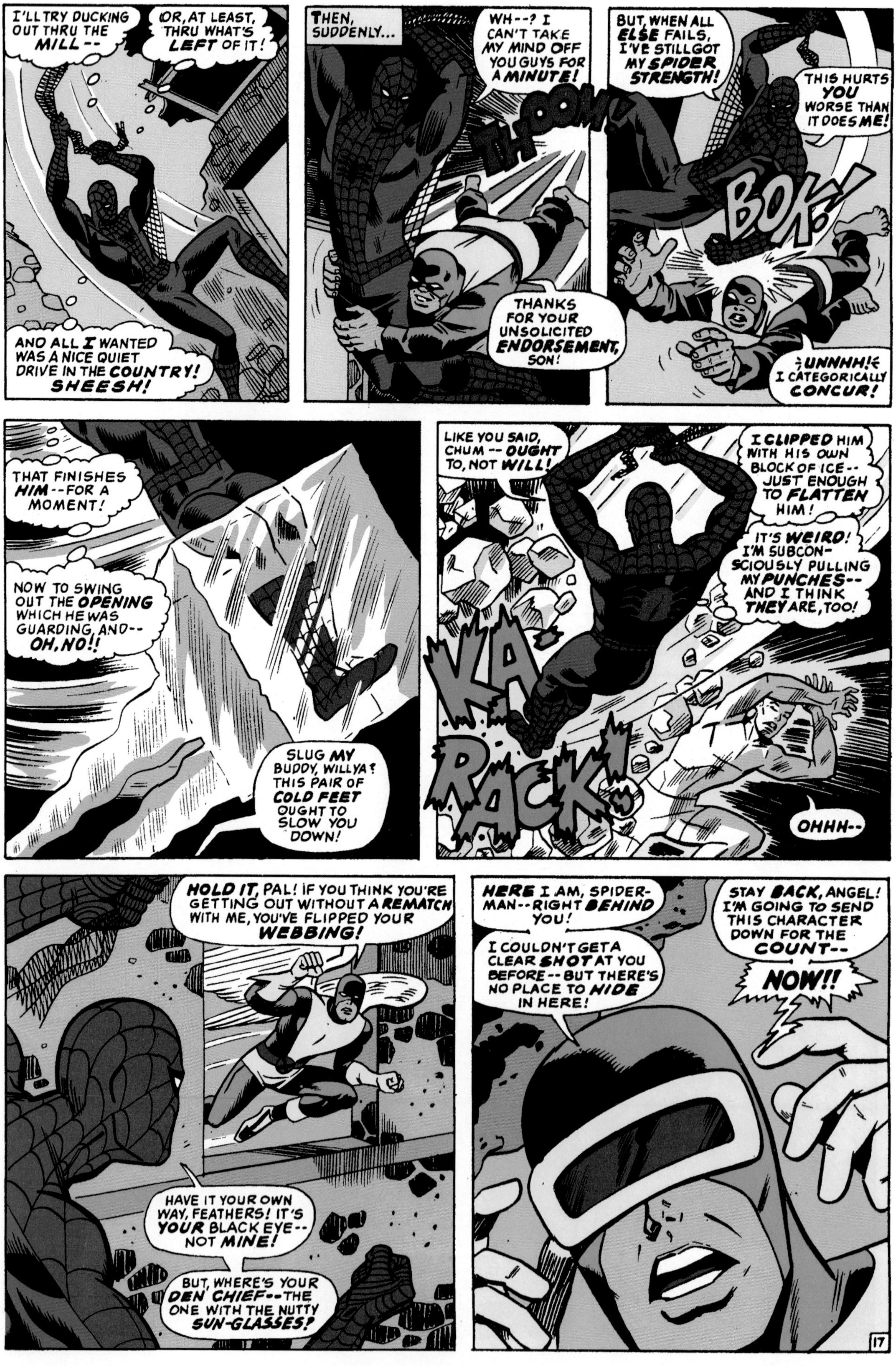
I'LL TRY DUCKING OUT THRU THE MILL --
OR, AT LEAST, THRU WHAT'S LEFT OF IT!
AND ALL I WANTED WAS A NICE QUIET DRIVE IN THE COUNTRY! SHEESH!
THEN, SUDDENLY...
WH--? I CAN'T TAKE MY MIND OFF YOU GUYS FOR A MINUTE!
THOOOM!
THANKS FOR YOUR UNSOLICITED ENDORSEMENT, SON!
BUT, WHEN ALL ELSE FAILS, I'VE STILL GOT MY SPIDER STRENGTH!
THIS HURTS YOU WORSE THAN IT DOES ME!
BOK!
UNNHH! I CATEGORICALLY CONCUR!
THAT FINISHES HIM -- FOR A MOMENT!
NOW TO SWING OUT THE OPENING WHICH HE WAS GUARDING, AND -- OH, NO!!
SLUG MY BUDDY, WILLYA? THIS PAIR OF COLD FEET OUGHT TO SLOW YOU DOWN!
LIKE YOU SAID, CHUM -- OUGHT TO, NOT WILL!
I CLIPPED HIM WITH HIS OWN BLOCK OF ICE -- JUST ENOUGH TO FLATTEN HIM!
IT'S WEIRD! I'M SUBCONSCIOUSLY PULLING MY PUNCHES -- AND I THINK THEY ARE, TOO!
KA RACK!
OHHH--
HOLD IT, PAL! IF YOU THINK YOU'RE GETTING OUT WITHOUT A REMATCH WITH ME, YOU'VE FLIPPED YOUR WEBBING!
HAVE IT YOUR OWN WAY, FEATHERS! IT'S YOUR BLACK EYE -- NOT MINE!
BUT, WHERE'S YOUR DEN CHIEF -- THE ONE WITH THE NUTTY SUN-GLASSES?
HERE I AM, SPIDER-MAN -- RIGHT BEHIND YOU!
I COULDN'T GET A CLEAR SHOT AT YOU BEFORE -- BUT THERE'S NO PLACE TO HIDE IN HERE!
STAY BACK, ANGEL! I'M GOING TO SEND THIS CHARACTER DOWN FOR THE COUNT --
NOW!!
17

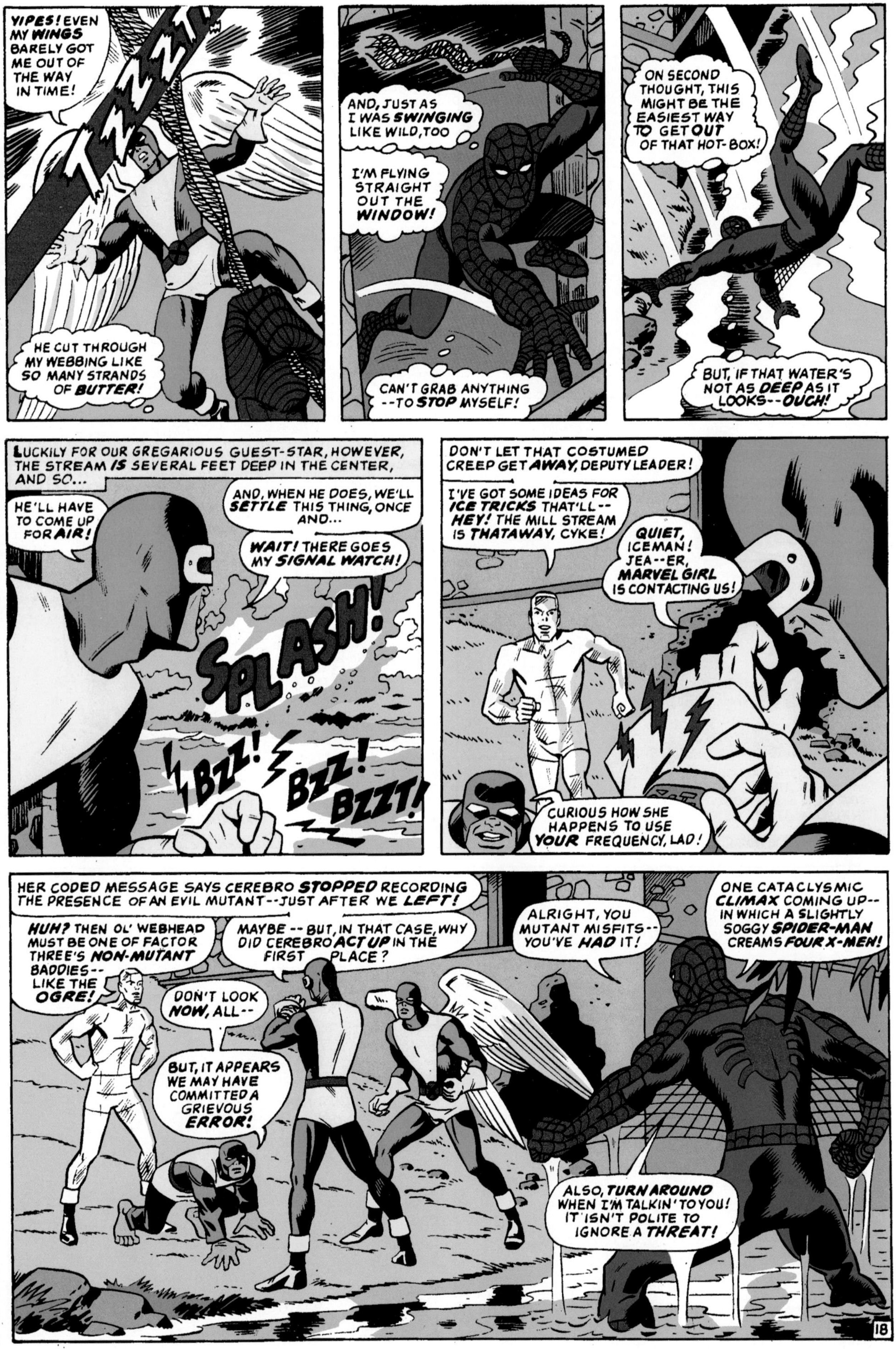
YIPES! EVEN MY WINGS BARELY GOT ME OUT OF THE WAY IN TIME!
HE CUT THROUGH MY WEBBING LIKE SO MANY STRANDS OF BUTTER!
AND, JUST AS I WAS SWINGING LIKE WILD, TOO
I'M FLYING STRAIGHT OUT THE WINDOW!
CAN'T GRAB ANYTHING --TO STOP MYSELF!
ON SECOND THOUGHT, THIS MIGHT BE THE EASIEST WAY TO GET OUT OF THAT HOT-BOX!
BUT, IF THAT WATER'S NOT AS DEEP AS IT LOOKS--OUCH!
LUCKILY FOR OUR GREGARIOUS GUEST-STAR, HOWEVER, THE STREAM IS SEVERAL FEET DEEP IN THE CENTER, AND SO...
HE'LL HAVE TO COME UP FOR AIR!
AND, WHEN HE DOES, WE'LL SETTLE THIS THING, ONCE AND...
WAIT! THERE GOES MY SIGNAL WATCH!
SPLASH!
BZZ! BZZ! BZZT!
DON'T LET THAT COSTUMED CREEP GET AWAY, DEPUTY LEADER!
I'VE GOT SOME IDEAS FOR ICE TRICKS THAT'LL-- HEY! THE MILL STREAM IS THATAWAY, CYKE!
QUIET, ICEMAN! JEA--ER, MARVEL GIRL IS CONTACTING US!
CURIOUS HOW SHE HAPPENS TO USE YOUR FREQUENCY, LAD!
HER CODED MESSAGE SAYS CEREBRO STOPPED RECORDING THE PRESENCE OF AN EVIL MUTANT--JUST AFTER WE LEFT!
HUH? THEN OL' WEBHEAD MUST BE ONE OF FACTOR THREE'S NON-MUTANT BADDIES-- LIKE THE OGRE!
MAYBE -- BUT, IN THAT CASE, WHY DID CEREBRO ACT UP IN THE FIRST PLACE?
DON'T LOOK NOW, ALL--
BUT, IT APPEARS WE MAY HAVE COMMITTED A GRIEVOUS ERROR!
ALRIGHT, YOU MUTANT MISFITS-- YOU'VE HAD IT!
ONE CATACLYSMIC CLIMAX COMING UP-- IN WHICH A SLIGHTLY SOGGY SPIDER-MAN CREAMS FOUR X-MEN!
ALSO, TURN AROUND WHEN I'M TALKIN' TO YOU! IT ISN'T POLITE TO IGNORE A THREAT!
18

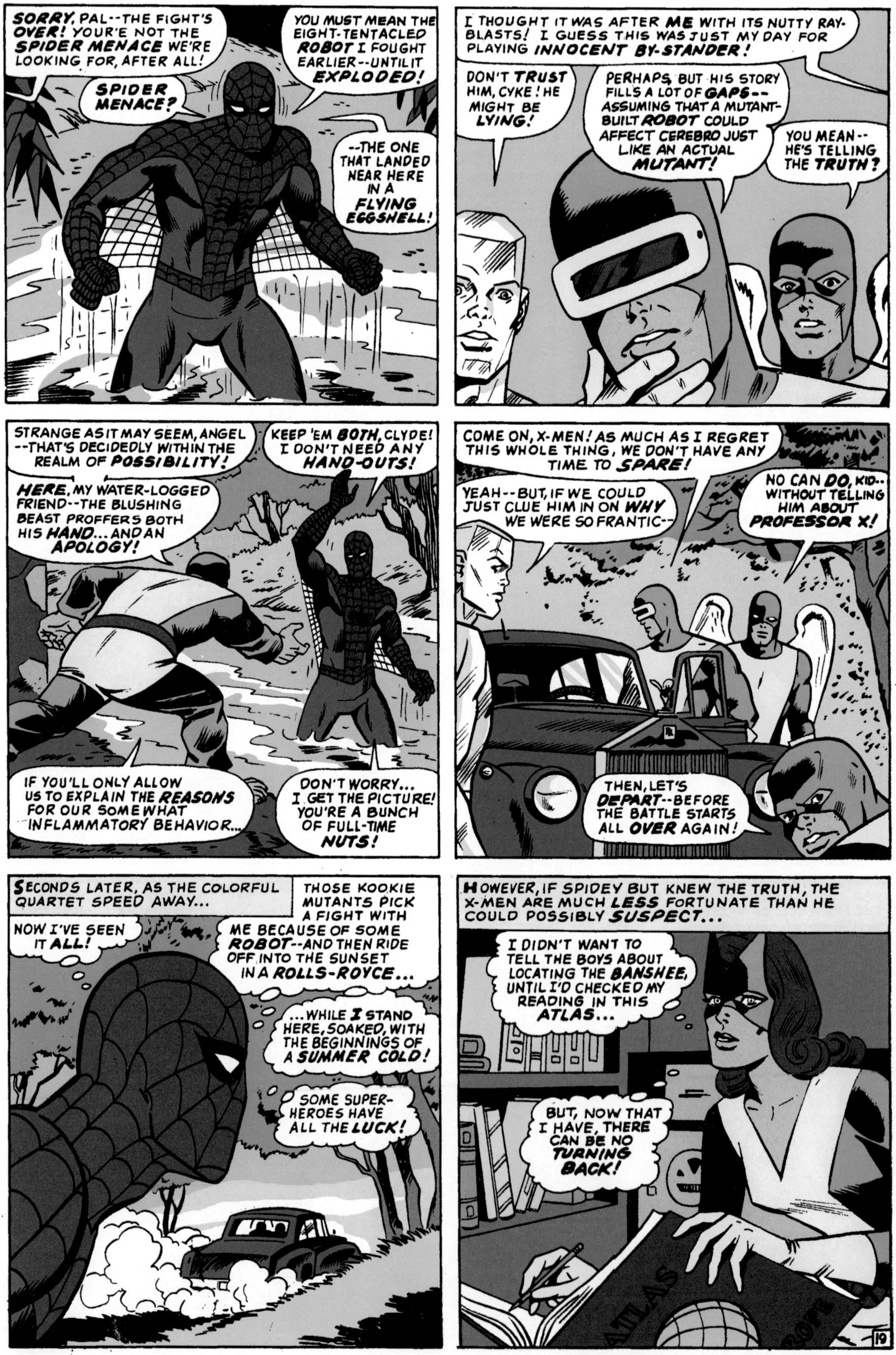
SORRY, PAL--THE FIGHT'S OVER! YOU'RE NOT THE SPIDER MENACE WE'RE LOOKING FOR, AFTER ALL!
SPIDER MENACE?
YOU MUST MEAN THE EIGHT-TENTACLED ROBOT I FOUGHT EARLIER--UNTIL IT EXPLODED!
--THE ONE THAT LANDED NEAR HERE IN A FLYING EGGSHELL!
I THOUGHT IT WAS AFTER ME WITH ITS NUTTY RAY-BLASTS! I GUESS THIS WAS JUST MY DAY FOR PLAYING INNOCENT BY-STANDER!
DON'T TRUST HIM, CYKE! HE MIGHT BE LYING!
PERHAPS, BUT HIS STORY FILLS A LOT OF GAPS--ASSUMING THAT A MUTANT-BUILT ROBOT COULD AFFECT CEREBRO JUST LIKE AN ACTUAL MUTANT!
YOU MEAN--HE'S TELLING THE TRUTH?
STRANGE AS IT MAY SEEM, ANGEL--THAT'S DECIDEDLY WITHIN THE REALM OF POSSIBILITY!
HERE, MY WATER-LOGGED FRIEND--THE BLUSHING BEAST PROFFERS BOTH HIS HAND... AND AN APOLOGY!
KEEP 'EM BOTH, CLYDE! I DON'T NEED ANY HAND-OUTS!
IF YOU'LL ONLY ALLOW US TO EXPLAIN THE REASONS FOR OUR SOMEWHAT INFLAMMATORY BEHAVIOR...
DON'T WORRY... I GET THE PICTURE! YOU'RE A BUNCH OF FULL-TIME NUTS!
COME ON, X-MEN! AS MUCH AS I REGRET THIS WHOLE THING, WE DON'T HAVE ANY TIME TO SPARE!
YEAH--BUT, IF WE COULD JUST CLUE HIM IN ON WHY WE WERE SO FRANTIC--
NO CAN DO, KID--WITHOUT TELLING HIM ABOUT PROFESSOR X!
THEN, LET'S DEPART--BEFORE THE BATTLE STARTS ALL OVER AGAIN!
SECONDS LATER, AS THE COLORFUL QUARTET SPEED AWAY...
NOW I'VE SEEN IT ALL!
THOSE KOOKIE MUTANTS PICK A FIGHT WITH ME BECAUSE OF SOME ROBOT--AND THEN RIDE OFF INTO THE SUNSET IN A ROLLS-ROYCE...
...WHILE I STAND HERE, SOAKED, WITH THE BEGINNINGS OF A SUMMER COLD!
SOME SUPER-HEROES HAVE ALL THE LUCK!
HOWEVER, IF SPIDEY BUT KNEW THE TRUTH, THE X-MEN ARE MUCH LESS FORTUNATE THAN HE COULD POSSIBLY SUSPECT...
I DIDN'T WANT TO TELL THE BOYS ABOUT LOCATING THE BANSHEE, UNTIL I'D CHECKED MY READING IN THIS ATLAS...
BUT, NOW THAT I HAVE, THERE CAN BE NO TURNING BACK!
ATLAS
19

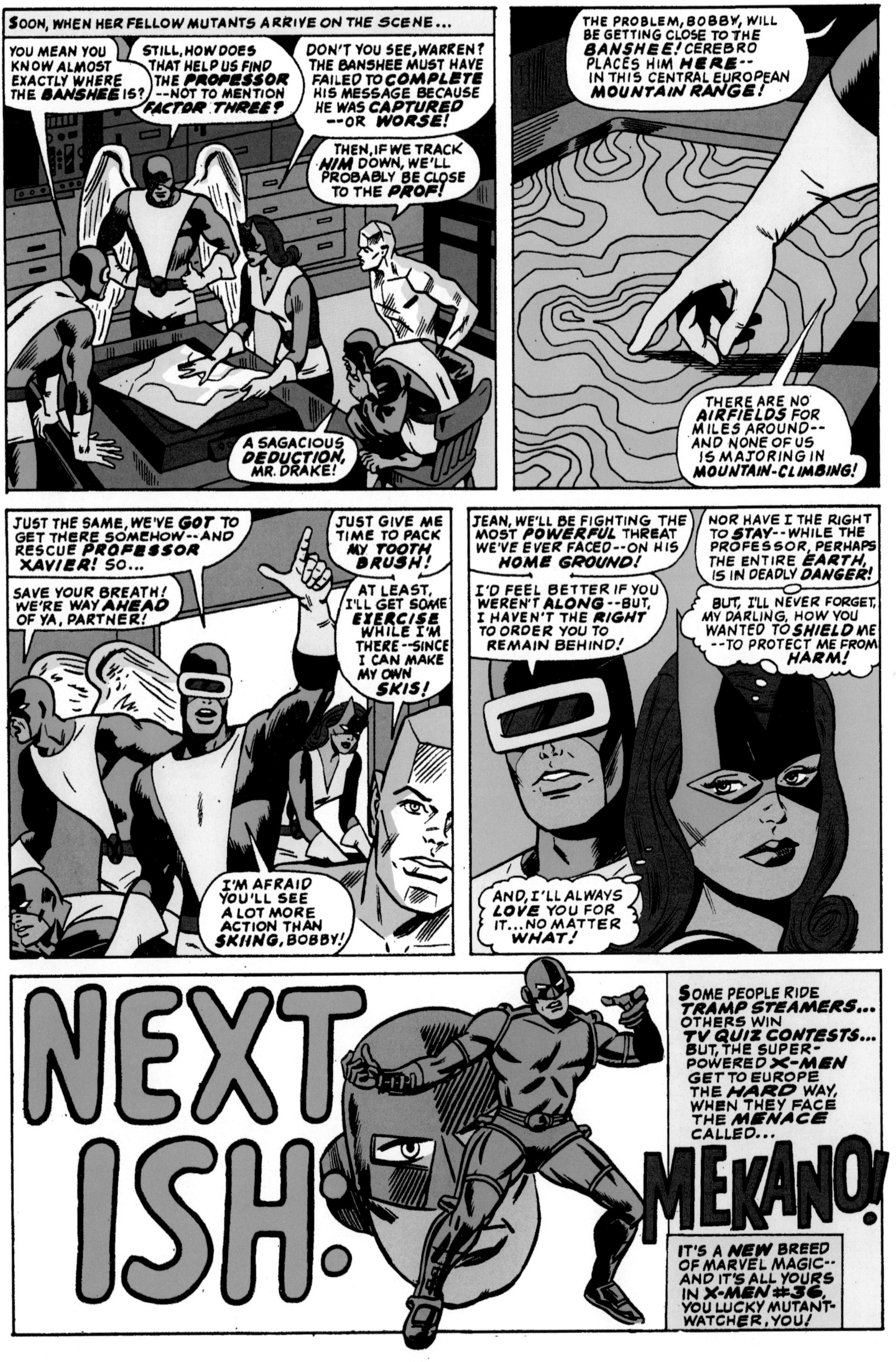
SOON, WHEN HER FELLOW MUTANTS ARRIVE ON THE SCENE...
YOU MEAN YOU KNOW ALMOST EXACTLY WHERE THE BANSHEE IS?
STILL, HOW DOES THAT HELP US FIND THE PROFESSOR --NOT TO MENTION FACTOR THREE?
DON'T YOU SEE, WARREN? THE BANSHEE MUST HAVE FAILED TO COMPLETE HIS MESSAGE BECAUSE HE WAS CAPTURED --OR WORSE!
THEN, IF WE TRACK HIM DOWN, WE'LL PROBABLY BE CLOSE TO THE PROF!
A SAGACIOUS DEDUCTION, MR. DRAKE!
THE PROBLEM, BOBBY, WILL BE GETTING CLOSE TO THE BANSHEE! CEREBRO PLACES HIM HERE-- IN THIS CENTRAL EUROPEAN MOUNTAIN RANGE!
THERE ARE NO AIRFIELDS FOR MILES AROUND-- AND NONE OF US IS MAJORING IN MOUNTAIN-CLIMBING!
JUST THE SAME, WE'VE GOT TO GET THERE SOMEHOW--AND RESCUE PROFESSOR XAVIER! SO...
SAVE YOUR BREATH! WE'RE WAY AHEAD OF YA, PARTNER!
JUST GIVE ME TIME TO PACK MY TOOTH BRUSH!
AT LEAST, I'LL GET SOME EXERCISE WHILE I'M THERE--SINCE I CAN MAKE MY OWN SKIS!
I'M AFRAID YOU'LL SEE A LOT MORE ACTION THAN SKIING, BOBBY!
JEAN, WE'LL BE FIGHTING THE MOST POWERFUL THREAT WE'VE EVER FACED--ON HIS HOME GROUND!
I'D FEEL BETTER IF YOU WEREN'T ALONG--BUT, I HAVEN'T THE RIGHT TO ORDER YOU TO REMAIN BEHIND!
NOR HAVE I THE RIGHT TO STAY--WHILE THE PROFESSOR, PERHAPS THE ENTIRE EARTH, IS IN DEADLY DANGER!
BUT, I'LL NEVER FORGET, MY DARLING, HOW YOU WANTED TO SHIELD ME --TO PROTECT ME FROM HARM!
AND, I'LL ALWAYS LOVE YOU FOR IT...NO MATTER WHAT!
NEXT ISH:
SOME PEOPLE RIDE TRAMP STEAMERS... OTHERS WIN TV QUIZ CONTESTS... BUT, THE SUPER-POWERED X-MEN GET TO EUROPE THE HARD WAY, WHEN THEY FACE THE MENACE CALLED...
MEKANO!
IT'S A NEW BREED OF MARVEL MAGIC-- AND IT'S ALL YOURS IN X-MEN #36, YOU LUCKY MUTANT-WATCHER, YOU!